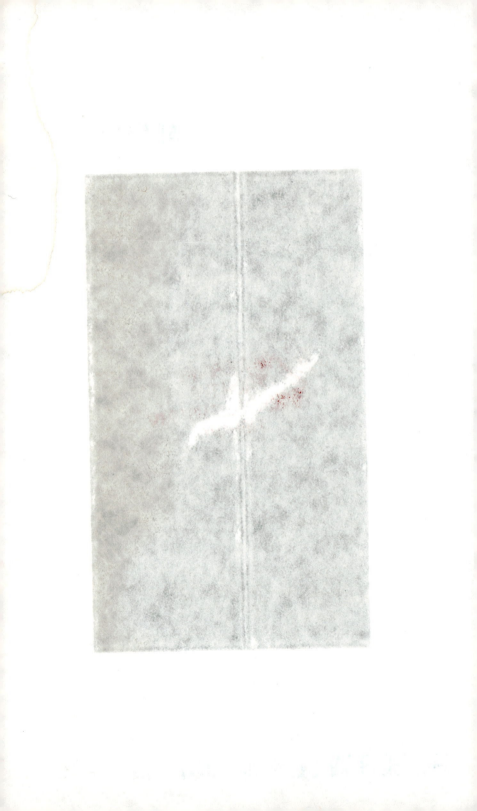

Tourism and heritage attractions

Issues in tourism series

Edited by Brian Goodall, *University of Reading* and Gregory Ashworth, *University of Groningen,* The Netherlands.

The growing significance of tourism as an economic activity is reflected in the increased recognition it has been given at national and local levels. There has been a rapid development of specialist educational and training facilities for academics and professionals, including widespread research activity, and the discipline could now be said to have 'come of age'. The books in this series provide rigorous, focused discussions of key topics in current international debates on tourism. They tackle the social, economic and environmental consequences of the rapid developments, taking account of what has happened so far and looking ahead to future prospects. The series caters for all those wanting to understand what is happening at the forefront of the field and how it will filter through to general tourism practice.

Other titles in the series

Tourism Research
Critiques and Challenges
Edited by Douglas Pearce and Richard Butler

The Economics of Tourism
Thea Sinclair and Mike Stabler

Tourism for the Environment
Colin Hunter and Howard Green

Tourism and heritage attractions

Richard Prentice

London and New York

10-14-93

First published 1993
by Routledge
11 New Fetter Lane, London EC4P 4EE

Simultaneously published in the USA and Canada
by Routledge
29 West 35th Street, New York, NY 10001

© 1993 Richard Prentice

Typeset in Times by Witwell Limited, Southport
Printed and bound in Great Britain by
Mackays of Chatham PLC, Chatham, Kent

British Library Cataloguing in Publication Data
A catalogue record for this title is available from the British Library.

Library of Congress Cataloging-in-Publication Data
Prentice, Richard (Richard C.)
    Tourism and heritage attractions/Richard Prentice.
        p. cm. — (Issues in tourism series)
    Includes bibliographical references and index.
    ISBN 0-415-08525-X
    1. Historic sites—Great Britain—Conservation and
restoration.   2. Cultural property, Protection of—Great
Britain.   3. Historical museums—Great Britain.   4. Tourist trade—
Great Britain.
    I. Title.   II. Series.
    DA655.P74   1993
    363.6'9'0941—dc20
                                                92-19910
                                                CIP

To that sense of place and past
and that landscape of colours
which remains Ellen Vannin.

Contents

List of figures		viii
List of tables		ix
Preface		xiii
Acknowledgements		xvi

1 Tourists' demands for heritage consumption   1

2 The heterogeneity of the heritage product   21

3 The socio-demographic characteristics of tourists at heritage attractions   51

4 Tourist decision-making and heritage attractions   75

5 Tourist trip making and visits to heritage attractions   94

6 The promotion of heritage attractions to tourists   119

7 The retailing role of heritage attractions   136

8 Tourist disposition towards conservation and commitment to heritage   154

9 Tourist assessment of heritage presentation   171

10 Benefits gained by tourists from visiting heritage attractions   202

11 Conclusion: the heritage market place summarised   222

Bibliography   235
Index   243

Figures

2.1 Linking heritage places – Nova Scotia.   30

2.2 Location of the major heritage attractions on the Isle of Man.   48

7.1 Locational clustering of gift shops around abbey attractions in heritage towns.   140

7.2 Locational clustering of gift shops around castle attractions in heritage towns.   141

7.3 'Dualistic' locational clustering of gift shops in heritage towns.   142

Tables

2.1 Sample sizes of Manx surveys. 46

3.1 The social class profile of adult holiday tourists visiting Manx heritage sites. 54

3.2 The social class profile of adult holiday tourists at different Manx heritage sites. 56

3.3 The age at which adult holiday tourists visiting Manx heritage sites had completed their full-time education. 59

3.4 The age profile of adult holiday tourists visiting Manx heritage sites. 61

3.5 The age profile of adult heritage tourists at different Manx heritage sites. 63

3.6 The presence of a child or children in the personal groups of adult holiday tourists visiting Manx heritage sites. 64

3.7 The presence of a child or children in the personal groups of adult holiday tourists at different Manx heritage sites. 65

3.8 The group size of adult holiday tourists at different Manx heritage sites. 67

3.9 Country of residence of adult holiday tourists visiting the Isle of Man and those visiting Manx heritage sites. 68

3.10 Holiday type of adult holiday tourists visiting the Isle of Man and those visiting Manx heritage sites. 70

3.11 Length of stay on the Isle of Man by adult holiday tourists visiting the island and those visiting Manx heritage sites. 71

3.12 Type of accommodation used by adult holiday tourists visiting the Isle of Man and those visiting Manx heritage sites. 73

4.1 Holiday tourists giving heritage tourism 'likes' in response to questioning in the Manx Passenger Surveys. 77

4.2 Reasons given for their visit to a heritage site by adult holiday tourists visiting heritage sites on the Isle of Man.   80

4.3 Main reasons given for their visit to a heritage site by adult holiday tourists at different heritage sites on the Isle of Man.   82

4.4 Main reasons given for their visit to a heritage site by adult holiday tourists of differing educational backgrounds at heritage sites on the Isle of Man.   84

4.5 Number of repeat visits made to specific heritage sites on the Isle of Man by adult holiday tourists visiting heritage sites on the island.   85

4.6 Repeat visiting to specific heritage sites on the Isle of Man by adult holiday tourists visiting the different heritage sites on the island.   86

4.7 Extent to which adult holiday tourists visiting the Isle of Man visit heritage sites on the island.   88

4.8 Number of specified heritage sites visited in the previous seven days by adult holiday tourists visiting Manx heritage sites.   89

4.9 Extent to which adult holiday tourists visiting heritage sites on the Isle of Man had visited other heritage sites on the island.   90

4.10 Extent to which adult holiday tourists visiting heritage sites on the Isle of Man had visited heritage sites elsewhere in the previous twelve months.   91

4.11 Effect of social class on the extent to which adult holiday tourists visiting heritage sites on the Isle of Man had visited heritage sites elsewhere in the previous twelve months.   92

5.1 Length of stays at heritage sites on the Isle of Man by adult holiday tourists.   97

5.2 Length of stays at different heritage sites on the Isle of Man by adult holiday tourists.   99

5.3 Area of origin on day of visit of adult holiday tourists visiting heritage sites on the Isle of Man.   102

5.4 Area of accommodation of holiday tourists on the Isle of Man.   104

5.5 Areas of the Isle of Man over-supplying and under-supplying adult holiday tourists to Manx heritage sites.   105

5.6 Means of transport to heritage sites on the Isle of Man by adult holiday tourists.   109

5.7 Visits made or intended to another attraction on the day of visit to Manx heritage sites by adult holiday tourists. 111

5.8 Disposition of adult holiday tourists visiting Manx heritage
sites to visit other heritage attractions on the island during
their holiday. 114

6.1 Main perceived influence on decision to holiday on the
Isle of Man by holiday tourists staying in paid
accommodation. 124

6.2 Main sources of information about heritage attractions of
of adult holiday tourists visiting heritage attractions on the
Isle of Man. 127

6.3 Single main source of information about heritage
attractions of adult holiday tourists visiting
heritage attractions on the Isle of Man. 128

6.4 Effect of awareness of heritage attraction prior to arrival
on Isle of Man for holiday on the main sources of
information about the attraction used by adult holiday
tourists visiting heritage attractions on the Isle of Man. 129

7.1 Expenditure distribution per head by holiday tourists to the
Isle of Man. 143

8.1 Main functions perceived of heritage sites by adult
holiday tourists to the Isle of Man. 158

8.2 Main functions perceived of different heritage sites by
adult holiday tourists visiting heritage attractions on the
Isle of Man. 159

9.1 Satisfaction of adult holiday tourists with the
presentational media at Manx heritage sites. 176

9.2 Satisfaction of adult holiday tourists at different Manx
heritage sites with the information provided on the displays
at the sites. 178

9.3 Satisfaction of adult holiday tourists with staff roles
at Castle Rushen. 179

9.4 Satisfaction of adult holiday tourists with the 'Story
of Mann' film at the Manx Museum. 181

9.5 Presentational media provided at attractions seen or
heard by adult holiday tourists visiting different Manx
heritage sites. 183

9.6 Attention paid to presentational media provided at
attractions by adult holiday tourists who had seen or heard
these media during visits to different Manx heritage sites. 185

9.7 Adult holiday tourists' views on the importance of
presentational media seen or heard to their understanding

of the sites at different Manx heritage sites.   194

9.8   Opinions of adult holiday tourists visiting different
       heritage sites on the Isle of Man that, 'Historic sites
       should be rebuilt to show their former splendour'.   198

10.1 Enjoyment of visits to different Manx heritage attractions
       by adult holiday tourists.   204

10.2 Recognition of interpretative information by adult
       holiday tourists when leaving Manx heritage sites.   214

10.3 Admitted prior knowledge of interpretative information
       by adult holiday tourists visiting Manx heritage sites.   216

Preface

It is perhaps symbolic, although by chance, that this author's preface to a book on tourism should be written by a tourist, for this preface is being thought out as jottings on what is strictly termed a secondary holiday or short break. The view from the hotel window sets the scene, overlooking what to the residents is a Saturday market place of stalls, but to tourists, a market place in an abbey town. This market place as a 'heritage' feature for tourists being notable for a medieval hexagonal conduit built for monks to wash in, and nearby a museum, and the abbey church.

What is 'heritage'? To reply that it is something which is passed down from previous generations suggests its heterogeneity, for much is passed from one generation to another. But such a reply ignores the way we as individuals each become aware of 'our' heritage, and claim it, emotively as inspiration, comfort or possession. As this preface is being written in the Dorset town of Sherborne, our initial question might seem singularly superfluous, for quaintness and built heritage as architecture and townscape are all around: the town's two castles, its fifteenth-century abbey church and its abbey gatehouse are only the grander features of this built heritage. Doubly superfluous it might be thought, as beyond the town itself are beautiful landscapes treasured by many if not designated as such officially. Dorset, of course, also has other associations, perhaps most prominently as the centre piece of Thomas Hardy's *Wessex*, itself an emotive landscape in a social world which was rapidly changing even as the author penned his words. Yet the Hardy theme also has commercial uses: for example, it even appears in the name of a Dorset beer, *Thomas Hardy Country Bitter*, presumably with which true Hardy followers may refresh themselves. As an epitomy of Englishness, Dorset well illustrates a more modern use of heritage, in product promotion. The apparent rurality and unchanging nature of its landscapes and villages are powerful associations, however unreal they are in contemporary 'post-modern' society.

Whose heritage is it that is represented by Dorset? Modern advertisers would imply that it is implicit in all our feelings, wherever in the British Isles we reside, for the associations its images convey are portrayed nationally, not just in England but in the other countries which constitute these islands. Yet Dorset is quite different as a place than, say the Isle of Man which features prominently in this book, or to the slate greyness of Snowdonia or the limestone greys and vivid greenness of meadows in the Yorkshire Dales. Are we to individually claim all these images, and more, as a collection of our heritage? More immediately, is Dorset the heritage of the folk who reside in the county? Presumably the past generations of people living in Dorset have passed an emotion for the county on to their descendants? Most probably, but as one of the English counties which rapidly expanded in population numbers in the 1980s, many Dorset residents have in fact been born elsewhere. Dorset is part of the 'counter urbanization' culture of population transfusion, with newcomers moving in and others moving out. The expectations and value systems of many contemporary Dorset residents have been formed elsewhere. Alternatively, is the heritage of Dorset for the tourist to consume? The promotion of the county to tourists is vigorously full of heritage imagery. Tourists arrive in the county in their cars and by the coach load – and, if postcards displayed for sale are indicative of demand, frequently depart with images of Dorset as a series of places represented by tourist 'honey-pots', among which village scenes of thatched cottages feature prominently. And yet we should not over-readily ascribe Sherborne's, and Dorset's, heritage to tourists to consume, for the festooning of the town's inns, for example, in December with ivy, holly, mistletoe and other greenery along the oak beams of the buildings is not for tourists' consumption but for residents'.

Although situated in Dorset, Sherborne is half encircled by part of the county of Somerset. And yet Bruton and Wincanton, as neighbouring Somerset towns of similar quaintness, are unambiguously different *places* in terms of their townscapes than Sherborne, and yield a different sense of the past, of which their county heritage is part. The wetlands of the Somerset Levels are not spatially distant either, but as a place are unambiguously distinct in landscape and lore. However, how the tourist equates these neighbouring heritages of undulating lowlands and wetland moor is less clear: indeed, such images may be seen as distinct spatially as well as in landscape terms for they are promoted to tourists separately.

As a shopping centre for comparison and specialist goods in a quaint and relaxed environment of small shops, Sherborne illustrates a further feature of heritage: its link with the physical consumption of goods. This has been termed 'leisure shopping', and can be seen elsewhere in Britain, for example, in the Swaledale town of Richmond, and internationally in the regeneration of city watersides with retailing as one land-use – the 'Historic Properties' refurbishment on the Halifax waterfront in Nova Scotia comes immediately to mind. Those towns of Europe which avoided much nineteenth- and twentieth-century modernisation clearly have a resource in their quaint townscape for such retailing changes, particularly where this coincides with an affluent local or tourist population. Retailing in such centres, relying as it does on the ambience of place, thereby becomes part of heritage consumption.

Sherborne further illustrates a further aspect of heritage. Its industrial heritage is not prominently presented to visitors. Its railway line, incongruously – despite its West Country location – now part of *Network South East*, was part of many Londoners' holiday experiences in the 1950s, as a main line to the Devon resorts. A feature which was recognised in the names – such as *Exmouth, Budleigh Salterton*, and *Ilfracombe* – of some of the passenger locomotives of the former Southern Railway and its successor. The town could also present a lost railway heritage for nearby Templecombe was a centre point of the former railway which bisected north to south the counties of Somerset and Dorset and brought many holiday-makers from the English Midlands to the South Coast. Undoubtedly other heritages could be presented too.

The essential point about heritage, therefore, is that it is both felt internally as *feelings of benefit* by its consumers and also *presented* implicitly and explicitly by producers who see a demand for such 'products'. Within this context, important questions for the understanding of heritage as a tourism experience derive from the transience of tourism. How far are such feelings transient, superficial or false, in contrast to leading to awareness, learning, insight and elaboration? Equally, how do the producers of heritage experiences respond to such demands? Ultimately, our understanding of heritage tourism must be founded on an understanding of the benefits gained by its consumers and how these are affected by the producers of heritage products. As the inspiration for this preface, Sherborne and its locality can in effect be presented and consumed in many ways by many different types of consumers.

Sherborne,
Dorset.

Acknowledgements

The author wishes to acknowledge, in particular, the help of Manx National Heritage in supporting the research reported in this book.

The author wishes also to acknowledge the assistance of the Atlantic Canada Opportunities Agency in the author's collation of research material in Atlantic Canada.

However, the views advanced in this book are those of the author and should not be assumed necessarily to be those of the sponsoring or assisting agencies.

1 Tourists' demands for heritage consumption

FEATURES OF TOURISM DEMAND

Tourism has been described as 'the export that doesn't go anywhere' (Atlantic Provinces Economic Council 1987). Not only is it ill defined, spreading over many industries such as hotel and food services, arts and crafts and the like, the things that attract tourists to a destination are not taken away with them. Taking Atlantic Canada as our example, 'The things which bring them here, however (scenery, lobster suppers, theatre, sandy beaches), don't leave with them. The only things they take home are photographs, purchased souvenirs, perhaps a sunburn, and memories' (Atlantic Provinces Economic Council 1987: 135).

Defining tourists as persons who stay overnight at a destination (Seekings 1989), the size of the tourism market is impressive. Because of the ill-defined nature of tourism estimates of the size of the sector have to include estimates of the proportion of time spent by employees serving tourists rather than other customers. Tourism not only creates direct employment, as in hotels and shops, but also in those industries supplying these industries. The employment created is invariably seasonal, and often requiring low skill levels. It may also be part time rather than full time. However, such jobs can be attractive to certain groups for whom permanent full time employment is impossible, such as students or mothers of small children wishing to earn extra money for their household without a commitment to longer term employment. Taking first Atlantic Canada as our example, tourism is estimated during peak periods in Prince Edward Island and Newfoundland to account for 15 and 8 per cent of all jobs respectively (Atlantic Provinces Economic Council 1987). Across the other side of the North Atlantic, and taking the United Kingdom as our example, United Kingdom residents are estimated in 1990 to have made some 95.5 million tourism trips of one night or more away from home, involving an expenditure of £10,500 million (Wales Tourist Board 1991a). In Wales it is estimated that nearly one in ten jobs, or 9.5 per cent to be more precise, are dependent upon tourism (Medlik 1989).

Tourism principally includes holiday trips, visits to friends and relatives, and business trips, involving at least one night away from home. Of the 95.5 million estimated tourism trips by United Kingdom residents within the United Kingdom in 1990, 61 per cent were thought to be holiday trips, involving an expenditure of some £7,350 million. As well as domestic tourism trips within the United Kingdom, United Kingdom residents were thought to have made over 30 million tourism visits overseas, including visits to the rest of Europe. The United Kingdom in 1989 also received 17 million overseas tourists, with estimated expenditure within the United Kingdom of nearly £7 million. Only with the exception of 1988 did overseas tourism to the United Kingdom fail to increase in volume in the 1980s, rising by an estimated 38 per cent between 1980 and 1989. In 1987 alone, overseas tourists to the United Kingdom are thought to have increased in number by 12 per cent over the previous year.

Tourism has been one of the growth industries of the countries of the European Community of the past three decades. For example, although in Britain the proportion of the adult population taking at least one holiday has hardly increased since 1965, and since the mid-1970s has remained at about six out of ten of the population, the proportion taking more than one holiday has trebled (Wales Tourist Board 1991b). In 1990 it is estimated that 15 per cent of British adults took two holidays, and that 8 per cent took three or more. However, whereas in 1965 British destinations predominated for holidays, accounting for more than eight out of ten holidays by British adults, in 1990, as is well known, many Britons flew to the Mediterranean 'sun belt' for their main holiday. However, whereas in 1990 an estimated 21 per cent of British adults holidayed abroad (including the rest of Europe) with no British holiday at all, 29 per cent holidayed only in Britain, with a further 8 per cent holidaying in both Britain and abroad. As such, despite the retraction of British domestic demand for holidays within Britain, Britain still remains a major destination for much of its population. This residual market share has not occurred without large scale restructuring of the British tourism industry towards new tourism products, such as second and additional holidays, as demand for these has increased. For example, in 1989 it is estimated that 68 per cent of holiday trips to destinations within Wales were second or otherwise additional holidays (Wales Tourist Board 1991b), seven out of ten of these additional holidays being described as 'secondary' holidays. It is restructuring of demand of this kind which has driven the domestic tourism industry within Britain, and similarly in North Western European countries, to develop new attractions, or to promote places to several markets in distinctive ways. In the 1990s it should no longer be assumed that the place–customer relationship is uniform to any place (Pattinson 1990). A 'place-product' can be sold in more than one tourism market, emphasing different aspects of a place to different groups or *segments* of tourists. Even where for operational reasons a product is essentially the same for all customers, there are generally different ways to promote it to different segments and opportunities to enhance the product around the differing needs of segments (Middleton 1988). As Goodall has commented, 'Place products need to be matched to holidaymakers: formulating the place product therefore has its mirror image in market segmentation, i.e. positioning that place product to serve a particular target market' (Goodall 1990: 268). A place's historic buildings, its landscape and the culture of its inhabitants become resources for exploitation in this way.

Despite the recession of the early 1990s the British Tourist Authority (BTA) expects tourism to expand within Britain in the five year period up to 1995 (British Tourist Authority 1992). Between 1990 and 1995 the BTA expects overseas tourists to Britain to increase in number by 21 per cent, despite a decline betweeı 1990 and 1991. These estimates are based on the assumption that visits from each country to Britain will rise at about the same rate as happened in the 1980s, but modified to take into account the views of the BTA's overseas managers and others. The BTA further expects the domestic market of British residents visiting British destinations to increase by 8 per cent in the same period, but that the numbers of Britons going abroad also to increase, but by 22 per cent. If these projections materialise in reality the continued restructuring of the United Kingdom tourist industry as occurred in the 1980s can be expected.

However, it would be wrong to assume that all sectors of society equally form the demand base for tourism in Britain. Spending by United Kingdom households on hotels and holiday expenses is directly related to income (Central Statistical Office 1991). The strength of the effect is very marked. For example, in 1989 households with a weekly income of between £225 and £274, when compared to all households surveyed, on average spent the national average amount on hotels and holiday expenses. But households with weekly incomes of between £100 and £124 spent on average only a third of the national average on hotels and holidays, and those with weekly incomes of between £80 and £99 less than a tenth of the national average on these services. In contrast, those households with weekly incomes of between £550 and £624 spent on average twice the national average on hotels and holidays, and those with weekly incomes of £750 or more, four times the national average. Tourism is unambiguously an income related demand, as a self-fulfilment need other more pressing needs tend to be met first, such as food, heating and housing. Although the two decades from 1970 saw an increase overall in real disposable income per head of population in Britain of around 60 per cent, these increases have been socially divisive. Those groups most likely to spend on tourism, the better off, have been the recipients of a disproportionate share of this increased income. Since 1975, and particularly since 1977, those in Britain with weekly incomes in the top tenth of earnings have experienced much greater increases in real incomes than even those on average earings (Northcott 1991). In contrast, those in the bottom tenth of the earnings league were in 1990 in real terms no better off than fifteen years before. In the two decades beginning in 1970 in Britain, in real terms the weekly earnings of those in the top tenth of earnings almost doubled, whereas those on average earnings rose by a half, compared to the poorest whose situation remained constant. This differential was even more marked when real income was calculated after the deduction of housing costs. Social inequalities of this nature in a large part explain the continued increase in tourism demands by British residents in the 1980s: those households more likely to take holidays were those most benefited by the income changes of that decade, and before. Projections based on past expansion of demand are only appropriate, therefore, if unequal increases in real income continue to be the situation. In particular, if the British economy in the 1990s becomes more redistributive than in the past two decades, past rates of increase in domestic demand are unlikely to be sustained.

Spatial differences in tourism demand can also be of importance. Within the United Kingdom, in 1988–9 on average households in Northern Ireland spent least on hotels and holidays, and those in East Anglia and the South East of England the most. These differences were quite marked. On average, Northern Ireland households spent half the average amount spent by United Kingdom households on hotel and holiday expenses in 1988–9, whereas those in East Anglia and South East England spent nearly a third more than the national average. Other low spending areas of Britain in terms of hotel and holiday expenses were Wales, the Midlands, Scotland, Yorkshire and Humberside. The regional inequalities in tourism spending clearly mirror the more general divisions in Britain, often summarised by the term, 'North–South Divide' (Lewis and Townsend 1989).

These features of tourism demand set an overall context for the particular discussion of the role of heritage attractions in contemporary tourism within the British Isles, and more widely, its implications for European tourism more generally. However, it would be wrong to equate the potential market size, or other demand characteristics, for heritage atractions as those generally pertaining to tourism demand in Britain. As noted above, 'place-products' are sold to different markets as consumers demands may vary. Some tourists may want a beach or poolside holiday, others may want to visit cathedrals or castles, yet others may wish to walk across the uplands of Europe. For their main holiday some tourists may want a different type of holiday than for their secondary holidays. In short, the *experiences* sought by tourists differ, and in consequence, the general parameters of demand already discussed need to be refined in terms of the *types* of holiday demanded by tourists. Similarly, it is unlikely that business tourists will demand similar products to holiday-maker tourists. This differentiation of demand is an essential further analytical step in understanding demand for tourism products.

SEGMENTING THE DEMAND FOR HERITAGE PRODUCTS

In the previous section it was concluded that the overall parameters of tourism demand had to be refined, as it would be unreal to assume implicitly that all tourists want similar 'place-products'. This refinement needs to be made by reference to the motivations, preferences and behaviours of tourists, and structured not only in terms of main holidays, but, of particular importance to North West European destinations, for secondary holidays also. Our interest in the present book is with *heritage* attractions. 'Heritage' is in the literal sense something that is inherited, 'The word "heritage" means an inheritance or a legacy; things of value which have been passed from one generation to the next' (Parks Canada undated: 7). However, this is only loosely how this term has in the past fifteen years come to be used in tourism. Essentially in tourism the term 'heritage' has come to mean not only landscapes, natural history, buildings, artefacts, cultural traditions and the like which are either literally or metaphorically passed on from one generation to the other, but those among these things which can be portrayed for promotion as tourism products. For example:

Nature and cultural heritage, particularly architecture, constitute
Europe's tourist resources. Touristic (sic) interest in Europe is its
variegated landscapes, historic sites and artistic monuments. The
work undertaken to preserve this shared heritage therefore also has
a more directly economic aspect . . . the architectural heritage is
behind such international tourism and as such it is a valuable asset
which brings considerable dividends to many areas of the Community. It therefore deserves to be preserved as a source of their wealth.
                (Commission of the European Communities 1982: 8–9)

The demand for tourism products based upon the presentation of
heritage has therefore to be measured in terms of the motivations,
preferences and behaviours of tourists for visits to landscapes, natural
environments, historic houses and the like, and, in the absence of
information relating specifically to tourists, to the motivations, preferences and behaviours of the population in general from which tourists
are supplied. Strangely in view of its importance to demand analysis,
motivational and activity analysis and the like has not until recently
been at the forefront of tourism research: 'the whole area of motivation and demand has been one of the least researched areas of tourism
to date' (Pearce 1987: 21).

One aspect of demand which has received some attention concerns
the images tourists hold of destination areas. From small group
discussions, for example, with residents of English regions important
in supplying tourists to Wales, the Wales Tourist Board have
identified the following positive attitudes towards Wales as a second
or additional holiday destination: Wales is thought of as offering a
relaxed atmosphere, a sense of peace, good scope for walking and
other outdoor pursuits, a fine sense of history, beautiful beaches, and
is associated with fresh air and health (Wales Tourist Board 1985).
This heritage image, however, holds negative value for main (summer)
holidays, with the slate greyness of Wales seen as giving a sense of
coldness, the weather as wet, a lack of entertainment; boredom
remembered from holidays in Wales when children, and the lack of
affordable modern accommodation of the kind found in the
Mediterranean. The importance of heritage as an attraction for short
break holidays has also been found for domestic tourism within
Scotland (Mew Research 1990). Whereas beautiful unspoilt scenery
and peacefulness were both rated among the five most frequently given
requirements of a short break holiday in Scotland by Scottish
residents, only the scenic requirement featured among the top five
requirements for a main holiday.

As noted earlier, the disaggregation of demand should be into market *segments*, sub-classes of the market. As O'Shaughnessy has stressed, market segmentation should be into sub-classes of the market which reflect sub-classes of wants, 'The aim of market segmentation is not just to divide the market into sub-classes based on product differentiation but to distinguish want-categories that correspond to the distinct demands of various groups in the market' (O'Shaughnessy 1984: 91).

To assume that all tourists buying a particular holiday are one segment is to assume that the *benefits* gained from that holiday in terms of its uses and generated functions, such as prestige felt or demonstrated, remain the same across all the tourists purchasing that holiday. That this is unlikely implies that even at the same destinations or on the same types of holidays, motivations will potentially differ between tourists. As Frain has commented, 'An individual product is many things to many people' (Frain 1986: 129). A comparison with another leisure activity may be illustrative. The consumer of a pint of beer (or in the true heritage context, let us suppose, 'real ale') may drink that pint to quench his or her thirst, to gain peer esteem, to be with friends, to taste the hops from which it is made, or to get merry. Our consumer may combine some of these benefits or have others we have not considered. The pint of beer, therefore, may be drunk to gain any of a variety of benefits, and likewise may holidays be consumed.

What limited work has been published on segmentation in tourism would suggest the inadequacy of simply segmenting by main purpose of trip, such as holiday, business or to visit friends or relations (Kaynak and Yavas 1981). A segmentation by Vanhoe (1989) of Belgian holiday-makers across twenty-nine dimensions of benefit from holidaying is a further pioneering study in seeking to understand the clusters of demand represented by different types of holiday tourists. Seven segments of demand are identified by Vanhoe on the basis of these benefits perceived by holiday-makers. The importance of benefits in segmentation, rather than main purposes of trip, would concur with marketing theory of the 1980s which promoted the primacy of techniques of segmentation to delimit preferences and expectations, and the benefits gained from holidaying. Middleton (1988), for example, proposed a segmentation first by purpose of travel and then within these purposes by the needs of buyers and the benefits they sought, supplemented as necessary by analyses of buyer character-istics, demographics, attitudes, lifestyles or reaction to price. Mid-dleton's purposes of travel included, within the holiday market, the enjoyment of beach-type holidays in the sun, participation in active water sports, to meet people, and participation in cultural activities. The importance given by Middleton to benefits as a means of segmentation was within these broad types of motivationally defined holidays: 'Segmentation by benefits makes it possible for marketing managers to fine tune their products within the broad requirements of purpose' (Middleton 1988: 71). O'Shaughnessy, likewise, emphasised the importance of the benefits gained by consumers, benefits which included intrinsic preference, use-value and generated functions. As with Middleton's technique, other categorisations were to supplement understanding of benefits, 'Once we have categorised those in the market on the basis of the benefits they seek, they can be identified by what they *are* and/or *do*' (O'Shaughnessy 1984: 93). Benefit segmentation of this kind is not, however, without its problems. The benefits sought by consumers are not easily identified, particularly as a market matures. In the latter case, the major use-functions and generated-functions of holidaying may be taken for granted and minor benefits become the basis of preference. These may be legion. However, at present the problem is largely one of insufficient applications of benefit segmentation to tourism, and, particularly, to heritage tourism.

Both Pearce (1987) and Kent (1990) have divided influences on holiday choice into 'push' factors and 'pull' factors, a division paralleled in traditional migration theory. In his summary of the past literature on tourism motivation Pearce interprets 'wanderlust' as a push factor, the need to escape from boredom, and 'sunlust' as a pull factor. The latter implicitly ignores other attractions of a destination area, and is not particularly appropriate to heritage tourism unless it is to be assumed that all motivation is of the 'push' variety. Pearce's summary of push factors of the 'wanderlust' kind includes travel to seek different cultures, institutions or cuisine, and that travel should be an important ingredient throughout the visit. Other push factors summarised include escape from a perceived mundane environment, exploration and evaluation of oneself, relaxation, prestige, less constrained behaviour, enhancement of kinship relationships and social interaction. Kent's push factors likewise include the motivations of tourists, but his 'pull' factors are the images held by potential tourists both of places and of types of holidays. In this way Kent expands imagery away from 'sunlust' alone. Pearce also summarises work by Plog on the psychographic positions of selected tourism destinations for North American tourists. This divided tourists into 'psychocentrics' and 'allocentrics', the former liking commonplace and familiar atmospheres, with sun and fun opportunities, the latter preferring 'non-touristy' areas, seeking a sense of discovery and wanting to meet people of a foreign culture. The latter would presumably include heritage tourists, but again such a division has limitations for it implies that psychocentrics (or 'sunlust' tourists to use the other terminology) do not represent a market for heritage attractions, with visits as one part of their holiday, rather than as the dominant aspect. However, the importance of such studies to an understanding of heritage tourism is to suggest that at least some heritage tourists are seeking different experiences, or to use the segmentation terminology, benefits, to other types of tourist. For example, some tourists may go to beaches to relax in the sun, others may go to admire the beauty of sandscapes or be inspired by the power of the waves breaking against rocks. This would in turn imply that heritage tourism needs to be defined as a *means* of consumption and not solely by the types of products consumed.

Attitudinal analysis of tourists is one means of investigating the means of heritage consumption. A pioneering study by Solomon and George (1977) into the attitudinal profile of the 'American Bicentennial Traveler' is worthy of particular note. Its limitation for the present purpose is that this study divided tourists into only two groups, what today would be termed heritage enthusiasts and non-enthusiasts, but termed by Solomon and George as historians and non-historians. Solomon and George divided the two groups in terms of their aggregated responses to six opinion statements, measured on six point scales. The statements were:

- visiting historical locations is an important consideration in planning my vacation;
- on vacation, I rarely pass up an opportunity to make a side trip to a historical location;
- I enjoy travelling to a historical location on my vacation;
- a vacation to a historical location is more satisfying to me than other types of trips;
- Virginia's (the state surveyed in) history is very exciting;
- history is Virginia's greatest attraction.

Fifty other opinion statements were used to elicit any differences in attitudes between heritage enthusiasts among the tourists and non-enthusiasts. The differences found by Solomon and George between the two groups of tourists largely related to their educational orientation. The heritage enthusiasts were significantly more likely than the non-enthusiasts to want to use their holiday to learn about local customs and culture, to increase their personal knowledge of places, to put fun second to learning when on holiday, to seek to get to know people, and to find educational holidays most fun and rewarding. This study would imply that at least among the less casual heritage tourist, or tourist visitor to a heritage site, unambiguous motivational differences pertain when compared to tourists generally. Equally, these findings cannot be interpreted as implying that all tourists fit neatly into two classes: the analysis only identified tendencies in educational orientation between the two groups of tourists. It should also be remembered that this was only a single study and it may or may not be possible to generalise. However, it offers clear pointers to motivation which will be developed in later chapters of this book.

A wider debate on the uses of history and the relationship of people to the past is also of relevance here. Stonehenge has been characterised as a monument to *our* age as well as to its builders (Chippindale 1990), with debates and disputes over who can use the site and for what purposes having resulted in scenes of violence (Fowler 1990a). As to many people a conscious, if ill-defined, awareness of the past is part of their intellectual environment, the past is not merely something which *has* happened, but a contemporary phenomenon (Fowler 1981). Of itself the past is unimportant, 'it is the presence of the past and our attitude to it that matters' (Laenen 1989: 94). The contemporary importance of the past can be described as a sense of the past equivalent to, and interacting with, a sense of place. In this sense the ethnography of locality (Cohen 1982), that is, how people experience and express their difference from others in terms of place, and how their sense of difference becomes incorporated into their social organisation, may properly be given a temporal dimension too. As such, preservation of artefacts of the past and the appreciation of heritage depends on some feeling that earlier epochs in one's own culture and those of others have something to offer the present (Hunter 1981), however confused and uncritical this feeling might be to most people. At the individual's level, whereas authenticity may derive from an object being conserved, heritage derives from its user (Ashworth and Tunbridge 1990). Such prevalent awareness of the past would further suggest that heritage tourism motivations may well be compared on a continuum from enthusiast for authenticity through to the tourist actively dismissive of heritage.

In terms of socio-demographic segmentations certain groups of consumers may be identified as more likely to require heritage products. For Scottish domestic tourism, for example, households aged over thirty-five years but without children have been identified through their expressed holiday requirements as a disproportionate market for heritage-based main summer holidays, especially the over forty-fives as disproportionately demanding beautiful, unspoilt scenery and historic castles and houses, and the over fifty-fives as disproportionately demanding peace and beautiful gardens (Mew Research 1990). Socio-economically, these demands were greatest among non-manual households, and skilled manual households without children.

DEFINING DEMAND BY BEHAVIOUR

In the absence of a substantial literature on motivations demand has to be defined in terms of behaviour. The number of visits recorded at historic buildings, gardens and museums and galleries in the United Kingdom in 1990 gives some indication of the scale of demand for heritage. Visitor figures do not distinguish between tourist and leisure visitors, and as such it would be wrong to equate visitor figures with tourist demand alone. However, in 1990 some fifty-seven historic buildings in the United Kingdom were each visited by in excess of 200,000 visitors, and likewise thirteen gardens and sixty-three museums and galleries (English Tourist Board *et al.* 1991a). Within Scotland, fifteen out of the twenty most visited attractions in 1989 where admission had to be paid for could be described as heritage attractions, including six castles (Scottish Tourist Board 1990a). In Wales, in 1990 eight castles were visited by upwards of 100,000 visitors, and similarly eleven museums, art galleries, industrial and craft attractions recorded like numbers of visitors (Wales Tourist Board 1991c). The fifty historic properties, including castles, for which the Wales Tourist Board collated visitor numbers for 1990 were visited by 2.3 million visitors; the eighty-five museums, art galleries, industrial and craft attractions, by 4.1 million visitors.

Although such figures give some indication of the scale of demand for heritage within the United Kingdom, they give no indication of the proportion of tourists expressing their desire to visit sites of the kind described. Some indication of background demand can be gained from surveys of people's participation in types of activities. For example, for 1986 it was estimated that on average each adult in Great Britain was involved in walking (including rambling and hiking) over two miles as an outdoor activity on twenty days of the year, visiting historic buildings or like sites on 3.7 days and visiting museums and art galleries on 0.8 days (Office of Population Censuses and Surveys 1989). Expressed in terms of the average participation rate in these activities over the year, 19 per cent of the adult population had walked over two miles as a form of outdoor activity in the previous four weeks, 9 per cent had visited historic buildings and 4 per cent had visited museums and galleries. Both walking and visits to historic sites, museums and galleries showed quite marked differences by social class. Non-manual adults were more likely to have engaged in these activities than manuals, and in particular, professionals were notably more likely to have been involved in all these activities than other groups. For example, 18 per cent of professionals were found to have visited a historic building in the four weeks prior to being interviewed, compared to about one in eight other non-manuals and under one in fourteen manuals. For museum and gallery visiting the differences recorded were even greater, with professionals being nearly twice as likely to have visited a museum or art gallery in the preceding four weeks than were other non-manuals, and four times as likely than were manual respondents. A similar social class gradient may be identified for days out in general, with, at the extremes, 72 per cent of professionals and managers in Scotland in an average month having had a day out, but only 41 per cent of those from unskilled manual worker households (Scottish Tourist Board 1991a). The Sports Council for Wales has provided similar evidence to that for Britain generally for long distance walking. For Wales it is estimated that approximately a third of non-manual adults annually make a leisure walk of two miles or more, compared to a quarter of non-manual adults (Sports Council for Wales 1989). Whereas not all of these walks may be supposed to have been taken in treasured townscapes or landscapes, many will have been. Evidence from the Countryside Commission further confirms the predominance of this more informal countryside activity over visits to specific historic sites. In 1990, whereas 14 per cent of countryside recreational trips in England were estimated to have been walks of over two miles, 6 per cent were estimated to have been made to historic buildings (Countryside Commission 1991a). These figures confirm earlier estimates for 1984 (Countryside Commission 1989). Likewise, in an average month the Scottish Tourist Board estimate that whereas 17 per cent of day trips taken in Scotland involve driving for sightseeing, and 12 per cent long walks or hikes, only 6 per cent involve a visit to a stately home and only 5 per cent a visit to a museum (Scottish Tourist Board 1991a). Even if only half of these drives or walks have been made in townscapes or landscapes treasured by the participants, to equate demand for heritage with recorded visits to historic buildings, museums and the like would result in a substantial under-estimation of expressed demands for heritage experiences in Britain. In short, despite their impressive volume, recorded visitor totals at heritage sites are insufficient indicators of background demand for heritage consumption.

The Countryside Commission has developed the following segmentation of the market for countryside heritage. *Frequent visitors*, who constitute a quarter of the English population, *occasional visitors*, who constitute half of the population, and people who visit *rarely or not at all*, the remaining quarter of the population (Countryside Commission 1989). The frequent visitors are characterised as often being well off, living in or near the countryside, and members of countryside related organisations such as the National Trust or the Royal Society for the Protection of Birds. The occasional visitors are characterised as non-manuals or skilled manuals, living up to three miles from the countryside, having young children and a car. Those persons rarely visiting the countryside, or not visiting it at all, are characterised as the elderly, persons on low incomes, the unemployed and ethnic minorities. These people tend to live several miles from the countryside, in poor housing, and are dependent on public transport. Once again, it should be noted that this segmentation is a general description of countryside users: some individuals will not fit well into the segments. However, the categorisation provides a useful if broad perspective, integrating as it does several characteristics into three segments.

So far our discussion has dealt with visitors, including both tourist and day trip visitors, or persons involved in activities, whether on holiday or from home. These background attributes of demand can in some cases be made more specific to tourists. The parameters of tourists' demand for heritage consumption can be impressive. For example, in the decade 1973–82, four out of ten Swiss adults are estimated to have made at least one holiday involving circular tours or 'discovery trips', just under a quarter had taken a holiday in this period to visit a city, one in eight to visit the countryside other than mountains, and one in ten for cultural or study purposes (Schmidhauser 1989). Similarly, for 1990 alone it is estimated that 7 per cent of holiday trips in the United Kingdom involved as their *main* purpose hiking, hill walking, rambling or orienteering, that 4 per cent of trips involved as their main purpose a visit to a castle, monument or church and like heritage site, and that 2 per cent of trips included as their main purpose visits to museums, galleries and heritage centres (English Tourist Board *et al.* 1991b). Such figures imply substantial reductions in the expressed demand by tourists for heritage when compared to the total volume of United Kingdom tourism. However, the importance of these activities and attractions as main purposes of holidays is set in a more favourable context when it is realised that over three quarters of tourism trips involved no particular activity at all as the main purpose of the holiday: hill walking and like walks were in fact the most frequently reported activities as main purposes of holidays, nearly twice as important as swimming, for example. Visits to heritage sites as attractions were particularly important as activities undertaken as the main purposes of holiday trips in Scotland and Northern Ireland in 1990. However, a division into short holidays (one to three nights away) and long holidays (over three nights away) to some extent counters the motivational evidence reviewed above. Although hiking and like walks, for example, were three times more popular among short stayers than long stayers in Northern Ireland as the main purpose of the holiday, in Scotland such activities were more frequently cited by long stayers as the main purpose of their holiday. Visits to heritage sites were four times more likely to be cited as the main purpose of their holiday by long stayers than short stayers in Northern Ireland, and similarly twice as likely to be cited by long stayers than short stayers in Scotland. The earlier motivational discussion, and, indeed, much professional comment in the tourism industry, might have led us to expect the opposite to be the case: namely, that heritage activities were more likely to be features of secondary, often short break, holidays. Such an inference would also concur with the social profile of United Kingdom short break holiday-makers in 1990, 32 per cent of whom were from professional and managerial households, compared to a quarter of holiday-makers staying away from home for four nights or more.

If all activities pursued on holiday, whether the main purpose of the holiday or not, are considered, the extent of expressed demand for heritage experiences increases. However, half of United Kingdom holiday trips in 1990 are estimated to have involved no particular activity at all (English Tourist Board *et al.* 1991b). Of all holiday trips, 17 per cent were estimated to involve hiking or like walking, 14 per cent visits to heritage sites and 7 per cent visits to museums and galleries. Although along with swimming and hiking, visits to heritage sites were the most frequently reported activities, these rates of expressed preference substantially reduce the expressed demand for heritage experiences that could be assumed from aggregate tourism volumes. Equally, it is unknown how many tourists undertaking no specific activities in fact engaged in some sightseeing, if only from their cars and thus experienced landscape heritage in a manner unrecorded by the English Tourist Board's survey. With the exception of Northern Ireland long stay holiday-makers were more likely than their short stay counterparts to go hiking or engage in like walking activities when on holiday. Likewise, visits to heritage sites and to museums were generally twice as likely to be reported by long stayers than short stayers (English Tourist Board *et al.* 1991b; Scottish Tourist Board 1992). Again this is contrary to what the motivational analysis would have led us to expect. The explanation may lie this time in the fact that on longer holidays tourists principally interested in other benefits from their holiday, such as relaxing on a beach or eating and drinking with friends, supplement these main demands by some heritage activity, if only of a casual or general interest nature. However, this explanation cannot apply to the previous case of main holiday purpose, and so it would seem over-hasty to assume its sole pertinence in this case. It may be that a heritage environment is a necessary backcloth to short break holidays for some tourists who intend no further expression of their demand for a heritage experience, in particular, having little or no intention of visiting specific heritage sites.

Further survey evidence may be had from Wales. This enables a comparison between the activities undertaken by British tourists holiday-making in Wales, and their overseas counterparts. The database was collected for summer tourists only. However, it must be noted that as the survey aggregated intentions to visit (as planned visits) and actual visits made, the frequencies reported are greater than those of the United Kingdom survey of 1990 already reported, for it is unlikely that all plans were kept and all visits actually made. However, the findings are important in indicating the differences in *preferences* for attractions and activities by British and overseas tourists. For example, whereas 47 per cent of British holiday-makers to Wales said that they had visited or planned to visit a castle, 78 per cent of their overseas counterparts holidaying in Wales said likewise (Survey Research Associates 1988). Whereas 15 per cent of domestic holiday makers said that they had visited or planned to visit a museum or art gallery, 29 per cent of overseas tourists gave such an attraction as visited or planned to visit. Similar differences were recorded for stately homes, 15 per cent compared to 33 per cent; Roman sites, 6 per cent compared to 25 per cent; cathedrals, churches and chapels, 13 per cent compared to 30 per cent; and ruined abbeys and monasteries, 9 per cent compared to 29 per cent. These differences were all recorded in the same direction: namely that heritage experiences were more popular among overseas tourists to Wales than among British tourists. However, steam railways formed an exception, with slightly more domestic tourists either having visited a tourist railway or planning to do so than had overseas tourists. This may in some part result from demands of children among the families of British tourists to Wales, Wales being a family holiday destination for domestic tourists in the summer. This exception apart, in Wales at least, overseas tourists are disproportionately attracted for the heritage experiences of specific attractions their holiday can bring.

The attractiveness of specific sites as heritage experiences for overseas tourists to Wales is not however mirrored in scenic heritage demands. Although overseas tourists were nearly as likely as British tourists to report hill walking as a holiday activity planned or undertaken, rambling was less frequently reported (Survey Research Associates 1988). Similarly, overseas tourists were less likely than British tourists to Wales to rate scenery or peacefulness as the best parts of their visit to Wales. This would suggest some differences in how overseas and domestic tourists interpret the heritage of a country. How far this is a more general characteristic of tourism demands than for Wales alone is in itself worthy of research. Its more general applicability would seem plausible from the honeypots of demand for heritage tourism represented by the cathedrals and like built sites of Europe.

Further evidence from Wales may be found in surveys of tourists to areas of high landscape quality, although, clearly, such studies cannot be generalised to tourists visiting other areas. More than eight out of ten tourists interviewed in the Vale of Usk and Wye Valley in 1986, for example, were found either to have taken part in long walks or hill walking on their holiday, or intended to do so (Monmouth District Council 1987). The area's scenery gained the highest rating of the facilities and services rated, 47 per cent of tourists rating the scenery as excellent. In terms of visits made on the holiday, the five most frequently named sites by staying visitors were all built heritage sites, namely, Chepstow Castle, Tintern Abbey, Llanthony Priory, Caerleon Roman Sites, and Raglan Castle. Studies of this kind serve to emphasise that in some areas heritage experiences are the dominant demand made by tourists and, in consequence, general estimates of demand for heritage experiences by tourists may be hopelessly inadequate as estimates of local demand. As such, heritage demand needs to be *spatially* disaggregated, and related to the *places* which attract tourists.

OTHER CONSUMPTION OF HERITAGE

A feature of heritage consumption is that as its benefits are experiences and feelings, 'consumption' may be divorced in spatial terms from the heritage place itself. For example, conservationists may be concerned about environmental degradation in places which they have never visited or which, although visited, are distant from where they now reside. The demands of conservationalists, in extending beyond their immediate areas, are increasingly for representation in the management of areas of which they are not a geographical constituency (Kaye 1990). Demands of this kind add an additional consumption to the estimation of demand for heritage experiences than is indicated by visitor figures at sites or participation in activities.

Likewise, retailing, office and residential demands for heritage environments in urban areas are a similar additional aspect of demand. Indeed, urban refurbishment of vernacular architecture and townscape has in many instances been led by commercial and residential demand, to which tourism demand has followed (Gordon 1985; Clark 1988; Ashworth 1990), an alternative sequence of development to one of commercially-led heritage as a tourism initiated demand. At the height of the development 'boom' of the late 1980s in Britain, planning authorities in Britain sought to extract 'planning gains' from developers in the form of cultural facilities and the like; these facilities were seen also by developers as a means of attracting extra customers to prestige office and residential developments. Waterfront revitalisation in the 1980s in both Europe and North America was a case in point. In such developments leisure shopping in a quaint or otherwise heritage environment, including feigned vernaculars, has provided the opportunity for tourism development as one form of commercial development, but not always the lead sector. Halifax, Nova Scotia, provides a case in point with refurbished buildings converted to shopping malls, such as the 'Historic Properties', inter-mixed with modern office developments, and inter-spaced with museums, mooring spaces, restaurants and the like. Developments of this type offer leisure shopping (Jansen-Verbeke 1990) as one 'product' to tourists, residents and office workers alike. Tunbridge aptly describes such retailing, 'Retail and service uses are chiefly of the "festival market" type, which is explicitly recreation-orientated. The leisure atmosphere is typically enhanced by period festivals and special events' (Tunbridge 1988: 69).

Further emphasing the commercial stimulus to the refurbishment of built heritage are the demands of small businesses to facilitate competition with modern shopping malls and retail parks. The *Mainstreet* and *Village Square* street refurbishment programmes of Atlantic Canada are a case in point, having unambiguous commercial underpinnings to revitalise the commercial centres of settlements

(Nova Scotian Department of Small Business Development 1989a; 1989b). However, in some European cities policies of conservation of buildings pre-date such commercial considerations, and comme cialisation may be in some cases a *post hoc* justification of an already existing policy, as planners face a growing stock of protected buildings which need purposeful use (Ashworth and Tunbridge 1990). In such cases, commercial demands are secondary to a wider environmental demand for conservation expressed through the political and land-use planning systems of local government.

The importance of consumption of heritage away from the actual heritage place, our first example of additional demand noted in the previous paragraph, has been researched in Britain in terms of support for countryside policies. In particular, throughout the 1980s public support for policies of greater public intervention in agriculture generally increased, but with greatest support for the greater regulation of farming activities coming disproportionately from persons with higher educational qualifications (Young 1990). Perceptions of change in the countryside were found to be greatest among persons living there, and, second, among the residents of country towns and villages (Young 1988). However, the *use* made of the countryside by people was found to have done little to raise consciousness of change. *Concern* for the countryside was also found to be divorced from *caring* for it:

> Concern for the countryside – which may be rather arms length – is not the same as *caring* for the countryside, a feeling derived from personal enjoyment. . . . Overwhelmingly then, our respondents claim to care about the countryside, although about a quarter do not themselves get much or any pleasure from it.
>
> (Young 1987: 155–6)

For many people, perceptions of unwelcomed changes were not translated into political priorities, an immediate manner of expressing such demands:

> In general, it would be a mistake to overemphasise the political significance of the growing awareness that something unwelcome is happening in the countryside. Despite the shifts in people's perceptions of change, and in the levels of concern about it, the issue does not emerge as a highly political one.
>
> (Young 1988: 160)

and

As yet, then, the countryside is not seen by the overwhelming majority of the population as a cause for which they would actively crusade. Concern is relatively passive and seems likely to remain so for all but a minority of people who are already activists . . . who are typically highly educated and in non-manual occupations.

(Young 1987: 157)

The low priority of such demands for most people was clearly reflected in the 1992 General Election campaign in Britain, in which economic issues predominated.

These surveys of countryside demands provide some direct evidence on how tourism, and recreation generally, are perceived in Britain as mechanisms of countryside change. Increases in the number of tourists and trippers visiting the countryside are generally perceived as changes for the better, not for worse (Young 1986). Strong objection among the British public has been found to the idea of stopping too many people from visiting the countryside (Young 1988). Increasingly, the British countryside has been perceived as a popular resource for mass leisure by the British population, changing notions of the private use of the countryside frequently assumed:

Greater opportunities to visit the countryside were also welcomed, even to the extent that these opportunities were used by other people. This suggests a popular perception of the countryside as essential for mass leisure activity, in which solitude figures less prominently than in earlier romantic notions of rurality.

(Young 1986: 63–4)

These perceptions of the countryside would concur with the behavioural evidence of demand already discussed, and principally that of walking.

These additional heritage demands to those evidenced by visitor numbers at heritage sites set a wider context of political economy within which tourism demands should be considered. That these additional demands are less easily estimated does not mean that they are less relevant or important to our understanding of demand for heritage experiences.

CONCLUSIONS

In this chapter demands for heritage have been defined as demands for heritage *experiences* which generate *benefits* that tourists and others enjoy. It would be foolish to equate heritage demand by tourists with the volume of tourism within an economy for clearly other forms of tourist activity also exist. However, the likely extent of heritage tourism demand within the aggregate total volume of tourism is less easy to estimate. Reference to visitor totals at sites not only include all visitors, not only tourists, they also neither include all sites nor all heritage activities. Walking in treasured landscape is an obvious heritage experience unenumerated by visitor counts at specific sites. But more generally, if a population sees its countryside as an asset for recreation, many leisure experiences will have some heritage content.

Can a heritage tourist be defined in terms of motivations or behaviour? This is an issue to which we will return in subsequent chapters of this book. However, for the present, the few segmentation analyses which have been undertaken into types of heritage tourists have tended to seek to divide heritage 'enthusiasts' from other tourists, the latter frequently assumed to be beach tourists. Such an approach ignores the wider demand for heritage experiences shown by sightseeing and concern for heritage issues among the wider population, and the tourists produced by that population. In seeking to define the characteristics of a heritage tourist a diversity of interests and enthusiasms may need to be allowed for, a theme also returned to later in this book. It is perhaps more appropriate to consider *all* tourists visiting heritage attractions or otherwise consuming heritage as 'heritage tourists', but of differing motivations and varying interests. It is the latter definition which will be adopted in the following chapters of this book unless otherwise qualified in the discussion.

2 The heterogeneity of the heritage product

THE HETEROGENEITY OF HERITAGE

'Heritage' was a term which came to the fore in the 1970s in Europe, and throughout the 1980s expanded increasingly to encompass other aspects and to be used increasingly for commercial purposes. If a benchmark for the start of heritage consumption as a popular demand is desired, however imperfect this benchmark might be, European Architectural Heritage Year of 1975 is probably the best claimant for this, for not only was building conservation promoted, 'heritage centres' were frequently founded on the North American model to 'tell the story' of a historic town (Dower 1978). However, popular demands for access to upland landscape in Britain predate 1975 by four decades or more. Likewise, the Isle of Man was promoting its wooded glens as popular tourist attractions in the late Victorian era (Prentice 1990a & b), and so our benchmark may itself need to vary to reflect the heterogeneity of heritage as popularly defined. However, as a demand of the richer sections of society, heritage consumption has a much longer antecedence. In the late eighteenth and early years of the nineteenth century, the artist, J.M.W. Turner toured landscapes to gain inspiration for his paintings (Irwin *et al.* 1982; Wilton 1984). The English town of Tewkesbury was trading as a tourist centre, for example, in the late nineteenth century on its links with historical events and persons, and its timber framed burgage houses (Jones 1987), relying in part on its important associations with Shakespeare's play, Richard III. Likewise, nineteenth-century novelists frequently used heritage imagery in their writings. The following comment by Brasnett on Thomas Hardy's use of Stonehenge is apposite in illustrating this tradition:

> By choosing Wessex's most remarkable temple as the scene for his heroine's dawn arrest Hardy was being more than merely dramatic, for the parallel between the innocent Tess's fate and that of a

selected victim slaughtered to the sun god is hard to overlook. For her final hours of freedom with the man she loved and who had failed her, the author set Tess against the prehistoric background of ritualistic sacrifice; a hapless victim of society.

(Brasnett 1990: 52).

In this way, Hardy was appealing to the imagery held by the late Victorian middle class about the past function of Stonehenge, and linking heritage with his commentary on then contemporary life. Use of heritage imagery in novels of this kind may be thought of as an early form of 'tourism without travel', akin to the travel books and diaries popular in the same era to British middle-class readers, the latter dealing with the newly found heritage of distant countries, the novels of Hardy and like authors with a distant heritage from past Britain.

In so much as heritage consumption is an appreciation of aspects of the past, the expansion of heritage consumption in the 1980s might be interpreted as an indication of enhanced nostalgia, that is, a 'home-sickness' for aspects of the past seen as convivial, reassuring and permanent. Such interpretations have been made:

> Dissatisfaction with the present and malaise about the future induce many to look back with nostalgia, to equate what is beautiful and livable with what is old or past.
>
> (Lowenthal 1981: 216)

and

> Nostalgia is profoundly conservative. Conservatism, with its emphasis on order and tradition, relies heavily on appeals to the authority of the past.
>
> (Hewison 1987: 47)

If such interpretations are correct, the increased heterogeneity of heritage in the 1980s is explicable by a widespread demand to recreate feelings for things past across almost all dimensions of human experience in the European communities and their former dominions and colonies throughout the world.

The extent of the physical manifestation of a nation's heritage in its current landscape may be seen from Ireland. In the mid-1980s more than one-sixth of the land area of the Republic of Ireland was designated as areas of outstanding landscape, and in one county, Wicklow, half its land area (An Foras Forbartha 1985). The country was thought to have some 200,000 known archaeological sites and monuments, of which around three-quarters were only recorded on maps but not otherwise identified. An Foras Forbartha, at that time, estimated considerable destruction to have taken place to field sites of this kind, particularly to ring-forts and medieval moated sites. During the decade 1970 to 1980, the number of monuments given state protection in Ireland all but doubled, to 2,055 sites, with substantial increases in listing and preservation orders, but little increase in direct management through ownership or guardianship. As well as archaeological sites and monuments, Ireland at the time had around 60,000 buildings thought to be of architectural or historic interest, one in ten of which were considered to be of national or international significance. These buildings were considered to 'make a major contribution to the visual appearance' (An Foras Forbartha 1985: 79) of Irish country towns and the countryside. The state of these buildings was, however, unknown. As well as these heritage aspects of the Irish physical environment, in 1985 Ireland had over a thousand designated areas of scientific interest, small areas of land totalling 3 per cent of the country's land area, of botanical, zoological, ornithological or geological value. Many were thought to be damaged or threatened with damage by 'development'. Eighty of these one thousand sites were considered to be of international importance. Of larger scale, Ireland had four national parks, those of Killarney, Glenveagh, Connemara and Burren. It had also an extensive but largely unenumerated wildlife heritage. This 1985 audit of the Irish national heritage of physical environment was produced as part of a wider physical environmental audit, and, as such, did not attempt an audit of the nation's cultural heritage.

Figures for England are equally as impressive. In 1990 there were 12,550 scheduled ancient monuments in England, 437,040 listed buildings and 7,157 conservation areas (English Tourist Board 1991). At least 946 town trails with an architectural or general theme were also known to the English Tourist Board, as well as 8,054 hotels, guest houses, bed and breakfast premises, farmhouses offering accommodation, and inns claiming a particular historic, literary or architectural importance. Added to this, approximately 8,500 Anglican churches date from pre-Reformation times.

A recognition of the heterogeneity of national heritage under threat from the modern economy prompted the definition of dimensions of a national heritage inventory for Ireland more than two decades ago. This inventory separated what was termed 'scientific' heritage from 'historic and artistic' heritage, the former including plants, birds, animals, rocks and national habitats, the latter fixed physical relics, ranging from holy wells to modern churches, and from hill forts to modern towns (An Foras Forbartha 1969). The aspects of scientific heritage thought to be of significance were differentiated largely by habitat rather than by species, and included: first, terrestrial habitats of woodland, scrub, grassland, heath and moor; second, freshwater habitats of ponds, lakes, rivers, callows, turloughs, marshes, fens and bog; third, marine habitats; and fourth, sites of geological interest. Ireland's historic and artistic heritage was differentiated largely by age and type, to include, prehistoric and early Christian sites, medieval sites, and recent civil, military, industrial and 'traditional' sites, the latter sub-group including house clusters, villages, workshops, piers, farm gates and the like. These heritage forms were considered to be of recreational, educational, research and tourist importance. The inventory avoided landscape as a class of heritage, largely because of the subjectivity involved in its evaluation. This omission was corrected in 1977 with the differentiation of outstanding landscapes into those of high terrestrial relief, of low terrestrial relief, lakes, rivers, high marine relief, low marine relief and islands (An Foras Forbartha 1985). With the addition of cultural heritage, such as language, customs, and performing, folk and fine arts, these dimensions of heritage form the heterogeneous core of what until recently was commonly thought of as 'heritage' by tourist and other agencies alike. The four main dimensions being natural ('scientific' in the Irish inventory), built ('historic and artistic' in the Irish inventory), cultural and landscape heritage. Similar inventories of heritage have been proposed elsewhere, in the case of natural heritage, for example, in Nova Scotia around which policy guidelines have been drawn (Nova Scotian Department of Lands and Forests 1987; 1988).

It should also be noted that what might be termed an 'official' heritage of state monuments increasingly expanded into 'popular' culture, which, again taking an Atlantic Canada example, may include folk art and domestic architectural styles, of which fifteen colonial house styles have been identified in Nova Scotia alone (Nova Scotian Department of Culture, Recreation and Fitness published sometime in the 1980s, exact date unknown; Art Gallery of Nova Scotia 1989). Similarly, on the other side of the North Atlantic rim, in Scotland the National Trust for Scotland's *Little Houses* projects have sought to conserve the vernacular domestic architecture of the burghs of the country (National Trust for Scotland c.1985; Mair 1988): an architectural tradition of pantile roofs, dormer windows, crowsteps on gables, corbels, forestairs, harling and chambered corners (Fraser 1982). From the nineteenth century, the painted tiled closes of Glasgow tenements are similarly part of a popular heritage (Russell

1992). Even Scottish graveyards can be counted among this lore (Willsher 1985). In the Irish case, the distinctive Carrickmacross embroidered net lace, for example, is as much part of popular heritage as the country's distinctive round towers (Barrow 1979; O'Cleirigh 1985). This is not to say that all popular heritage is so well promoted: folklore is a particular example. Few tourists visiting Wales or the Isle of Man, for example, are likely to be made aware of the folklore of fairies which predominates in traditional Celtic cultures (Moore 1971; Simpson 1976). At most, on the Isle of Man, coach parties may be invited to say 'hello' to the fairies as they speed over Fairy Bridge en route to Castletown from Douglas. In effect, some popular heritage remains forbidden and unpromoted.

From such core dimensions, 'heritage' expanded in usage by the mid-1980s and today has become a term to represent an even greater heterogeneity of things for a similar diversity of motives. In Great Britain, as an unusual example of motivation, the remaining 30 year old diesel multiple units of British Rail are now frequently referred to in the press as 'heritage units', as a form of derogation. Such motivation is quite unusual in the use of the term or what may be considered, the *heritage technique*: more common is its use in enhancement. Usage can range from the more established preservationist or inspirational, to the more recent, commercial. In England, state monuments are promoted by *English Heritage*, which from its inception has had a changed role to that of the Department of Environment before, 'The passive role of guardianship was to be cast aside in favour of the active promotion of heritage properties and their preservation' (Eastaugh and Weiss 1989: 60).

The owners of thirteen castles, historic houses and gardens in the Scottish Borders now promote themselves collectively as *Scotland's Border Heritage*. Similarly, the National Trust for Scotland titles its magazine, *Heritage Scotland*: the editorial of the Spring 1992 issue well illustrated the heritage technique, with a discussion of the *current* planning debate over the proposed bridge from mainland Scotland to the Isle of Skye including reference to Dr Johnson's and James Boswell's visit in the *eighteenth century*, and the route taken by these historic notables being determined by 'the prospect of a good meal'. Inspirational uses can be illustrated by the Northern English landscape guidebooks of A. Wainwright who enhanced what anyway would have been invaluable walking guides, with three dimensional plans of fellsides, into kindly art forms of personal insights and comments in the forms of both drawings and words. The strong, but detailed, three dimensional pen and ink images of such guidebooks were recognised in 1983 with the publication of a composite sketchbook, *Wainwright in Lakeland* (Abbot Hall 1985). In 1986 Ulster Television produced a series of programmes setting out the lore of Ulster buildings, entitled *A Heritage from Stone*, seeking to promote public interest in building and townscape conservation (Boyd 1986).

Commonly, heritage has increasingly had commercial employments. In advertising and sales promotion an area's heritage is used to enhance the consumer's image of a product through association. For example, in 1988 it was proposed that tourist information centres within Wales should be retitled as 'Welcome Centres', and to redevelop them as 'cultural gateways' to Wales (European Centre for Traditional and Regional Cultures 1988). In the Netherlands, historic buildings, monuments, historic town trails and walks have been shown to feature prominently in the promotional image of destinations (Ashworth and Voogd 1990a). Such heritage associations are frequently developed through revived links with an area's past, particularly with a historic person. Ashworth and Tunbridge (1990: 26) have spoken of the 'hijacking of literature by places' to gain themes. Examples are legion. The English district of Huntingdonshire has sought to promote itself as a tourist destination in terms of Oliver Cromwell's birthplace. The following is taken from a handbill produced by Huntingdonshire District Council in 1987:

> Oliver Cromwell, Lord Protector of the Commonwealth, was born in Huntingdon on 25th April 1599. He lived in Huntingdon until 1631 and then in St. Ives until 1636. So the 'most powerful man in England' was truly a son of Huntingdonshire. The relics of that period have not entirely vanished, important buildings, articles and records can still be seen to recall the world of Oliver Cromwell. In Huntingdonshire you can discover the issues and environment that influenced Oliver Cromwell and so shaped the destiny of Britain.
>
> Huntingdonshire is Cromwell Country. Come and explore the trail of treasures that await you in friendly market towns, attractive villages and down quiet country lanes. Look for the sign of the Cromwellian Helmet on your trail and call in at the Tourist Information Centre for your Cromwell Country Booklet and other information about staying and enjoying Cromwell Country.

The neighbouring district of Ely is similarly promoted to tourists as 'Hereward Country', after the English leader who challenged the Norman Conquest. As the fens of Ely have markedly changed since the eleventh century, not least by their drainage, this might be thought a difficult heritage to promote. Not so, as the following quotation from a Fenland District Council promotional booklet, *Around Hereward Country*, (1987) shows, further well illustrating the heritage technique:

Hereward the Wake, a legendary hero. The last of the Saxon leaders to hold out against the Norman invaders. The seat of his resistance was the Isle of Ely and the surrounding Fenlands, an area of mystery and alien beauty. Protected by the treacherous and uncharted marshes, Hereward opposed William the Conqueror's oppressive reign until betrayal by the monks of Ely lead to his flight and obscure death.

No other area of rural Britain can have changed so much as the Fens in the 900 years since Hereward. What he would have recognised as fen and marsh for fishing and fowling has been transformed by massive drainage programmes to form some of the most fertile farmland in Britain. Using Dutch experience and ingenuity and generally against the wishes of the natives, the Fens have been drained. Waters pumped by wind and steam, dykes and drains carved through the landscape and the sea and flood waters held at bay all serve to create a land in contrast to 'the typical English landscape'.

Despite these changes many of the places Hereward would have known can still be identified.

The leaflet then listed these places, including Peterborough, Ely, Bourne, Upwell, Ramsey, Crowland and Thorney. While these cities and towns may still be 'identified' their Saxon character cannot be. Indeed, such has been the landscape transformation of the fenland, they could more appropriately be promoted as 'Vermuyden Country', after the seventeenth-century engineer responsible for their initial drainage. However, this would ascribe a Dutch rather than English heritage to this area of England.

Anniversaries of historic events can equally be included in the heritage technique for tourism promotion. For example, in 1991 the Mid Wales town of Machynlleth promoted itself in terms of the seven-hundredth anniversary of its market charter of 1291. Again, the heritage technique can be seen from a promotional leaflet produced by *Machynlleth 700*, linking implicitly the market charter to another event over a century later:

Famous for its clock tower standing in the centre of the town, Machynlleth has played a leading role in Welsh history. Owain Glyndwr led a rebellion against the English in the 15th century and held a Welsh parliament in the town in 1404. An earlier event in the town's history however was the granting of its Market Charter in 1291 – 700 years ago.

Market charter celebrations may not, it might seem, be sufficient in themselves for attracting tourists, especially as Wales is rich in medieval market towns (Soulsby 1983). In effect, tourism promotion in Britain is creating a new map of Britain, spatially described in terms of historic persons or like themes: a geography of heritage in a quite literal sense. A danger of such theming is the potential 'bowdlerisation' of history, reducing complexity to a few simple characteristics: as Ashworth and Tunbridge (1990: 54) have commented, 'Nottingham becomes exclusively the city of Robin Hood'. Certain associations have developed their own literary tradition for tourists to interpret the landscape remnants and places associated with particular persons or their writings. Perhaps most notable of these is the literary tradition induced by Thomas Hardy, which represents a secondary literature to that of the author, interpreting Dorset to the tourist through Hardy's life and writings (e.g. Draper 1989; Edwards 1989; Brasnett 1990).

The use of links with persons to promote places to tourists also extends into linking places together. In 1987, what is now Historic Scotland promoted *A Queen's Progress*, linking buildings associated with Mary Queen of Scots as a theme (Historic Buildings and Monuments 1987), Mary Queen of Scots having been executed in 1587, four hundred years before. The year after the Scottish theming, *Cadw* (Welsh Historic Monuments) promoted places linked to Gerald of Wales as a theme, describing the places visited by this cleric on his journey through Wales in 1188 (Kightly 1988). Theming of this kind seeks to associate places in different spatial locations, rather than to associate contiguous places. Further variants are to use associations with legend or with animals rather than of those with people: as a case in point, part of Somerset is now 'Camelot Country'. Likewise, part of Devon is now promoted as 'Tarka Country', after the story of *Tarka the Otter* (Oliver 1991). Such theming need not stop with local agencies seeking to promote tourism, for in 1991 passengers riding Regional Railways's Exeter to Barnstaple railway line were riding the 'Tarka Line'.

The use of historic associations with persons as a means of promoting areas for tourism is not only a Western European phenomenon. The same may be found, for example, in North America. Nova Scotia illustrates this point well. It has been promoted to tourists as a series of areas or 'trails' (Figure 2.1), several of which pertain to historical associations. For example, the Cabot Trail is named after John Cabot, the navigator who sighted Cape Breton island in 1497, the Evangeline Trail after the heroine of Longfellow's poem about the expulsion of the Acadian French in 1755, and the Glooscap Trail after the legendary divine warrior of the Micmac Indians of Nova Scotia. The heritage technique abounds in promotional literature of these trails and the places they join. For example, in a promotional leaflet of 1989 the Cape Breton Highlands National Park introduced the Cabot Trail to the tourist as the 'Memory trail', and aptly illustrates a further variant of seeking to overcome the impacts of modernisation through image creation, this time in seeking to promote the trail as a wildscape experience:

> From 'worst road in the Dominion' to scenic winding highway, the Cabot Trail has come a long way. In 1881, a narrow footpath connected Ingonish with Cape North and Cheticamp with Pleasant Bay. Only a hapless few made the journey – mailmen struggling through the mire, a doctor on the way to answer a sick call. By 1932, the entire route from Cheticamp to Ingonish was open to vehicles. Paving was completed in 1961!

Antigonish, on the Sunrise Trail, has been promoted to tourists by the Antigonish Chamber of Commerce as the 'Heart of the Highlands', with appropriate Scottish imagery, including the Gaelic welcome, *Ciad Mile Failte* (One hundred thousand welcomes). The Scottish highland heritage of Antigonish is vigorously promoted, rather than its Micmac or Acadian French past.

Moreover, the use of heritage to create images in advertising does not stop with tourism promotion. Welsh and Southern European cultures were juxtapositioned in the 'Coracle Kebabs' promoted as a leisure product by an international hotel in Swansea as an innovation for 1992 (a coracle being a small boat made by covering a wicker frame with leather or oil-cloth used for traditional river fishing in South West Wales). To take a Manx example, Tynwald Mills on the Isle of Man promote their 'Isle of Man Tartan' with the following lines to evoke associations with a landscape of Manx colours:

> The Misty-Blue for the seas that surround
> The Reddy-Brown for the rocks which abound
> The Green for the Grass and the Green for the trees
> The Gold for the gorse that waves in the breeze
> The White for the cottages, homely and gay
> The Red for the sunset at close of the day

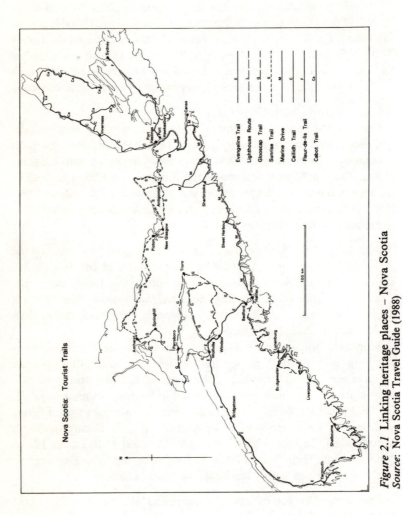

Figure 2.1 Linking heritage places – Nova Scotia
Source: Nova Scotia Travel Guide (1988)

The Purple, the heather that covers the hills.

Not all such employment of heritage imagery is recent, however. The Isle of Man Post Office has used similar imagery, although in visual form, to promote the island via its postage stamps since 'postal independence' from the United Kingdom in 1973. Initially this was with a series of definitive stamps representing Manx places by the island's famous contemporary artist, J. H. Nicholson, followed by a series in 1983 by the same artist on marine birds in Manx seaside settings, and in 1988 by a series depicting vintage scenes of Manx railways and tramways, these by the artist A. D. Theobald. In this way, images of Manx heritage have for the past twenty years been distributed internationally as a promotion for the island.

Essential to the so-called 'post-modern' era of contemporary Western civilisation is diversity. Part of this diversity is a heterogeneity of heritage both as populations move within countries and between them, and as the physical attributes of foreign cultures are replicated elsewhere as a form of leisure experience. The Mediterranean 'sun-belt' has increasingly attracted North European population as settlers, either as new permanent residents or as time-share residents, principally from England and Germany. Clear enclaves of such settlers are now identifiable in Mallorca, for example. In Britain, in the 1980s, the South East of England acted as a kind of population 'escalator' (Fielding 1989), attracting younger migrants from elsewhere in Britain, promoting the incomers to more highly paid jobs, and then losing some of them to elsewhere in Britain. Even prior to this era of intensive population circulation, in 1981 three out of ten, or more, of the population of a quarter of the thirty-seven districts of Wales had been born outside of Wales, in most cases, in England (Prentice 1992a). In contrast to the Welsh case which has occurred through economic and social factors, the Isle of Man's government has actively promoted a population transfusion through immigration as an economic development strategy, attracting largely English 'new residents' (Prentice 1990c; Robinson 1990). In cases such as these the question of 'whose heritage?' becomes of increasing pertinence for that of the indigenous population can no longer be promoted as unambiguously universal nor necessarily dominant. Facetiously one might ask, 'Whose heritage do you want to claim?' However, this heterogeneity need not result from large scale population transfusions. In the 'post-industrial' era cultural attributes may be replicated for sale in other places. For example, in the English provincial city of Manchester in the early 1990s it is possible to dine within the city's central area in restaurants of at least sixteen cultures other than English: namely: American, Bangladeshi, Cantonese, Dutch, French, Greek, Indian, Italian, Japanese, Korean, Mexican, Middle Eastern, Nepalese, Persian, Thai, and Turkish. Culinary diversity of this kind is not only indicative of the increasing heterogeneity of consumer taste among those able to afford to seek new experiences, without the necessity of foreign travel to achieve them, but possibly also of the beginnings of a weakening of the attachment of cultural heritage to specific places.

Nor is this diversity solely a feature of the post-modern era. The colonial era in North America, for example, has left a like diversity of heritages which may be presented. Not only is this a clash between indigenous and colonial cultures, but also between colonial traditions. In the case of Atlantic Canada, for example, of the colonial legacies, should the Acadian French tradition (Clark 1968; Daigle 1982) be presented to tourists or should that of the British (Conrad 1988) be presented? In the case of Atlantic Canada both heritages are jointly presented as tourist products, the potential incongruity resolved for tourists by presenting this clash of traditions as a past event and not a current process. The wider issue of 'whose heritage?' has also been prompted by recent celebrations of anniversaries of European colonisation in an era when the reassertion of aboriginal rights has come to the fore:

> The Australian bicentennial early in 1988 commemorated both the 200th anniversary of European settlement there, and the taking of the continent by the colonists from those already living there, as archaeologists now know, upwards of 30,000 years. 'Who owns the Australian past?' is now an uncomfortable question, and it begins to become, 'Who ought to own Australia?' 'Who owns the American past?' will be a common and uncomfortable question in 1992, the 500th anniversary of the European discovery of the New World and its first taking from the aborigines. The New World was, of course, only 'New' to we Europeans who had chanced to be ignorant of it.
> (Chippindale *et al.* 1990: 7)

The recognition and promotion of heritage has moral implications of which colonisation and subjection are unambiguously part.

The possible heritage of the future needs also to be remarked upon. With the potential expansion of oil production in the Commonwealth of Independent States (formerly the Soviet Union), in Venezuela, China, Cambodia, Iran, Myanmar (Burma), Colombia, Algeria, Mexico and Kuwait, will for example the oil era of Scotland of the 1980s become by the early twenty-first century a heritage theme rather than a primary industry? With the potential rise in coal imports into Britain in the 1990s and the switch to gas fired power stations will the heartland of today's coal industry in Yorkshire and Nottinghamshire be largely a heritage resource by the turn of the century? Industrial change will inevitably continue, and may render current industrial structures little more than memories or images to be reconstructed as heritage in future years. No longer may it be scurrilous to suggest that the era is upon us when investment strategies should include the heritage potential of industries once they become no longer viable, extending the 'product life cycle' so to speak beyond the use of the product into a generated use subsequent to its demise. Other heritage of the future may include resources currently inaccessible, such as those in the deep oceans, for example. At present wrecks are only accessible to, at most, a minority of people, but in the future the sea bottom may become accessible to all as technology changes. In such a context, the dangers of destruction, deliberate or otherwise, become potential threats, both to the relics of human endeavor, such as wrecks, and also to the natural environment. Only if technology fails to evolve or the popular taste for heritage changes will the most inaccessible parts of the earth not be threatened by future heritage tourists.

Heterogeneity is also to be found in the manner in which at least five basic needs of heritage consumers are to be met. These needs range from awareness, orientation, participation, skills and dialogue (Sealey 1987). Different tourists may seek to consume heritage and so to define it in any combination of these five needs. The first is to be aware of a heritage, the second to be able to orientate oneself to heritage resources. The third need is participation, to be able to come into contact with and to perceive heritage values. The fourth need, that of skills, is to be able to learn about how a country's heritage is presented and conserved, and the fifth, that of dialogue, to have a say in these processes of heritage presentation and conservation. Heritage can thus be understood in a heterogeneity of ways as needs are perceived differently by different groups.

In so far as heritage reflects a heterogeneous nostalgia for the past as imagined or presented, how far does it represent a retreat from the future across a diverse range of dimensions of human life? Laenen (1989) has referred to the 'retro climate' of the past decade. Commenting about historical re-enactments, Light has used similar imagery, 'The basis of the visit experience is thus a *retreat* [emphasis added] from the modern, technological world into that of a supposedly simpler past. This movement is known as "living history" ' (Light

1991: 8). Hewison in particular has termed the change from producing goods to producing heritage as a 'climate of decline':

> The growth of a heritage culture has led not only to a distortion of the past, but to a stifling of the culture of the present.
>
> (Hewison 1987: 10)

> As the past solidifies around us, all creative energies are lost.
>
> (Hewison 1987: 10)

and

> As the past begins to loom above the present and darken paths to the future, one word in particular suggests an image around which other ideas of the past cluster: the heritage.
>
> (Hewison 1987, 31)

Lowenthal (1981) commented that the use of the past is now to preserve it, not to look to it for models as sources of contemporary aspiration. In contrast, for example, are past vernacular architectural revivals, such as the Scottish Baronial Style of crow-steps, dormers and heavy chimney stacks, with plain soaring wall surfaces which was applied even to tenement housing in late-nineteenth-century Scotland, a revival finding inspiration in past architectural styles in Scotland (Walker 1985), or the Gothic revival likewise in England of the same era. For the purpose of preservation noted by Lowenthal, Hewison has substituted economic revival but offers a similar message. Charges that the consumption of heritage has displaced forward looking endeavour, first, ignore the heterogeneity of heritage; in particular, they ignore the conservational objective of preserving species diversity in 'natural' environments which is unambiguously forward looking. This omission results from the interpretation of heritage in terms of past things. In terms of attention to the future in other human enterprise, creative recreation or less structured leisure, may be argued to enhance production through enhancing the quality of life of the producers. An essential link which Hewison assumes rather than demonstrates is that leisure and tourism which involves heritage consumption not only *affects* human enterprise, but does so in a *negative* sense. Hewison also ignores the fact that as material needs are met, those of self-fulfilment may be more important to consumers. However inauthentic some heritage presentations may be, and however imprecise and uncritical may be the interpretation of past-type heritage by tourists and others, such consumption yields benefits, presumably of self-fulfilment, which consumers are prepared to pay for instead of other goods, services or experiences. Hewison may himself be charged therefore with equating what may simply be a leisure experience with a perverse attitude of mind.

THE HETEROGENEITY OF HERITAGE ATTRACTIONS

The heterogeneity of present day heritage is mirrored in the heterogeneity of heritage *attractions*; that is, sites, themes and areas promoted as heritage products for 'consumption' by tourists and day-trippers visiting from home. This is a broader definition of attraction than that used by tourist boards in Britain, of which that used by the Scottish Tourist Board is an example; an attraction being defined by the Scottish Tourist Board as:

> A permanently established excursion destination, a primary purpose of which is to allow public access for entertainment, interest or education, rather than being principally a retail outlet or a venue for sporting, theatrical or film performances. It must be open to the public without prior booking, for published periods each year, and should be capable of attracting tourists or day visitors as well as local residents.

> (Scottish Tourist Board 1990b)

The Scottish Tourist Board's definition would, for example, exclude much landscape heritage as an attraction, as well as locations for field sports and many cultural events. The exclusion of landscape is particularly inappropriate in a discussion of heritage tourism, in view of the importance of landscape demands demonstrated in Chapter 1. Equally, the Scottish Tourist Board's exclusion of principally retailing sites is important, although perhaps less easy to apply in practice. Likewise, the present definition is broader than that used by Walsh-Heron and Stevens:

> A visitor attraction is a feature in an area that is a place, venue or focus of activity and does the following:
>
> 1. Sets out to attract visitors (day visitors from resident and tourist population) and is managed accordingly.
> 2. Provides a fun and pleasurable experience and an enjoyable way for customers to spend their leisure time.
> 3. Is developed to realize this potential.
> 4. Is managed as an attraction, providing satisfaction to its customers.

5. Provides an appropriate level of facilities and services to meet and cater to the demands, needs, and interest of its visitors.
6. May or may not charge admission for entry.

(Walsh-Heron and Stevens 1990: 2)

The Walsh-Heron and Stevens definition emphasises management and development as aspects of attractions, as well as a fun experience: landscape and townscape, although they may be promoted as attractions, are not necessarily managed or developed as such. Likewise, many museums do not offer fun experiences, although such experiences may be pleasurable. Walsh-Heron and Stevens further refine their definition of attractions to include staffing and on-site management, aspects which do not always apply to heritage attractions. It is perhaps not by accident that opposite the definition of attraction offered by Walsh-Heron and Stevens in their book is a photograph of a Disneyland landmark, for this type of attraction well fits their definition of attraction. However, Walsh-Heron and Stevens in their further discussion of the hallmarks of an attraction also include the feature that an attraction needs to be recognised as such by its visitors. This is an important feature for it emphasises a consumer element to the definition of attraction.

Walsh-Heron and Stevens comment that, 'Attractions come in all shapes and sizes, catering to a wide variety of tastes and leisure requirements' (Walsh-Heron and Stevens 1990: 2). Much the same comment has been made about heritage attractions, which have been described as 'a bewildering variety' (Light 1989: 130). However, this heterogeneity has been masked by the prevalence of the term, *heritage industry*, to describe heritage attractions. The categorisation of this diverse group of attractions as one 'industry', the heritage industry (Hewison 1987), groups together attractions of varying compatibility in terms of size, theme, management objectives and funding. Categorisation of all attractions as one 'industry' can easily lead to the limitations of some attractions being universally inferred to all, the confusion in particular of educational and leisure objectives, and the uncritical castigation of authentic sites as implicitly contrived and historical interpretation as inherently fantastic rather than factual. It is illustrative to compare some British heritage attractions. It would seem unlikely that major attractions which are superficially similar such as the North of England Open Air Museum at Beamish, Wigan Pier in Wigan, the Jorvik Viking Centre at York, Tullie House in Carlisle, Black Gold at the Rhondda Heritage Park at Trehafod, Morwellham Quay near Tavistock, or the Timewalk at Brewers Quay in Weymouth, for example, each share all of each others' strengths and weaknesses in their interpretation of history through the 'production' of heritage from our knowledge and reading of the past. Likewise, major attractions of this kind are unlikely to share the same strengths and weaknesses in their 'production' of heritage as small museums of a traditional 'cabinet of curiosities' type run on shoestring budgets, or ruined castles and abbeys in the care of State agencies. It would, further, seem curious to imply that the theming of areas of England such as 'Catherine Cookson Country', 'Hadrian's Wall Country' or 'Captain Cook Country' in the North East, or as already mentioned of Huntingdonshire as 'Cromwell Country', brought with it similar problems of historical interpretation as those present in industrial museums. In sum, the so-called 'heritage industry' is in reality diverse and has been ill-served by over-hasty adoption of its labelling as one industry.

The heterogeneity of heritage attractions implies the desirability of classifying them into types, so that comparison may be made between attractions of like type, and between types of attraction, in any discussion of the 'production' of heritage, and in particular in any discussion of the processes and impacts of 'production'. Such a classification, or typology, needs to have the advantages of being concise and manageable, reducing numerous attractions into types of manageable number, but not the disadvantage of over-generalisation. The typology can be based either on the *means of presentation* used at the attractions or on the *main subject presented* at them. The former has the advantage of allowing comparison of attractions in terms of media used, but the disadvantage that many, if not most, attractions are today multi-media in terms of their presentation, with, for example, wall panels, displays, exhibitions and demonstrations frequently used in contemporary museums. The alternative of basing a typology on the main subject presented has the advantage of grouping like contents together, such as social history attractions, but the disadvantage that some attractions are of multiple content, such as stately homes with gardens. Equally, if most attractions can be classified by their main subject presented, it may be possible through consumer surveys of tourists and others visiting such attractions, to relate reasons for visiting, the benefits gained and other consumer characteristics to particular types of attractions. That is, to relate demand characteristics to supply characteristics through relating the characteristics of visitor segments (Chapter 1) to the attractions with the main subject type of the attractions. Such a typology also has a commercial application in attraction promotion. Not only may it allow promotion to be based on an understanding of the markets for attractions by main subject type, but also it may prompt a greater production of promotional literature and the like for areas themed by attraction subject. Existing classifications have generally been hybrids of the types discussed here. For example, that suggested by Middleton (1988) included ten categories of managed attraction, namely: ancient monuments, historic buildings, parks and gardens, theme parks, wildlife attractions, museums, art galleries, industrial archaeology sites, themed retail sites, and last, amusement and leisure parks. Not all of these categories are fully appropriate to heritage tourism, notably amusement parks. An alternative, relating specifically to heritage tourism, is that used by the National Trust for Scotland which has nine categories by which its properties are advertised: castles and large houses, countryside, gardens, historic sites, islands, Little Houses Improvement Scheme, famous Scots, museums, and, finally, social and industrial heritage (National Trust for Scotland 1992a).

The following typology is based on main subject types, and is offered as a means not only of countering any impression that heritage attractions are inherently alike but also as a means of transcending a country basis to classification, so concurring with the emergent European Community ideal of 'producing' a common European heritage independent of national constraints. The typology which follows is far from perfect, but is offered as a model which may be further refined as research effort throughout Europe focuses on heritage issues, heritage tourism among them. The typology has of necessity to reflect the range of 'attractions' which are visited by tourists and other visitors; as such, it has to include some 'attractions' for which this very term may seem inappropriate, and the inclusion of some types of site may be distasteful to some. Foremost among such sites are those commemorating genocide, particularly the extermination camps retained as memorials to the dead of continental Europe in the Second World War and other eras of genocide. The heritage of Europe is, regrettably, one of bloodshed, subjection, division and cruelty, as well as one of achievement, triumph, solidarity and compassion. As Uzzell has commented:

> Our museums and interpretive sites should be centres of excellence for telling the story of our cultural heritage in all its dimensions. Of course, we want them to be a celebration of the finest achievements of man, but if they are to be of educational value they must also honestly re-present the more shameful events of our past . . . . If

interpretation is to be a source of social good then it must recognize the continuity of history and alert us to the future through the past.

(Uzzell 1989: 46)

The word 'attraction' is singularly inappropriate in the context of genocide, but can be found used by some of the 'producers' of heritage. Others may take objection to the inclusion of blood sports among fieldsport attractions; but for many these sports are attractive, however repulsive to others. In developing this typology the term 'attraction' is meant in no other way than to describe a site, theme or area which attracts visitors; that is, the definition given above. It should not be taken to imply that these sites and the like are otherwise thought to be attractive. The typology proposed as a basis for the emergent research agenda into heritage issues is as follows:

Natural history attractions, including nature reserves, nature trails, aquatic life displays, rare breeds centres, wildlife parks, zoos, butterfly parks, waterfowl parks; geomorphological and geological sites, including caves, gorges, cliffs, waterfalls.

Science based attractions, including science museums, technology centres, 'hands on' science centres, 'alternative' technology centres.

Attractions concerned with primary production, including agricultural attractions, farms, dairies, farming museums, vineyards; fishing, mining, quarrying, water impounding reservoirs.

Craft centres and craft workshops, attractions concerned with hand made products and processes, including water and windmills, sculptors, potters, woodcarvers, hand worked metals, glass makers, silk working, lace making, handloom weaving, craft 'villages'.

Attractions concerned with manufacturing industry, attractions concerned with the mass production of goods, including pottery and porcelain factories, breweries, cider factories, distilleries, economic history museums.

Transport attractions, including transport museums, tourist and preserved railways, canals, civil shipping, civil aviation, motor vehicles.

Socio-cultural attractions, prehistoric and historic sites and displays, including domestic houses, social history museums, costume museums, regalia exhibitions, furnishings museums, museums of childhood, toy museums.

Attractions associated with historic persons, including sites and areas associated with writers and painters.

Performing arts attractions, including theatres, street-based performing arts, performing arts workshops, circuses.

Pleasure gardens, including ornamental gardens, period gardens, arboreta, model villages.

Theme parks, including nostalgia parks, 'historic' adventure parks, fairytale parks for children (but excluding amusement parks, where the principal attractions are exciting rides and the like).

Galleries, principally art galleries.

Festivals and pageants, including historic fairs, festivals 'recreating' past ages, countryside festivals of 'rural' activities.

Fieldsports, traditional fieldsports, including fishing, hunting, shooting, stalking.

Stately and ancestral homes, including palaces, country houses, manor houses.

Religious attractions, including cathedrals, churches, abbeys, priories, mosques, shrines, wells, springs.

Military attractions, including castles, battlefields, military airfields, naval dockyards, prisoner of war camps, military museums.

Genocide monuments, sites associated with the extermination of other races or other mass killings of populations.

Towns and townscape, principally historic townscape, groups of buildings in an urban setting.

Villages and hamlets, principally 'rural' settlements, usually of pre-twentieth century architecture.

Countryside and treasured landscapes, including national parks, other countryside amenity designations; 'rural' lanscapes which may not be officially designated but are enjoyed by visitors.

Seaside resorts and 'seascapes', principally seaside towns of past eras and marine 'landscapes'.

Regions, including pays, lande, counties, or other historic or geographical areas identified as distinctive by their residents or visitors.

These twenty-three types of heritage attraction, and their potential subdivisions, clearly illustrate the diversity of the heritage 'product', and frustrate the meaningful classification of attractions as a single 'industry'. Aspects of places found attractive by tourists but which are not site-specific, such as the Welsh language in Wales, add further to this heterogeneity. The distinctiveness of an area may be its language, and to hear it spoken and to see roadsigns written in it can be a significant part of an area's attractiveness to tourists (European Centre for Traditional and Regional Cultures 1988). Nor can we assume that the types of heritage attractions defined above are equally distributed across the countries of Europe, nor, for that matter, within parts of Europe, such as Great Britain. In the absence of a European, or British, inventory of heritage attractions it is difficult to quantify this national and regional diversity. However, within Britain, Wales is frequently promoted by images of its military heritage, principally its medieval castles, its transport heritage, including its tourist railways, its countryside and its townscapes. Scotland is frequently promoted by images of its residential castles or ancestral homes, its countryside landscapes, mainly its mountains and wildness, and its townscapes. In contrast, the North of England is frequently promoted by its social history and transport heritage, but the South West of England by its natural and social history attractions. The Midlands of England are different, again, being frequently promoted by images of their stately homes, natural and social history attractions, countryside and performing arts. It is this essential heterogeneity which forms the backcloth to heritage tourism.

Further heterogeneity of attractions results from the differing philosophies through which they are presented. These values can range from preservationist, regulative, redistributive and marketing (Ashworth and Voogd 1990b). Preservationist philosophies have as their orientation the object to be preserved, the goal of protection, and value heritage for its cultural significance. Monuments are generally a good example of the application of preservationist philosophies. Regulative philosophies have spatial patterns as their orientation, a goal of resolving conflicting demands, and value heritage in terms of legal norms. The conservation of townscape is a good example of regulative philosophies applied. Redistributive philosophies have needs as their orientation, often the goal of equity, and value heritage in social terms. Access to treasured landscape for popular recreation is a good example of redistributive philosophies applied. Marketing philosophies are orientated towards the customer, have the goal of sales development, and value heritage through the market place. Tourism promotion of heritage resources is a good example of marketing philosophies applied. Thus, not only may attractions vary by type, they may also vary in terms of the philosophies inherent in their management.

Two further final comments need to be made on the heterogeneity of attractions not by type but by their authenticity and by their size in terms of visitor numbers. Built attractions range in authenticity from field monuments unprotected other than by designation, through preserved ruins, to 'restored' houses, and to the outright contrived. It is a lack of authenticity which has fuelled the so-called 'heritage debate' as to the desirability of heritage consumption. For example, Lowenthal commented that re-enactments of historic events were apt 'to turn venerable places into self-conscious replicas of themselves' (Lowenthal 1981: 226). However, such a castigation should not be generalised uncritically to all 'events' for this would ignore the range of 'events' now promoted, which can include plays and garden walks (National Trust for Scotland 1992b), and in fact 'events' are quite a diverse activity (Walsh-Heron and Stevens 1990). Hewison has charged that 'museums are turning into theatres for the re-enactment of the past' (Hewison 1987: 83), and that 'the ultimate logic of the new type of museum is the museum that has no collection' (Hewison 1989: 19), but offers instead a pleasurable experience. The absence of authenticity is also to be seen in the separation by critics of contemporary museums and the like, of history (implicitly authentic) from heritage (implicitly inauthentic):

> My objection is that Heritage is gradually effacing History, by substituting an image of the past for its reality. Our actual knowledge and understanding of history is weakening at all levels, from the universities to primary schools. At a time when the country is obsessed with the past we have a fading sense of continuity and change, which is being replaced by a fragmented and piecemeal idea of the past constructed out of costume dramas on television, re-enactments of civil war battles and misleading celebrations of events.
>
> (Hewison 1989: 21)

Such a clear cut dichotomy between history and heritage assumes that both are uniform collections of ideas and methods, and quite distinct one from the other: such a dichotomy is false for history is as much our relationship with the past as is heritage a relationship with the past, only the means and quality of understanding may differ. The absence of authenticity may, however, also be more subtle than costumed dramas and re-enactments; for example, of Scottish seaside towns, 'Tourists can demand historic images which a town has never possessed, and pampering to their tastes by creating pseudo-Scottish scenes for the camera lens undermines the integrity of old towns' (Edwards 1986: 11).

Authenticity and inauthenticity add a further dimension to the heterogeneity of heritage attractions, and in terms of tourists' expectations need to be appraised in terms of how these expectations are met. Indeed, how likely are different types of heritage tourist to mistake the contrived for the authentic, or the reverse? It may be that some tourists expect to be fooled, for this is seen as part of the tourist experience and enjoyable to such tourists all the same.

The second comment concerns the diverse size of attractions in terms of their popularity when measured by counts of visitor numbers. Visitor numbers, as shown in Chapter 1, include both tourists and day-trippers, so to measure the size of attractions by recorded visitor totals should not be equated with the tourist markets of those attractions so measured. However, in the absence of other statistics, visitor totals have to be used. Even similar types of attraction vary substantially in size in terms of numbers of visitors attracted. For the present using the Wales Tourist Board's classification of attractions, in 1990 the eighty-five museums, galleries, industrial and craft attractions for which the Wales Tourist Board collated visitor numbers, ranged in size from 433,977 visitors recorded at James Pringle Weavers, at the village with the longest name in Britain, Llanfairpwllgwyngyllgogerychwyrn-drobwyllllantysiliogogogoch, to 520 estimated at the Llandudno Museum (Wales Tourist Board 1991c). The top fifth of these attractions in terms of visitor numbers accounted for two-thirds of all visits recorded for the eighty-five attractions, and the bottom fifth, just over 1 per cent of visits. Objection might be raised to the diversity of attractions grouped together by the Wales Tourist Board. Their class of historic properties is less heterogeneous in attraction type, although it includes castles and houses together. In 1990 visitor numbers ranged from 282,160 at Caernarfon Castle to 7,255 at White Castle. The top fifth of historic properties in terms of visitor numbers accounted for 57 per cent of all visitors recorded at the fifty properties for which visitor figures were collated; the bottom fifth only 1.5 per cent. This heterogeneity of size may be found more locally, also. Of the thirty-two heritage attractions which tourists and day visitors to the Vale of Usk and Wye Valley could have visited in 1986, eight had been visited by more than three out of ten tourists on their present holiday or day trip; Tintern Abbey heading the list with 46 per cent of all visitors to the area surveyed claiming to have visited it on their current holiday or day trip (Monmouth District Council 1987). In contrast, six attractions had been visited by fewer than 15 per cent of visitors to the area on their current holiday or day trip. Heterogeneity in terms of size is a further argument countering the uniformity implied by the term 'heritage industry'.

THE MANX SUMMER HOLIDAY TOURIST DATABASE

Heritage tourism needs to be studied not just in terms of its 'production' as a system of meanings and attractions, but also in terms of its consumers, namely, tourists. With the exception of surveys undertaken at Welsh heritage attractions in the 1980s (Herbert *et al.* 1989), systematic review of heritage production and consumption across a range of heritage attractions has been lacking: despite much having been written on European heritage, and with the 'Single Market' within Europe from 1992, European cultural integration having become a central feature of European Community policy, systematic research needed to monitor integration has been lacking. Although outside of the European Community, despite its geographical location between Great Britain and Ireland, a series of studies undertaken on the Isle of Man provide invaluable case evidence in this regard, and form a central resource from which the ideas of this book may be illustrated. The island has eight major heritage sites, and innumerable smaller ones, including many archaeological field monuments. The eight major sites are major tourist attractions on the island and form the basis of the holiday tourist database frequently referred to in subsequent chapters of this book, they are:

Peel Castle	Grove Museum
Castle Rushen	Laxey Wheel
Manx Museum	Cregneash
Nautical Museum	Odin's Raven

These form a diverse range of sites, mirroring in a small area some of the diversity apparent in heritage attractions already noted. Moreover, these attractions are all of the conventional 'core' of heritage, and would likely be unambiguously so classifed by almost all in the tourist industry. The two castles and Odin's Raven may be classified as military attractions, the museums and Cregneash as socio-cultural attractions, and Laxey Wheel as an attraction concerned with primary production. Although these attractions mirror some of the heterogeneity of type found in European heritage attractions, clearly many types of attraction are not represented among them, and await research elsewhere. In that only three of the types of heritage attraction identified by the foregoing typology are represented in the database, generalisation to other types of heritage attraction is likely to be fraught with error, and inferences should be made with caution in the absence of empirical comparison.

The database derives from surveys of visitors to the island's major heritage attractions designed by the author and undertaken by Manx National Heritage (formerly, the Manx Museum and National Trust). For clarity, the current name of this agency will be used throughout the book, irrespective of the actual name applicable at the dates of survey. Manx National Heritage has been progressively developing the presentation of its sites, some of which were only acquired in 1989 from another department of the Isle of Man Government. In particular, Castle Rushen and the Manx Museum have been substantially refurbished in the past few years, and plans have been prepared for the presentational refurbishment of Peel Castle. The database derives from the ongoing commitment on the part of Manx National Heritage to monitor the effects of their developments.

The database comprises five interview-based surveys of adult tourists, four undertaken at the island's major heritage attractions, mostly when under the ownership of what is now Manx National Heritage, but also in 1988 at some attractions then to be transferred to it. A fifth survey involved on-street interviewing in the sea front area of Douglas, the island's main town and major holiday accommodation resort. All surveys were undertaken in the summer holiday months of July, August and early September when the island is a destination area mainly for tourists from England and Ireland. The surveys included interviews with Manx residents as well as with holiday and other types of tourists. The interviews with Manx residents are excluded from the analysis presented in this book which focuses on tourists (in this case, staying visitors to the Isle of Man). However, as so few business tourists were interviewed these are also excluded from the database, as their behaviour and characteristics are known to be different to those of many holiday-makers, the island now being an off-shore financial sector attracting what may be termed 'hop-overs', business tourists island 'hopping' by plane around the off-shore financial centres of the British Isles. As such the database is based on interviews with summer holiday tourists to the island, and makes no reference to out of main season holiday tourism, nor to day visitors to the island (who are often holiday-makers staying at the Lancashire resorts in England). Other than for the on-street interviews, the database refers to what may be loosely termed 'heritage' tourists, in that it is based on interviews with tourists visiting heritage attractions. The aptness, or otherwise, of this term will be returned to in the subsequent chapters of this book. The more general applicability of the arguments made in this book from the Manx database to European heritage tourism and the ideal of heritage integration derive from the island attracting all but a few of its tourist visitors from Great Britain and Ireland, rather than from

Table 2.1 Sample sizes of Manx surveys

	Site surveys:		Castle Rushen Marketing	Castle Rushen Interpre-tation	All site surveys	Douglas Sea Front Survey
	1988	1990	1991	1991		1988
Total number of respondents	2,383	614	258	300	3,555	438
Number of holiday tourists among the total sample	1,942	547	146	192	2,827	342

outside of Europe. As Manx cultural traditions are distinct from those of the countries which surround the island, although at the same time mirroring aspects of these different cultures, it provides a useful case study of the impacts on tourists of being exposed to a differing European but not distant culture.

In total, the four surveys undertaken at the Manx heritage attractions which are reported in this book involved interviews with 3,555 visitors to the attractions, of whom 2,827 were holiday-maker tourists (Table 2.1). All visitors were interviewed when leaving the attractions. The on-street survey in Douglas involved a further 438 interviews, 342 of which were with holiday-maker tourists.

Further reference to Table 2.1 indicates the overall sample size of each survey. The Site Survey of 1988 included all of the island's eight major heritage sites either in the ownership of what is now Manx National Heritage or then soon to be. From the 1990 Site Survey data are available on three of these sites, representing in part a re-survey of three sites first surveyed two years earlier. In 1991 two surveys were undertaken at the then recently refurbished Castle Rushen. One survey considered general marketing issues and the other was directed to issues of interpreting the castle to its visitors. For ease of reference in this book these site surveys will be termed:

• *Site Survey 1988;*
• *Site Survey 1990;*
• *Castle Rushen Marketing Survey 1991*; and
• *Castle Rushen Interpretation Survey 1991.*

The on-street survey in Douglas will in similar fashion be termed:

• *Douglas Sea Front Survey 1988.*

It should be noted that, as the surveys did not include all the same questions between years, reference in the chapters which follow will not always be made to all surveys, but will be dependent on the particular data available. As the surveys represent the evolution of research ideas, they can usefully provide guidance for future research elsewhere in Europe in moving from general assessments to more specific assessments framed by a perspective from the earlier surveys.

As noted above, the eight heritage atractions which provide the basis of the database are somewhat diverse. They include two castles (Peel Castle; Castle Rushen), three museums (the Manx Museum; Nautical Museum; and Grove Museum), one industrial monument (Laxey Wheel), a folk village or *clachan* (Cregneash), and a reproduction Viking boat (Odin's Raven). These attractions are located throughout the island (Figure 2.2). The 1988 Site Survey was undertaken at all the attractions, and this forms the base survey. Data are further available from the Site Survey of 1990 for the two castles (Peel Castle and Castle Rushen) and for the folk village of Cregneash. As noted above, both the 1991 surveys refer to a single castle, Castle Rushen. As such, in total, data are available from the database from interviews with 1,269 adult holiday tourists at castles on the island, and likewise from interviews with 640 adult holiday tourists visiting the island's museums, 230 visiting its major industrial monument at Laxey, 486 visiting the folk village at Cregneash, and 202 visiting the reproduction Viking boat.

A further contextual source of information on the island's tourist visitors may be found in the successive *Isle of Man Passenger Surveys* undertaken by the Economic Advisor's Office of the Manx Government. Unfortunately, the Passenger Surveys do not differentiate heritage tourists from others, and as a result this source at best provides some context for the specific site surveys which comprise the database. The Passenger Surveys have involved quite substantial samples (for example, in the four years from 1985 to 1988 respectively 14,885, 14,659, 11,805 and 9,049 interviews were undertaken) and enable a breakdown of tourists by broad type of tourist in particular, principally holiday-makers staying in paid accommodation, those staying with friends or relatives, and business tourists. For purposes of compatibility with the site surveys wherever possible when reference is made to the Passenger Surveys it will be to the months of July and August.

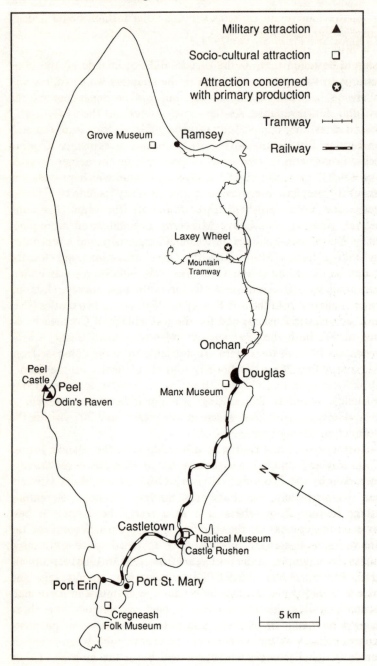

Figure 2.2 Location of the major heritage attractions on the Isle of Man

Tourism on the Isle of Man has had to restructure away from a reliance on main summer holidays and towards secondary holidays, often promoted by special 'events', of which the Manx Tourist Trophy motor cycle races are perhaps the most well known example, although these races in fact substantially predate the restructuring of the island's tourism industry in origin. The experience of tourism on the island in the past two decades has been one of declining numbers of tourists and shortened stays (Cooper *et al.* 1987; Prentice 1990a). The decline in volume terms is substantial enough: for example, in the fifteen year period from 1972 to 1987, passenger arrivals on the island declined from 626,057 in number to 483,460 (Isle of Man Economic Advisor's Office 1988). The shortened stay of visitors has compounded this decline, as increasingly fewer hotel bedrooms would have been required to cater for even a constant demand. In the period 1969–70 to 1987–8 the proportion of the island's gross domestic product generated by the tourist accommodation industry declined from an estimated 5.6 per cent to an estimated 1.6 per cent (Isle of Man Treasury 1989). In this dual context of decline and restructuring the island's heritage has become increasingly seen as a tourism as well as a cultural asset, particularly to attract disproportionately more higher social class tourists on secondary holidays (Cooper *et al.* 1987).

CONCLUSIONS

The discussion of this chapter has centred on the heterogeneity of heritage and of heritage attractions. In particular, the notion of a single, uniform 'heritage industry' has been rejected. 'Heritage' as a phenomenon has been shown to have expanded in the past decade or so from its core of natural, built, cultural and landscape features into more diverse dimensions. The heterogeneity of heritage has in effect been increased not so much by our increased scientific knowledge but through an increased awareness of change, a desire for conservation and a nostalgia for the past. In particular, heritage has become a commercial 'product' to be marketed to customers seeking leisure and tourism experiences. The demands of heritage customers now substantially define what can be included under the heritage label. 'Coracle kebabs' and the bowdleristic theming of places represent responses to what are perceived as customer demands by tourism and leisure businesses. However, whether such departures from the core of heritage represent a constraint on the economic and cultural development of Britain, or other Western countries, as has been charged by others, is less readily demonstrated. It is one thing to castigate the presentation of heritage as the antithesis of history, it is another to infer that such presentation represents a perverse frame of mind for the communities of Europe and their former dominions and colonies.

The question of whose heritage is being claimed will remain a pertinent issue. Conquest, subjection and liberation have both their losers as well as their victors. While some of the castles of Europe, for example, represent the supremacy of the military might of the ancestors of the communities now living in their vicinity, others are monuments to past defeats or dispossessions. The so-called 'post-modern' era has already enhanced cultural diversity, and this process is likely to continue. In that a heritage has to be both recognised and claimed it is not an impertinent question to ask, 'Whose heritage do you recognise and whose do you claim?' The transitory nature of many leisure and tourism experiences may further modify this question into, 'Whose heritage do you recognise and whose do you claim today or on this holiday?' In an extreme form, the increased culinary diversity in terms of restaurants in the post-modern era means that customers may claim different culinary heritages on a nightly basis if they have the means and desire to do so.

For all that has been asserted about the social and economic meaning of heritage and heritage attractions, over the past decade to date, there has been a deficiency of systematic studies of the consumers of heritage in terms of the heterogeneous 'products' they are consuming. This might be thought surprising for in the absence of such research informed debate is impossible. The database provided by the Manx National Heritage surveys provides an invaluable empirical base from which informed appraisal of some of these issues can begin. The database is of particular relevance to the core of built heritage. It is used in the following chapters to initiate a debate and to encourage similar empirical studies elsewhere in Europe.

3 The socio-demographic characteristics of tourists at heritage attractions

A SCARCITY OF KNOWLEDGE ABOUT HERITAGE TOURISTS

Comparatively little is known in a systematic manner about the characteristics of heritage tourists. This might be thought surprising in view of the importance of heritage tourism to the European economy, and the importance of a knowledge of the characteristics of these tourists to successful marketing and promotion. Vanhoe (1989) reports a segmentation of Belgian tourists into seven clusters based on the benefits of holidaying, although the socio-demographic character of these clusters are not reported. Prentice (1992b) has likewise attempted a preliminary segmentation of holiday-maker tourists, drawing from samples principally of owner–occupier residents of West Wales and the Isle of Man, combining behavioural and socio-demographic characteristics. This analysis has shown that heritage attractions are visited by many segments of tourists, and that in consequence 'heritage tourists' either have to be defined widely to include tourists making a visit to a heritage site as one part of their holiday (and possibly as a minor part of that holiday) or precisely to include only those tourists not undertaking activity, beach or pool-based holidays, but who visit heritage sites, townscapes or landscapes as their principal or sole holiday activity. In the former sense the market represented by heritage tourists is substantial, but in the latter much less so. Such a delimitation concurs with the conclusions reached in Chapter 1 about the prevalence of a sense of the past expressed as heritage demand.

The empirical segmentation discussed by Prentice (1992b) is very much in its infancy, and, in particular, segmentations require much wider field surveys to develop a generalised segmentation of heritage tourists, distinct from other types of tourists. This analysis as yet provides little guidance as to the size of the segments by socio-demographic characteristics. However, although our knowledge of the socio-demographic characteristics of heritage *tourists* has been to date lacking, this is less true for our knowledge of the socio-demographic characteristics of *visitors* to heritage attractions and *members* of heritage organisations. Tourists will figure among these visitors and members to varying extents, and, as such, projection of the characteristics of these groups to the tourists among them should be made with some caution unless tourists have been specifically identified by the authors of these studies. The need for caution is emphasised in particular if holiday activity patterns diverge from more usual leisure activity patterns, as would seem to be the case (Prentice 1992b; Light and Prentice 1993).

Visitor surveys at heritage attractions have been characterised by their definitional incompatibility and, often, their confidentiality. There has been a shortage of published studies of attractions in close proximity, and surveyed using comparable definitions and questions. Reference has instead largely to be made to disparate studies, for which variations may result from the diversity of places covered as well as attraction types. Frequently, however, such surveys have concentrated on the collection of socio-demographic data and a summary of findings from visitor surveys at heritage attractions, supplemented by those from membership surveys, such as summarised by Prentice (1989a). This summary has shown that visitors to heritage attractions are predominantly white-collar, and that membership of heritage organisations is biased substantially, not only to white-collar households in general, but also to professional and managerial households in particular. Visitors are not, in contrast, so readily characterised by age group, although it would seem from this summary of surveys that adult visitors to castles, folk parks, museums and galleries are on the whole younger than the members of the National Trusts or visitors to historic houses. This summary also suggested that the dominance of family groups among visitors to heritage sites should not be assumed.

The Manx summer holiday tourist database enables a comparison of the socio-demographic characteristics of holiday-maker tourists visiting the island's major heritage sites with the characteristics of holiday-maker tourists to the island. The database also enables a comparison to be made between the major sites on the island in terms of the socio-demographic characteristics of holiday-maker tourists visiting them, to see if any consistent differences may be identified by site type. The database further enables a comparison to be made over time for three attractions, enabling a check to be made on the consistency of the characteristics of holiday-makers visiting these sites. As such, the Manx database can help to rectify the deficiencies in our knowledge of the socio-demographic characteristics of heritage tourists. Equally, it should be remembered that comparison with fieldwork elsewhere in Europe is needed before general conclusions may be drawn about the socio-demographic characteristics of heritage tourists, and consideration needs to be given in particular in this wider comparison to the types of heritage tourist if such tourists are equated with tourists visiting heritage sites.

THE SOCIAL CLASS AND EDUCATIONAL PROFILE OF HOLIDAY-MAKER TOURISTS VISITING HERITAGE ATTRACTIONS

The summary of visitor surveys noted above (Prentice 1989a) would give strong support for a view that holiday-maker tourists visiting heritage sites are likely to be of a socially unrepresentative social class profile, with a substantial bias to non-manual worker social groups. Further support for such an inference is provided by other studies not summarised in this composite source. Only a quarter of tourists visiting Dylan Thomas's boathouse at Laugharne in Dyfed were found by a 1983 survey to be from manual worker households (Wales Tourist Board 1984a); in contrast, a third of all tourists surveyed at the attraction were from professional or senior managerial households. Despite developments to encourage a greater representation of those groups less likely to visit the site, at Audley End, English Heritage reported a changed profile away from professional and higher managerial households, but not towards the substantially under-represented manual worker households: instead, a greater proportion of middle-managerial and skilled non-manual households were attracted (Easthaugh and Weiss 1989). Prior to these developments, visitors from professional and senior managerial households represented in excess of four out of ten visitors to Audley End; after the developments they represented only three out of ten, still a substantial over-representation compared to their prevalence in the population. Manual workers remained almost constant in their representation among visitors at Audley End, at just over three out of ten, although the proportion of skilled to other manual visitors changed towards the former group. Even at the primary production industrial heritage attraction of Big Pit, in Gwent, manual workers do not seem to have been disproportionately more prevalent than non-manuals among visitors in the 1980s. A survey undertaken in 1985 reported 26

Table 3.1 The social class profile of adult holiday tourists visiting Manx heritage sites

| Social class: | Holiday tourists visiting sites: | | | | Holiday tourists visiting IOM: |
	Site Survey 1988 %	Site Survey 1990 %	Castle Rushen Marketing Survey 1991 %	Castle Rushen Interpretation Survey 1991 %	Douglas Sea Front Survey 1988 %
Professional/ higher managerial	12.1	22.9	18.9	16.7	5.8
Intermediate managerial	36.3	36.3	26.6	34.4	22.0
Non-manual supervisory/ clerical	19.6	14.1	16.1	19.3	18.7
Skilled manual	17.0	15.4	26.6	23.4	30.6
Semi and unskilled manual	11.9	7.2	4.9	4.7	18.0
Student	3.1	4.0	7.0	1.6	4.9
N =	1,921	545	143	192	327

Source: unpublished surveys undertaken by author for Manx National Heritage
Note: N = sample size

per cent of this attraction's visitors to be Daily Telegraph readers compared to 16 per cent generally at the nine attractions surveyed throughout Wales (Public Attitudes Surveys Research 1986): as the Daily Telegraph is predominantly a newspaper read by non-manuals, this industrial attraction would appear to have disproportionately attracted non-manual visitors, and not manual visitors as might have been expected. A survey of the same attraction in the first year of its operation confirms this. This survey found that three out of ten of its tourist visitors were from professional or senior managerial households, and a further third were from other other non-manual households (Wales Tourist Board 1984b).

The socially unrepresentative profile of heritage consumption is in fact confirmed for holiday-maker tourists visiting the Manx attractions (Table 3.1). Upwards of six out of ten holiday tourists visiting these attractions were found to be from non-manual households (using the British Office of Population Censuses and Surveys classification, but classifying retired households by their last employment and supplementing the classification with the category 'student' for student households interviewed). This profile is quite distinct from that found from the Douglas Sea Front Survey also shown in Table 3.1. In particular, professional and managerial households would appear to be over-represented among holiday tourist visitors to the Manx heritage attractions compared to the holiday tourists interviewed in Douglas. In contrast, semi- and unskilled holiday tourists would seem to be substantially under-represented at the sites when compared to their frequency among the holiday tourists to be found in Douglas.

The Passenger Surveys provide data on the social class of holiday tourists, but is derived from the Institute of Practitioner's in Advertising's classification which is not fully comparable to the OPCS classification as amended for the Manx National Heritage surveys. The Passenger Survey classification essentially divides holiday tourists into one class of non-manuals and another of manuals, retired and unemployed persons. The Passenger Survey classification by social class of holiday tourists to the island indicates that in July and August 1988 about three-quarters of holiday tourists to the island were from manual, retired or unemployed households, and in the same months of 1990, approximately six out of ten were from these social groups. Because of the allocation of retired households to the manual category in the Passenger Survey, caution is implied, in comparison with the social classification used in the site survey. However, the minority of non-manual holiday tourists found by the Passenger Survey would not seem to contradict a conclusion that heritage tourists, or strictly heritage site visitors among holiday tourists, to the island are distinctive in their social class profile when compared to holiday-makers generally. As this concurs with what has been found previously for visitors in general at heritage attractions, it would seem safe to conclude that a social class bias to the non-manual groups is a common feature of heritage tourism at the kinds of attractions represented among the Manx database. Equally, it would be wrong to conclude that heritage tourism is equated solely with higher social class tourists.

It could be assumed that different kinds of heritage attractions might attract different social profiles of holiday tourists. It is known, for example, that the National Railway Museum at York attracts a less formally educated, and thus by implication, lower social class, profile of visitors than do the Science Museum or Victoria and Albert Museum in London (Heady 1984). Equally, as noted above, the example of Big Pit in Gwent counters this inference. The Manx database would confirm a view of site specific variation within the general predominance of non-manual holiday tourists visiting the island's heritage sites (Table 3.2). However, some caution is implied in

Table 3.2 The social class profile of adult holiday tourists at different Manx heritage sites

Holiday tourists visiting sites:

Social class:	Peel Castle 1988 %	Peel Castle 1990 %	Castle Rushen 1988 %	Castle Rushen 1990 %	Manx Museum 1988 %	Nautical Museum 1988 %	Grove Museum 1988 %	Laxey Wheel 1988 %	Cregneash 1988 %	Cregneash 1990 %	Odin's Raven 1988 %
Professional/higher managerial	7.9	21.9	13.1	19.5	5.7	16.9	11.4	18.4	10.5	27.7	16.2
Intermediate managerial	37.4	41.0	36.3	33.5	35.5	37.3	34.7	26.5	41.3	34.5	39.9
Non-manual supervisory/clerical	28.7	13.1	18.3	14.1	15.1	18.1	28.0	9.9	20.7	15.3	18.7
Skilled manual	17.3	10.9	18.0	21.6	15.1	18.6	10.9	26.9	13.4	13.6	16.7
Semi- and unskilled manual	5.5	7.1	10.1	8.1	24.2	6.2	13.0	14.3	11.5	6.2	8.6
Student	3.1	6.0	4.2	3.2	4.5	2.8	2.1	4.0	2.6	2.7	0.0
N =	254	183	306	185	265	177	193	223	305	177	198

Source: unpublished surveys undertaken by author for Manx National Heritage
Notes: see Table 3.1 for 1991 profile of Castle Rushen
N = sample size

any interpretation by the substantial variation in social profile between years at two sites, with Castle Rushen providing somewhat of an exception in this regard. The one industrial heritage site among the eight, Laxey Wheel, would appear to attract a disproportionate number of manual holiday tourists; but equally so would the Manx Museum, which in 1988 did not have an industrial history orientation. It might be thought that the accessibility rather than the type of heritage site might be an alternative explanation of the social class variation between the Manx attractions, particularly as the Manx Museum is in Douglas (the island's major tourist accommodation centre), and the two sites outside of Douglas which disproportionately attract manual workers (Laxey Wheel and Castle Rushen) are accessible from Douglas by the island's vintage transport systems (Figure 2.2). However, accessibility cannot be a full explanation as the Nautical Museum is located in the same town as Castle Rushen. As such, accessibility and preference in attraction type may need to be seen as joint determinants of the social class profiles of holiday-maker tourists at sites. A fuller grouping of attraction types in terms of social class profiles of tourists attracted will need to await fuller surveys of tourists at attractions throughout Europe. A research agenda for heritage tourism could, therefore, usefully include a sampling framework involving attraction type, rather than the arbitrary selection of sites which commercially funded research may provide.

Similarly, only a little has been published about the educational backgrounds of heritage tourists in Europe and North America, and the rarity of these surveys would imply some caution in generalising from them. The comparative rarity of published studies is despite the importance of being aware of the educational attainments of the differing segments of tourists, and other visitors, attracted to sites in order to design interpretative displays and other media to explain to the visitor the significance of what is being seen. The disproportionate presence of higher social groups among the visitors to heritage attractions would suggest that they, and the tourists among them, are likely to disproportionately include persons having received further or higher education. This inference is confirmed for visitors to British cathedrals surveyed in the late 1970s, four out of ten being found to have undertaken higher education (Cathedral Tourism Advisory Group 1979). Similarly, eight out of ten visitors to Colonial Williamsburg were found to have received higher education (Alderson and Low 1986). The Manx database confirms this bias towards more highly educated tourists for summer hoiday tourists visiting at least some of the island's major heritage sites (Table 3.3). As a question on educational attainment was only asked in the 1990 and 1991 surveys data are not available for all of the Manx sites, and following on from the analysis above, Laxey Wheel is a notable omission in this context. At two of the attractions where educational attainment was asked of tourists visiting, upwards of four out of ten tourists had received continuous full-time education up to an age which in Britain would represent further or higher education, namely, to age nineteen or above. However, the third attraction, Castle Rushen, is an exception to the other sites, and this would concur with this attraction's social class profile as noted above. The recurrence of Castle Rushen as an exception in terms of the educational profile of its visiting tourists would imply some caution in our interpretation of a further and higher educational bias among tourist visitors to heritage attractions of the kinds surveyed on the island. It would also be wrong from the Manx samples of tourists to equate heritage tourists with more highly educated persons even if in general it is the case that the more highly educated are to be found disproportionately among tourists visiting heritage sites. Even at the two Manx attractions, Peel Castle and Cregneash, where a clear bias towards more highly educated tourists is apparent from Table 3.3, over half of the tourists interviewed had completed their education before the age of nineteen. Not only are more surveys into the educational attainments of heritage tourists needed in order to establish the general picture and its discordant site types, the present findings imply the need to design interpretative and other displays which inform visitors with a range of educational attainments in mind, as at some sites tourist visitors may differ substantially in their educational backgrounds.

AGE AND GROUP PROFILE OF HOLIDAY-MAKER TOURISTS VISITING HERITAGE ATTRACTIONS

Age is a commonly collected visitor characteristic when visitor surveys are undertaken at attractions. The summary of visitor surveys noted earlier (Prentice 1989a) suggested that visitors to historic houses show an older profile in terms of their age groups than do visitors to other heritage attractions. This is in part confirmed, for example, by a study at Stan Hywet Hall, a pseudo-Tudor mansion in Ohio, where visitors under the age of thirty were found to be under-represented (Achmatowicz-Otok and Goggins 1990). In contrast, at Colonial Williamsburg a bias in the attraction's visitor profile towards adult visitors in their late twenties and in their thirties has been reported, with most adult visitors aged between twenty-five and fifty-five years

Table 3.3 The age at which adult holiday tourists visiting Manx heritage sites had completed their full-time education

Age at which continuous full-time education completed/intended to be completed:	Site Survey 1990: Peel Castle %	Castle Rushen %	Cregneash %	All sites %	Castle Rushen Marketing Survey 1991 %	Castle Rushen Interpretation Survey 1991 %
16 or earlier	30.2	56.2	39.4	42.3	50.0	50.8
17 or 18 years	24.4	28.1	18.3	23.7	25.7	31.4
19 to 22 years	30.8	11.4	26.9	22.7	12.5	14.1
23 years or older	14.5	4.3	15.4	11.3	11.8	3.7
N =	172	185	175	532	144	191

Source: unpublished surveys undertaken by author for Manx National Heritage
Note: N = sample size

of age (Alderson and Low 1986). This is a similar age profile to that reported for Scottish folk festivals surveyed in 1990, 49 per cent of whom were found to be aged in their thirties or forties (Scottish Tourist Board 1991b). The under-representation of older adults has been noted at cathedrals: eight out of ten adult visitors to British cathedrals in the late 1970s were found to be aged under fifty-five years (Cathedral Tourism Advisory Group 1979). However, the 1983 survey of visitors to Dylan Thomas's boathouse found a wider representation of adult age groups, but with an under-representation of persons aged under twenty-five years and also of those aged over sixty-four years (Wales Tourist Board 1984a). A similar profile was found at Big Pit (Wales Tourist Board 1984b). At state monuments in Wales in 1986, young adults were found to predominate among adult visitors: with a fifteen to forty years age range accounting for over six out of ten adult visitors (Prentice 1989a). In some contrast, a survey in 1985 of visitors to nine heritage attractions in Wales found persons aged under twenty-five years to be *under-represented* among visitors, but those aged twenty-five years to forty-four years, over-represented (Public Attitudes Surveys Research 1986). As some of the 1985 and 1986 attractions surveyed were the same, these findings would imply that persons in their twenties and thirties form a disproportionate market for castles and abbeys and the like when presented as heritage products. Findings at English Heritage attractions would confirm this (Public Attitudes Research 1986). However, other than these Welsh studies, little has been known systematically about the age profile of tourists among visitors at *neighbouring* attractions. A substantial degree of heterogeneity in age profiles would seem apparent from the literature surveyed, but with aged adults the least likely to visit heritage attractions. The Manx summer holiday tourists database cannot help in investigating the distinction possibly existing between tourists visiting historic houses and those visiting other sites, as the eight Manx attractions do not include a historic house comparable to those, say, of the National Trust in England. However, the database does enable a comparison by age group, first, between holiday tourists visting heritage attractions and all holiday tourists visiting the island, and, second, between different attractions on the island.

Most adult holiday tourists interviewed at the Manx attractions were aged in their thirties and forties (Table 3.4). This profile is made more emphatic by comparison with the age profile of adult tourists visiting the island. Compared to the age profile of holiday tourists interviewed in Douglas in 1988, tourists in their twenties are clearly under-represented at the Manx heritage attractions, as were persons

Table 3.4 The age profile of adult holiday tourists visiting Manx heritage sites

| Age groups: | Holiday tourists visiting sites: | | | | Holiday tourists visiting IOM: |
	Site Survey 1988 %	Site Survey 1990 %	Castle Rushen Marketing Survey 1991 %	Castle Rushen Interpretation Survey 1991 %	Douglas Sea Front Survey 1988 %
15–20	3.5	2.8	6.2	1.6	4.4
21–30	15.5	12.5	11.6	8.9	20.8
31–40	29.1	29.5	20.5	21.5	24.0
41–50	28.3	29.9	27.4	27.7	13.2
51–60	12.7	14.8	13.0	19.9	13.2
over 60	10.9	10.5	21.3	20.4	24.3
N =	1,937	542	146	191	341

Source: unpublished surveys undertaken by author for Manx National Heritage
Note: N = sample size

aged in their sixties or older in the 1988 and 1990 surveys. In contrast, tourists aged in their forties are substantially and consistently across all three surveys over-represented among heritage site visitors when compared to their proportion among the Douglas sea front survey of tourists (Table 3.4).

The categorisation of age groups used in the Passenger Surveys differs from that used in the Manx National Heritage surveys, and as such makes comparison difficult for some age groups. However, a comparison between the age profiles found by the Passenger Survey and site surveys would confirm the under-representation of young adults at the heritage sites, and give support to the argument that elderly adults are also under-represented at the sites compared to their proportion among holiday-makers generally. In 1988 tourists aged sixteen to twenty-three years comprised around one in eight of the summer tourists surveyed leaving the island by the Passenger Survey, a significantly greater proportion than interviewed at the heritage attractions in that year, even allowing for the strict incomparability of the age ranges used. In 1988 the Passenger Survey recorded between one in eight and one in six summer holiday-makers as aged over sixty, substantially more than recorded by the site surveys at the island's heritage attractions. In 1990 a similar difference was also recorded. Because of the categorisation used in the Passenger Surveys the over-representation of tourists in their forties found by the Manx National Heritage surveys cannot be further considered.

The Manx database enables some discussion of the effect of attraction type on the age profile of tourists attracted to heritage sites. It would suggest that broad generalisation is as yet premature. Both Cregneash folk village and the Nautical Museum would seem to attract fewer young adults than the other Manx heritage attractions (Table 3.5), in contrast, particularly, to Peel Castle, the Manx Museum and Laxey Wheel. Castle Rushen and the Grove Museum would seem to attract a disproportionate number of tourists aged over sixty. The visitor surveys summarised from elsewhere would not lead us to expect an over-representation of elderly tourists at Castle Rushen. The general diversity in site types in terms of their popularity with different age groups of tourists on the island should warn us against hasty generalisation from limited numbers of surveys of age profiles by attraction type: instead, the heterogeneity of attractions in terms of age groups attracted is emphasised. The age profiles shown in Table 3.5 also serve as a reminder that the sites are varyingly popular to *all* age groups, further suggesting the heterogenity of the tourist market for heritage attractions of this kind. Taking the Manx and other findings together, a substantial degree of heterogeneity in visitor profiles would seem apparent, but with some consistent emphasis on tourists and other visitors in their late twenties, and in their thirties and forties. A future research agenda should include the age characteristics of heritage tourists, to see in particular if the Manx trends can be more generally confirmed, and to seek general profiles for attractions within the typology set out in Chapter 2.

Group size and composition are another common characteristic recorded on visitor surveys. For example, Big Pit has been found to be a popular destination for large groups, presumably coach parties (Wales Tourist Board, 1984b). Of tourists interviewed at Laugharne in 1983, only 43 per cent were described as family groups of adults with their children (Wales Tourist Board 1984a). At Big Pit the equivalent proportion was 42 per cent. Only a minority of visitors interviewed in the late 1970s at cathedrals in Britain were likewise found to have children in their group (Cathedral Tourism Advisory Group 1979). At English Heritage attractions surveyed in 1984, 69 per cent of all visitor groups surveyed were found to be comprised of adults only, as were 41 per cent of visitor groups interviewed at Welsh heritage attractions in 1985 (Public Attitudes Surveys Research 1986). The surveys of visitors to Welsh monuments reported by Prentice (1989a) suggested that

Table 3.5 The age profile of adult heritage tourists at different Manx heritage sites

| | Peel Castle | | Castle Rushen | | Holiday tourists visiting sites: Manx Museum | Nautical Museum | Grove Museum | Laxey Wheel | Cregneash | | Odin's Raven |
Age groups:	1988 %	1990 %	1988 %	1990 %	1988 %	1988 %	1988 %	1988 %	1988 %	1990 %	1988 %
15–20	2.8	6.1	3.9	1.6	8.2	2.3	4.1	3.1	1.9	0.6	0.5
21–30	20.1	16.0	15.7	11.4	16.5	11.3	15.9	18.9	10.1	10.2	15.8
31–40	34.6	35.9	27.1	26.1	25.8	29.9	24.6	33.3	27.9	26.6	30.2
41–50	28.0	26.5	30.1	27.7	22.5	31.1	27.2	28.5	33.4	35.6	24.8
51–60	7.9	10.5	10.1	19.0	17.2	14.1	13.3	10.1	15.6	14.7	13.4
over 60	6.7	5.0	13.1	14.1	9.7	11.3	14.9	6.1	11.0	12.4	15.3
N =	254	181	306	184	267	177	195	228	308	177	202

Source: unpublished surveys undertaken by author for Manx National Heritage
Notes: see Table 3.4 for 1991 profile of Castle Rushen
    N = sample size

Table 3.6 The presence of a child or children in the personal groups of adult holiday tourists visiting Manx heritage sites

	Holiday tourists visiting sites:		
			Castle Rushen Interpretation
	Site Survey 1988	*Site Survey 1990*	*Survey 1991*
	%	*%*	*%*
Child/children in group	49.9	46.3	21.5
No child/children in group	50.1	53.7	78.5
N =	1,942	546	191

Source: unpublished surveys undertaken by author for Manx National Heritage
Note: N = sample size

many visitors were without children in their groups, and that few had pre-school age children with them.

These visitor surveys summarised do not tell us whether or not heritage tourists are distinctive from other holiday tourists in terms of their group sizes or other group characteristics. For example, do heritage tourists more frequently have children in their personal group than tourists undertaking other activities, or is heritage tourism a disproportionately single adult or two adult group activity in which children are uninvolved? Does the type of heritage attraction affect this? For example, may castles disproportionately attract tourist families with children, but museums attract mainly adult tourists? The Manx holiday tourist database helps in answering questions of this kind.

Once again the Manx database suggests caution in seeking to generalise in terms of group type. All the attractions surveyed attracted a mix of tourists with children and of those without (Tables 3.6 and 3.7). Laxey Wheel would seem more popular than the other Manx attractions as a destination for tourists with children, and two of the museums least popular. Other than social history museums being less attractive to tourists with children the site differences are not readily generalised. Instead, the attractiveness of sites to both tourists with children and those without would imply the need to develop and present the sites in ways attractive to both types of tourist visitors.

The group sizes of heritage tourists can also be illustrated from the Manx database. The heterogeneity of heritage tourists in this regard is

Table 3.7 The presence of a child or children in the personal groups of adult holiday tourists at different Manx heritage sites

	Peel Castle 1988 %	Peel Castle 1990 %	Castle Rushen 1988 %	Castle Rushen 1990 %	Manx Museum 1988 %	Nautical Museum 1988 %	Grove Museum 1988 %	Laxey Wheel 1988 %	Cregneash 1988 %	Cregneash 1990 %	Odin's Raven 1988 %
					Holiday tourists visiting sites:						
Child/children in group	50.8	50.0	52.0	42.7	40.3	49.2	42.6	66.1	52.9	46.3	43.6
No child/children in group	49.2	50.0	48.0	57.3	59.7	50.8	57.4	33.9	47.1	53.7	56.4
N =	256	184	306	185	268	177	195	230	308	177	202

Source: unpublished surveys undertaken by author for Manx National Heritage
Notes: see Table 3.6 for 1991 profile of Castle Rushen
   N = sample size

again suggested. Of the holiday tourists visiting the Manx attractions the most common group size is two persons (Table 3.8), with only Laxey Wheel an exception. Equally, in only one case, that of Castle Rushen in 1991, do two person groups predominate among the tourist visitors. The Passenger Survey provides data on the average size of holiday tourist group to the island: in the months of July and August 1988 for tourists staying in paid accommodation this was three persons (the Passenger Survey rounds these figures). This compares to an average (mean) holiday tourist group size surveyed at the heritage sites of 3.47 persons. As such, we cannot conclude that, on the island at least, heritage tourists are distinctive in their group sizes to other holiday-maker tourists. In the absence of any more direct evidence, this may suggest that the profile of heritage tourists in terms of whether or not children are to be found among their groups is much the same as for holiday tourists generally to the island.

NATIONALITY OF HOLIDAY-MAKER TOURISTS VISITING HERITAGE ATTRACTIONS

It is as yet unknown how far heritage tourism is a truely European phenomena in terms of tourist behaviour. Whereas it is known that the former Eastern bloc countries are promoting their cultural and architectural heritage as tourist attractions for Western European visitors (the supply side), the corollary of tourist preference (the demand side) is unknown Europe-wide. Even within Western Europe variations by country in terms of tourist preference for heritage tourism are largely unknown, and should represent part of a future research agenda for heritage tourism.

The Manx database may be used to explore any differences in the demonstrated preferences of British and Irish tourists for heritage attractions. This is because as noted in Chapter 2 the Isle of Man receives most of its summer tourists from the countries bordering the Irish Sea. For 'nationality', the proxy of country of residence of tourists is used in the present analysis. Reference to Table 3.9 shows an unambiguous over-representation of holiday tourists from England at the island's heritage sites (Wales has been categorised with England in this analysis as few tourists to the island originate from Wales). This over-representation is apparent whichever of the two surveys of holiday tourists is used as the means of comparison. Correspondingly, Irish tourists are consistently under-represented at the island's heritage sites.

The findings shown in Table 3.9 would imply some caution in

Table 3.8 The group size of adult holiday tourists at different Manx heritage sites

| | Peel Castle | Castle Rushen | | Manx Museum | Nautical Museum | Grove Museum | Laxey Wheel | Creg-neash | Odin's Raven | All sites |
| | 1988 | 1988 | 1991(a) | 1988 | 1988 | 1988 | 1988 | 1988 | 1988 | 1988 |
Group sizes:	%	%	%	%	%	%	%	%	%	%
One person	4.7	4.9	13.7	11.9	5.6	6.2	1.3	2.6	6.4	5.4
Two persons	38.3	38.2	65.8	42.2	36.7	38.5	24.3	34.7	42.6	36.9
Three persons	20.3	16.3	12.3	17.5	19.2	16.9	20.0	17.9	16.8	18.1
Four persons	23.4	22.9	6.2	19.4	25.4	21.0	27.0	24.0	18.3	22.7
Larger	13.3	17.7	2.0	9.0	13.1	17.4	27.4	20.8	15.9	16.9
N =	256	306	146	268	177	195	230	308	202	1,942

Source: unpublished surveys undertaken by author for Manx National Heritage
Notes: (a) indicates Marketing Survey
N = sample size

Table 3.9 Country of residence of adult holiday tourists visiting the Isle of Man and those visiting Manx heritage sites

Country of residence:	Holiday tourists visiting sites:		Douglas Sea Front Survey 1988 %	Holiday tourists visiting IOM:			
	Site Survey 1988 %	Site Survey 1990 %		Passenger Survey 1988		Passenger Survey 1990	
				July %	August %	July %	August %
England and Wales	73.9	} 80.9	56.5	40	44	50	58
Scotland	4.3		5.1	11	7	9	4
Northern Ireland	7.6	} 14.0	22.2	24	19	19	13
Irish Republic	9.4		15.0	23	27	19	23
Other	4.8	5.1	1.2	2	3	3	2
N =	1,923	543	333				

Source: unpublished surveys undertaken by author for Manx National Heritage and Isle of Man Passenger Surveys undertaken by Economic Adviser's Office

Note: N = sample size

assuming the generality of heritage tourism preferences across the nationalities of Europe. However, it may be that the Irish tourists to the Isle of Man are coming to the island for different reasons to those from Great Britain, and therefore seeking different benefits from their holidays. In consequence, the present findings may not reflect the preferences of either the full population of tourists from the two areas. If a different mix of market segments is being attracted from Ireland than from Great Britain to the island, differences in preferences as revealed in behaviour could be expected even if in the full population of tourists from these areas preferences were much the same. This proviso adds the dimension of destination to that of revealed preference. At the least, the Manx findings would suggest the potential importance of nationality as a demand side explanation of heritage tourism, and the need for the inclusion of nationality in a future research agenda.

HOLIDAY TYPE OF TOURISTS VISITING HERITAGE ATTRACTIONS

Both from the efforts of tourist boards in Northern Europe to extend the holiday season away from the summer months by promoting heritage resources as attractions and from the increase in the numbers of 'second' or other 'additional' holidays being taken at domestic destinations, heritage tourism might, at least in part, be equated with the market for second or additional holidays. However, our demand analysis in Chapter 1 suggested otherwise, as does the Manx database. As reference to Table 3.10 shows, we would be wrong to equate heritage tourists (or, strictly, tourists visiting heritage attractions) with largely second or additional holiday-makers on the Isle of Man: a visit to a heritage attraction is a frequent main holiday activity on the island. Nor may we conclude that heritage tourists, at least in the summer, are disproportionately second or additional holiday-makers compared to the number of such tourists among those visiting the island. At least in the summer months, holiday-maker tourists on the island are represented very much in the same proportions in terms of being on main or other holidays at the attractions as they are among tourists generally to the island. However, it would equally be incorrect to ignore the presence of second or additional holiday-makers among the tourists found at the island's heritage sites in the summer, its traditional main holiday season. In particular, Castle Rushen would seem to attract a sizeable proportion of second and additional holiday-makers among its summer tourist visitors.

Table 3.10 Holiday type of adult holiday tourists visiting the Isle of Man and those visiting Manx heritage sites

	Holiday tourists visiting sites:						Holiday tourists visiting IOM: Passenger Survey 1990	
	Peel Castle		Castle Rushen		Cregneash	All sites		
			Marketing Survey	Interpretation Survey				
	1990 %	1990 %	1991 %	1991 %	1990 %	1990 %	July %	August %
Main holiday	75.5	64.9	53.4	47.9	77.0	72.4	68	78
Second or additional holiday	24.5	35.1	46.6	52.1	23.0	27.6	32	22
N =	184	185	146	192	178	547		

Source: unpublished surveys undertaken by author for Manx National Heritage and Isle of Man Passenger Survey undertaken by Economic Adviser's Office

Note: N = sample size

Table 3.11 Length of stay on the Isle of Man by adult holiday tourists visiting the island and those visiting Manx heritage sites

| | Holiday tourists visiting sites: | Holiday tourists visiting IOM: | | |
| | | Douglas Sea Front Survey | Passenger Survey 1988 | |
Number of nights:	Site Survey 1988 %	1988 %	July %	August %
1	0.2	1.3	1	0
2–4	7.0	13.5	12	13
5–7	45.0	55.3	65	61
8–10	16.1	10.4	13	14
11–14	25.3	16.4	9	10
15–20	2.8	1.6	1	1
over 20	3.6	1.5	0	0
N =	1,915	318		

Source: unpublished surveys undertaken by author for Manx National Heritage and *Isle of Man Passenger Survey* undertaken by Economic Adviser's Office
Note: N = sample size

The impression, noted at the outset of this section, of heritage tourists often being second or additional holiday-makers may well result from their presence at heritage attractions outside of the main summer tourist season. As such, the holiday type taken by the heritage tourist may have important aspects of seasonality. What is unknown is how far these tourists are in fact the same people, in and out of the main season, and in particular whether out of main season heritage tourists on additional holidays undertake other activities on their main holidays. What is known for the Isle of Man from its Passenger Surveys is that very few main season holiday-makers who intend to return to the island, intend to do so for a second or additional holiday, whereas this is a more common intention for out of main season tourists when second and additional holidays to the island are most common. This would imply substantial segmentation between these markets, with any linkage in terms of second holiday-makers becoming subsequent main holiday-makers. However, a similar analysis cannot be undertaken for heritage tourists alone, and linkages may equally be between sports tourists (the island's other main out of season market) as between heritage tourists. Further research into linkages of this kind is clearly needed before conclusions can be drawn.

From the visitor surveys summarised by Prentice (1989a) little or nothing has been known about the length of holidays taken by the heritage tourist, and how this compares to other kinds of tourism. An association of heritage tourism out of main season with second or additional holidays might imply, out of main season at least, that heritage tourists might take shorter holidays than other types of tourist. The demand analysis in Chapter 1 has shown, however, that such an argument cannot be sustained generally to summer tourism. For the main season tourist the Manx database suggests such an inference similarly to be incorrect. Heritage tourism, in the summer at least, is in part associated with the longer staying tourist on the island (Table 3.11). Tourists staying five to seven nights on the island, although they represent nearly half of the tourists visiting the island's heritage attractions surveyed, are all the same under-represented compared to their numbers on the island. In contrast, heritage attraction visiting is over-represented among the minority of holiday tourists staying eleven to fourteen nights on the island. This might suggest that for some tourists visiting the island in the summer, heritage attractions are a secondary priority for visiting, to be visited if time permits. If so, the term 'heritage tourist', as a label for all holiday tourists visiting heritage needs, as noted in Chapter 1, refining by motivation into sub-classes; that is, to be itself segmented.

It might be thought that the social class bias among the tourists visiting heritage attractions, noted earlier in this chapter, would lead to a distinctive accommodation profile for heritage tourists, compared to others. In particular, it might be thought that heritage tourists would be more likely to stay in hotels, compared to other tourists. The Manx database does not support such an assumption (Table 3.12). In terms of accommodation tourists visiting the island's heritage attractions would seem to display a similar profile of accommodation types to holiday-makers generally on the island. This would imply some caution in equating the heritage tourist with the higher spending tourist, and with the tourist sector generally demanding higher quality accommodation: equations frequently heard in the tourism industry of recent years in Britain.

CONCLUSIONS

This chapter has demonstrated that, with the exception of the social selectivity of heritage consumption, the consumer profiles of attractions would seem to present a further dimension of heterogeneity. The impression given by the term 'heritage industry' of a comparatively

Table 3.12 Type of accommodation used by adult holiday tourists visiting the Isle of Man and those visiting Manx heritage sites

Accommodation:	Site Survey 1988 %	Douglas Sea Front Survey 1988 %	Passenger Survey 1987 July %	August %
Friends or relatives	20.9	7.9	14	19
Hotel	42.3	53.3	69	65
Guest house	16.3	28.1		
Self-catering	16.3	9.1	12	12
Camp site	2.5	1.3	4	3
Other	1.7	0.3	2	1
N =	1,923	317		

Source: unpublished surveys undertaken by author for Manx National Heritage and
  Isle of Man Passenger Survey undertaken by Economic Adviser's Office
Note: N = sample size

uniform profile of consumers would seem fictitious, suggesting further the inadvisability of this terminology.

In terms of the age distribution of their tourist visitors, heritage attractions would seem highly heterogeneous. One element of consistency would seem an under-representation of aged adults at most heritage attractions, and frequently also of young adults. But exceptions abound, notably Castle Rushen in the Manx case. Group types of visitors would also seem diverse in terms of character; one consistent feature is that the predominance of families with children cannot be assumed. Equally, some sites attract such visiting groups disproportionately. Nor can we assume that heritage consumption is essentially a secondary holiday activity as is frequently implied by tourism professionals: heritage is a form of consumption undertaken by many main holiday-makers.

The Manx surveys imply that the different nationalities of Europe may consume heritage to differing extents. As noted in the discussion, such a conclusion can only be preliminary, but from the analysis presented here Irish residents would appear less likely to visit a heritage attraction when on holiday on the Isle of Man than their English counterparts. The prospect of national heterogeneity in heritage demand is suggested.

The social selectivity of heritage consumption would appear the single homogeneous feature of the socio-economic characteristics of the consumers of heritage as demonstrated by visits to heritage attractions. Visits to heritage attractions are disproportionately an activity undertaken by tourists from non-manual households, and especially those from professional and managerial households. While manual worker households do not as a group totally exclude themselves from visiting attractions, their propensity to visit is much less, and preferences for other holiday experiences are implied. Although attractions are not exclusively visited by tourists who have received higher or further education, a similar if less consistent and pronounced bias would seem apparent.

In an era of market orientation where consumer preferences dominate, the social class and educational profiles of heritage consumption have important implications not just for the means whereby heritage is to be presented but also for its content. Equally, the heterogeneity identified in other socio-economic characteristics between attractions in terms of their visitor profiles implies, in an era of consumer dominance, the need for attraction managers to be aware of the particular characteristics of their tourist and other visitors, and by implication if they seek to expand their market share, of their non-visitors.

4 Tourist decision-making and heritage attractions

TOURIST PREFERENCES

Surveys of visitors, tourists and non-tourists, to heritage attractions have often identified a broad recreational context for visits to such sites (Thomas 1989a), that is, general interest reasons for visiting attractions and the linkage of such visits to other activities, such as drives through the countryside, visits to towns, leisure shopping and eating out. As such, visits to heritage attractions are frequently only part of a day's recreational activity for many who visit them.

Tourist boards throughout Europe have often undertaken studies of tourists' activities and ratings of their areas. Surveys of this kind provide data on the relative importance of heritage attractions compared to other attractions, and were utilised in this way to estimate the general parameters of heritage demand in Chapter 1. However, these surveys are usually destination area-specific and lack comparison with other surveys, or to surveys of tourist visitors to heritage attractions. These surveys may also lack in-depth attention to heritage attractions, as they are designed to gain a general overview of tourist activities and images. As such, specific attraction-based survey material is potentially useful in identifying aspects of decision-making which may in particular apply to heritage tourists, or strictly to those tourists visiting heritage attractions.

TOURIST IMAGES OF HERITAGE ATTRACTIONS ON THE ISLE OF MAN

Despite its potential usefulness in attraction promotion little has been known about the images of heritage attractions held by tourists. The Passenger Surveys of the Isle of Man provide only limited insight into tourist images of this kind. The Passenger Surveys have been concerned with measuring the overall satisfaction of tourists with facilities and entertainments, rather than with activities and preferences. For example, in July 1988, 39 per cent of holiday tourists to the island staying in paid accommodation rated the island's entertainments and facilities as 'good', with half of like tourists in August giving such a rating. A feature of these ratings, possibly resulting from their generality, has been their variation from year to year and from month to month. From 1985 until 1988 the Passenger Survey asked tourists for their 'likes' about the island, these replies being unprompted. In Table 4.1 the heritage 'likes' have been abstracted from the Surveys. Few summer holiday tourists to the island would seem to rate the island's heritage attractions sufficiently to warrant giving them as 'likes': a consistent exception is the island's scenery. From the responses tabulated in Table 4.1 it would seem incorrect to categorise the tourists to the island as substantially 'heritage enthusiasts'. As such, the information presented in Table 4.1 adds further to the discussion of Chapter 3 as to how a 'heritage tourist' may be appropriately defined.

The Manx database prepared from the Manx National Heritage surveys does, however, shed some light on tourist images of heritage attractions, both from the surveys undertaken at the island's major heritage sites and that undertaken on Douglas Sea Front. These images can be supposed to pertain more generally than to the island's heritage attractions alone, as they will have been formed in substantial part from the tourists' experiences in their countries of residence, largely England and Ireland. It is important in the analysis which follows to distinguish between the perceptions of tourist visitors to the island's heritage sites and those tourists interviewed in Douglas, the latter including visitors to heritage attractions, potential visitors and tourists quite unlikely to visit such attractions.

For many of the tourists interviewed on Douglas Sea Front, castles were mainly places to visit when on holiday, with over half of those interviewed agreeing with the statement, 'Castles are mainly places to visit when on holiday', and fewer than three out of ten disagreeing (the remainder of holiday-makers being unsure). This would imply that for most tourists, or at least for those visiting the island, visits to castles are not part of their leisure activities and are, at most, perceived to be part of a holiday experience. In contrast were the holiday tourists interviewed at the heritage sites in 1990, for most of whom a visit to a castle was not perceived as associated with holiday activities alone. Of these tourist visitors, two-thirds disagreed with the statement; only a quarter agreed. This would suggest that in terms of image, holiday tourists interviewed at heritage attractions are likely to be somewhat

Table 4.1 Holiday tourists giving heritage tourism 'likes' in response to questioning in the Manx Passenger Surveys

Survey	'Like' mentioned	July %	August %
1985			
All holiday-makers	Scenery	16	20
	Towns/places of interest	4	4
	Sea/coast/beaches	0	*
1986			
Holiday-makers			
(a) sea passengers	Scenery	11	14
	Places of interest	0	6
	Glens/walks	0	4
(b) air passengers	Scenery	21	18
	Sea/beaches/coastline	*	0
	Places of interest	3	*
1987			
Holiday-makers			
(a) sea passengers	Scenery	15	18
	Places of interest	4	0
	Trams/trains	*	*
(b) air passengers	Scenery	21	18
	Walks/glens	3	*
	Trams/trains	*	3
	Beach/sea	*	*
1988			
Holiday-makers staying in paid accommodation			
(a) sea passengers	Scenery	21	21
	Beach/sea	3	*
	Walks/glens	*	*
(b) air passengers	Scenery	24	20
	Trams/trains	9	3
	Walks/glens	*	4
	Beach/sea	0	4
	History	0	*

Source: *Isle of Man Passenger Surveys* undertaken by the Economic Adviser's Office, Douglas: Isle of Man Government
Note: * indicates a frequency so low that it is not separately tabulated in the Passenger Survey

distinct from tourists generally. For tourists, generally, heritage sites may be a separate part of their imagery associated with holiday-making. This would seem also to be the case for a minority of holiday-maker tourists visiting attractions, but not for the large majority.

The perceived boredom of visiting all but the most prominent heritage attractions by the majority of tourists might be thought one reason for the imagery noted above. The Manx database may be used to counter such an argument, however. Holiday tourists interviewed on Douglas Sea Front were asked for their reactions to the statement that, 'Museums are boring places'. Exactly two-thirds of tourists disagreed with this statement, and a further one in twenty strongly disagreed. It would seem clear that the perception of museums as boring places is uncommon among tourists and as such would not appear to be a general deterrent to holiday-makers in their decision-making about what to do when on holiday.

Athough not generally seen as boring for adults, it might be thought that some types of heritage attractions are perceived by tourists as generally of insufficient interest to children. This would seem from the Douglas Sea Front survey to be the case, with holiday tourists with children generally agreeing with the insufficiency of both castles and museums as attractions for children. Castles were seen as having insufficient for children by more than six out of ten tourists with children accompanying them on the island, and museums likewise by 55 per cent. This image was by no means universal, however, among holiday tourists, with minorities disagreeing with the statements asked: a quarter disagreeing about the inadequacy of castles in this regard and three out of ten tourists disagreeing with the like inadequacy of museums. Although not strictly comparable, a similar question was asked of holiday tourists interviewed at the sites surveyed in 1990. The findings from this survey would confirm that tourists visiting heritage attractions on the island tend to have different images of heritage sites than do tourists generally. Twice as many tourists with children interviewed at the attractions disagreed than agreed with the statement, 'In my experience there is generally insufficient at places such as this to keep children occupied', 52 per cent compared to 23 per cent. These findings would suggest that heritage tourists are distinctive in their images of heritage attractions and that for many holiday-makers with children heritage sites represent unattractive places to visit because of a perceived, or experienced, insufficiency of interest for children.

Any negative images of heritage attractions among tourists generally would not seem particularly strong, however, at least among the sample of holiday-makers interviewed on Douglas Sea Front. Overall, there would seem to be only slight adverse recommendation of heritage attractions by tourists, for fewer than one in twenty of the tourists interviewed in Douglas would not recommend a friend visiting the island to visit a castle or like historic site, and a similar proportion would not recommend a friend to visit a museum. Moreover, more than eight out of ten tourists interviewed in Douglas in 1988 disagreed with the statements asked, namely, 'I would NOT recommend a friend to visit a castle or like historic site/museum if visiting the island'. The opportunity for promoting attractions would seem to be clear: at worse many holiday-makers would, from the Manx evidence, appear to have a 'non-image' or passively negative image of heritage attractions, rather than an overtly negative image.

TOURISTS' REASONS FOR VISITING HERITAGE ATTRACTIONS

Surveys in Wales have shown that tourists visit heritage attractions at Easter out of general, rather than specific, interests or to enjoy sightseeing, with an interest in archaeology, architecture, culture or other specific interest in a site as only secondary reasons (Thomas 1989a). In these respects tourists were found to be similar to visitors generally at Welsh heritage attractions. Achmatowicz-Otok and Goggins (1990) report much the same for visitors to a mansion in Ohio. Similarly, at the primary production, coal mining, attraction of Big Pit in Gwent, only around a quarter of visitors surveyed in 1983 gave educational reasons for their visit and even fewer, about one in seven, gave an interest in industrial archaeology as a reason; in contrast, three-quarters of all visitors gave 'to see how coal is mined' as a reason (Wales Tourist Board 1984b). However, certain kinds of heritage attractions may be exceptions to this general rule. For example, tourist visitors to churches, although rarely visiting for religious reasons, have been reported as generally visiting out of an interest in history or architecture, with monuments, stained glass, towers, fonts and associations with people reported as frequent attractions (Hanna and Hall 1984). The extent of this reported interest is not clear, however, from the report. At Laugharne, more than eight out of ten visitors surveyed in 1983 gave an interest in Dylan Thomas or Welsh literature as their reason for visiting, the attraction having been the author's home (Wales Tourist Board 1984a). However, again it is unclear how far this interest was particular or general. These possible exceptions apart, the general interest thesis would seem more widely found. In view of the need to get some indication of the quality of tourists' interest among their reasons for visiting, in the Manx surveys an attempt was made to separate out these degrees of self-

Table 4.2 Reasons given for their visit to a heritage site by adult holiday tourists visiting heritage sites on the Isle of Man

	Holiday tourists visiting sites:			
	Site Survey	*Site Survey*	*Castle Rushen Marketing Survey*	*Castle Rushen Interpretation Survey*
Reasons important in decision to visit:	*1988* %	*1990* %	*1991* %	*1991* %
Enjoy sightseeing/general interest	66.6	68.9	78.1	84.9
Part of a day out	47.6	48.3	31.5	27.6
Particular interest in castles/historic places	45.4	57.6	45.9	38.0
Particular interest in Manx culture/history	33.3	25.4	15.8	6.8
Brought child(ren)/ child(ren) wanted to come	25.5	17.7	8.9	2.6
Education	21.5	12.2	4.8	4.7
Unable to go where originally planned	2.5	0.4	0.7	1.6
Just came to look	15.5	6.6	6.8	3.1
Special 'event' on	2.4	—	—	—
No particular reason	—	0.7	1.4	1.0
N =	1,942	547	146	192

Source: unpublished surveys undertaken by author for Manx National Heritage
Notes: more than one reason could be given as important
   N = sample size

rated interest, enabling the generality of the general interest thesis to be tested.

The Manx database refers to summer tourists. The dominance of sightseeing and a *general* interest is clear among the holiday tourists' reasons for visiting the Manx attractions (Table 4.2). A *particular* interest in castles or historic places and the visit as one part of a day out are secondary reasons given for visiting. In contrast, a particular interest in Manx culture and history forms only a third order reason for visiting the Manx attractions. As such, the appropriateness of categorising all tourists visiting heritage attractions as heritage specialists is once again raised. Equally, few holiday-maker tourists visiting the Manx heritage attractions were aimless in their reasons for visiting, few coming simply to look, and fewer still either coming because they had been unable to go where they had originally intended or coming out of no particular reason. The latter would concur with survey findings from tourists visiting Welsh attractions in 1985, only 37 per cent of whom were found to have decided to visit on impulse or no earlier than on their day of visit (Public Attitudes Surveys Research 1986). Equally, many visitors had only decided to visit an attraction on the day prior to their visit, although Caernarfon Castle, the Bishop's Palace at St Davids, and Big Pit had significantly higher rates of longer term pre-visit planning than others of the nine Welsh attractions surveyed in 1985.

The heterogeneity of heritage attractions would imply that it should not be assumed that the reasons given by tourists for visiting different types of heritage attractions are generally the same. As yet we have insufficient case studies to compile profiles of reasons by attraction types, but the Manx surveys provide some useful insights into likely differences. A particular interest in *Manx* culture and history was far more frequently given as a reason for visiting the folk village at Cregneash and the Manx Museum than for visiting the island's castles, the primary production industrial monument of Laxey Wheel or the reconstructed Viking boat, Odin's Raven (Table 4.3). In this case it would seem that tourists are equating Manx history with the island's social history. Sightseeing and general interest were particularly important among the reasons given for visiting the island's castles and the Grove Museum. As the latter is promoted as a museum of middle-class nineteenth century rural life a stronger representation of reasons similar to those given at Cregneash and the Manx Museum might have been expected. Odin's Raven was notable as being visited disproportionately as part of a day out. The differences shown in Table 4.3 are difficult to systematically explain. What they serve to emphasize is the variation within the general pattern of reasons for visiting given by holiday tourists visiting heritage attractions which may be expected as further site surveys are undertaken throughout Europe. The Manx survey data further emphasizes the limitations of asserting, for example, that visitors to heritage attractions are largely seeking 'nostalgia' (Chapter 2): such an assertion ignores substantial variations between attractions in the reasons tourists themselves give for their visits.

Differences in the educational attainments of tourists can be of some importance in explaining differences in the reasons for visiting heritage attractions. Although sightseeing is a pervasive reason given for visiting Manx heritage attractions, it is less common among the more highly educated tourists, for whom an interest in local culture or desire for personal education can be a disproportionately frequent

Table 4.3 Main reasons given for their visit to a heritage site by adult holiday tourists at different heritage sites on the Isle of Man

Reasons most frequently given as important in decision to visit:	Holiday tourists visiting sites:										
	Peel Castle		Castle Rushen		Manx Museum	Nautical Museum	Grove Museum	Laxey Wheel	Cregneash		Odin's Raven
	1988 %	1990 %	1988 %	1990 %	1988 %	1988 %	1988 %	1988 %	1988 %	1990 %	1988 %
Enjoy sightseeing/general interest	72.3	73.4	71.6	79.5	55.6	62.7	73.3	63.5	67.5	53.4	65.8
Part of a day out	37.5	54.9	49.3	43.2	26.1	49.2	48.2	45.2	52.9	46.6	78.7
Particular interest in castles/historic places	60.9	68.5	57.5	56.8	35.1	55.9	56.9	30.0	47.7	47.2	14.4
Particular interest in Manx culture/history	27.0	24.5	26.1	8.6	45.1	34.5	36.4	19.6	50.3	43.8	22.3
N =	256	184	306	185	268	177	195	230	308	178	202

Source: unpublished surveys undertaken by author for Manx National Heritage
Notes: (a) see Table 4.2 for 1991 profile of Castle Rushen; and
(b) more than one reason could be given
N = sample size

reason given for visiting (Table 4.4). However, we should take care not to exaggerate the extent of such differences resultant of educational backgrounds. For example, an interest in castles or other historic places would seem undifferentiated by educational background. Equally, although this may indicate a real absence of differences by education, it may also result from the imprecise nature of what actually constitutes a 'particular interest' in a site, which may range from an informed to a less informed interest. Ambiguities such as this may suggest the need for greater in-depth investigation of the reasons given for visiting attractions as part of a research agenda for heritage tourism.

TOURIST REPEAT VISITING OF HERITAGE ATTRACTIONS

Repeat visiting of heritage attractions might be thought to be an index of satisfaction or preference. Equally, if a tourist selects different destination areas for his or her successive holidays, repeat visiting of specific sites could be thought to be minimal or non-existant. Similarly, a tourist visiting the same destination for a series of holidays might not visit all of the heritage attractions of the destination on his or her first holiday, but visit the remainder on successive holidays. This would also imply low rates of repeat visiting of sites by tourists on holiday. If the latter two patterns of holidaying pertain, satisfaction or preference would be more appropriately measured through repeat visits not to specific sites but to types of sites, which may be in the same destination area but equally may not be.

Surveys in Wales have found that most visitors to heritage attractions are in fact on their first visit. For example, at the nine Welsh heritage attractions surveyed in 1985 just under three-quarters of visitors were found to be on their first visit (Public Attitudes Surveys Research 1986). At the state monuments surveyed in Wales in 1986 roughly seven out of ten visitors were found to be on their first visit (Prentice 1989a). At Laugharne only one in eight visitors surveyed were on a repeat visit (Wales Tourist Board 1984a). The Welsh findings generally concur with those for English Heritage attractions surveyed in 1984 (Public Attitudes Surveys Research 1986). However, a North American study suggests a different profile. At Colonial Williamsburg half of all visitors surveyed were reported to be repeat visitors (Alderson and Low 1986). Similarly, city centre museums and art galleries could in many cases be presumed to have higher proportions of repeat visitors among their visitors resultant of the changing of temporary exhibitions. It may be, therefore, that different

Table 4.4 Main reasons given for their visit to a heritage site by adult holiday tourists of differing educational backgrounds at heritage sites on the Isle of Man

Holiday tourists visiting sites by age at which continuous full-time education was completed or intended to be completed:

Reasons most frequently given (plus education) as important in decision to visit:	16 or earlier		17 or 18 years		19 to 22 years		23 years or older	
	Site Survey 1990 %	Castle Rushen Surveys Combined 1991 %	Site Survey 1990 %	Castle Rushen Surveys Combined 1991 %	Site Survey 1990 %	Castle Rushen Surveys Combined 1991 %	Site Survey 1990 %	Castle Rushen Surveys Combined 1991 %
Enjoy sightseeing/general interest	70.7	85.2	79.4	85.6	62.8	95.6	48.3	58.3
Part of a day out	47.1	29.0	50.8	29.9	52.1	26.7	36.7	29.2
Particular interest in castles/historic places	52.9	42.6	54.8	38.1	64.5	42.2	61.7	45.8
Particular interest in Manx culture/history	22.7	9.5	16.7	12.4	32.2	13.3	38.3	8.3
Education	8.0	—	7.9	—	15.7	—	28.3	—
N =	225	169	126	97	121	45	60	24

Source: unpublished surveys undertaken by author for Manx National Heritage
Notes: (a) the samples for Castle Rushen are combined for 1991 due to the small sample sizes of tourists educated to 19 years or older; and
(b) more than one reason could be given
N = sample size

Table 4.5 Number of repeat visits made to specific heritage sites on the Isle of Man by adult holiday tourists visiting heritage sites on the island

	Holiday tourists visiting sites:		
			Castle Rushen
Number of previous visits to site:	Site Survey 1988	Site Survey 1990	Marketing Survey 1991
	%	%	%
None	76.7	74.8	69.9
One	11.1	13.1	18.5
Two	3.6	4.4	4.1
More times	8.6	7.7	7.5
N =	1,942	544	146

Source: unpublished surveys undertaken by author for Manx National Heritage
Note: N = sample size

types of attractions will be be visited by repeat visitors in differing proportions, emphasing further the heterogeneity of heritage consumption.

The Manx holiday tourist database shows that most tourists visiting the island's heritage attractions are on their first visit to the site (Table 4.5). However, roughly a quarter had visited the attraction before, often once before. Some site variation is apparent with the Manx Museum and Laxey Wheel having disproportionate numbers of repeat tourist visitors, and the Grove Museum, Nautical Museum and Odin's Raven the fewest (Table 4.6). These differences may be interpreted, at least in part, as indicators of the popularity of the sites. Despite many tourist visitors to the island's heritage attractions being on their first visit to a site this is not so for tourists to the island, many of whom are repeat visitors. In July and August 1988 the Passenger Survey found that about half of the holiday-makers staying in paid accommodation had visited the island before; in the same months of 1990 the equivalent proportion was between two-thirds and 57 per cent of tourists. Indeed, the island attracts a sizeable minority of tourists who have repeatedly visited the island previously. In both July and August 1988 and 1990 more than half of the island's repeat holiday-makers were on their fourth visit or more. In July and August 1990 this group of tourists in fact represented more than four out of ten of all holiday-makers staying in paid accommodation on the island. These repeat visitors would not seem to be repeat visiting the island's heritage attractions, implying that for many tourists to the island, at most, one

Table 4.6 Repeat visiting to specific heritage sites on the Isle of Man by adult holiday tourists visiting the different heritage sites on the island

	Peel Castle 1988 %	Peel Castle 1990 %	Castle Rushen 1988 %	Castle Rushen 1990 %	Manx Museum 1988 %	Nautical Museum 1988 %	Grove Museum 1988 %	Laxey Wheel 1988 %	Cregneash 1988 %	Cregneash 1990 %	Odin's Raven 1988 %
					Holiday tourists visiting sites:						
Visited the site previously	25.8	23.6	27.5	27.6	29.9	12.4	8.7	35.7	25.3	24.3	11.4
Not visited the site previously	74.2	76.4	72.5	72.4	70.1	87.6	91.3	64.3	74.7	75.7	88.6
N =	256	182	306	185	268	177	195	230	308	177	202

Source: unpublished surveys undertaken by author for Manx National Heritage
Notes: see Table 4.5 for 1991 profile of Castle Rushen
    N = sample size

visit to a particular heritage attraction is sufficient, even if they repeatedly visit the island. How far this may be generalised into a statement that for many tourists a visit once to a specific heritage attraction is sufficient, even if they return several times to the holiday destination, must await research elsewhere, but it would seem a likely supposition, particularly as having visited an attraction before has been found to be a frequent characteristic of visitors who turn away at the gates of Welsh monuments (Prentice 1989b). This would imply the need to include research into the past behaviour of tourists at destinations when seeking to explain their current behaviour patterns.

Part of this multi-holiday behaviour would seem to include the common ranking of sites in terms of priority for visiting, along with other types of attraction on the island. Within a general context of all but one of the eight major heritage attractions on the island having not been visited by most holiday-maker tourists to the island on their present or previous holidays (Table 4.7), certain priorities in visiting may be inferred. Laxey Wheel has been clearly much more popular as an attraction to visit than the other seven major sites. Further, Laxey Wheel and Peel Castle would seem to be most likely to be visited on a holiday-maker's current holiday. The extent to which such effective ranking of attractions to visit occurs elsewhere should form part of a research agenda for heritage tourism, for its occurrence would seem plausible but its determinants unclear. Tourists returning to a destination would seem to be working through a retrospective 'shopping list' of attractions to visit over a series of holidays, only to return to the original attractions when most of the others have been visited. In this way, holiday tourists repeatedly visiting a destination, although not varying that destination, may effectively vary its content in terms of its attractions. This would also suggest that those tourists repeatedly visiting a particular heritage attraction or types of attraction should perhaps be most appropriately termed 'heritage enthusiasts', a discussion we return to in Chapter 8.

The concept of repeat visiting in terms of site *type* was outlined earlier. This may be defined either in terms of behaviour on a holiday or over a period of time longer than the tourist's present holiday. Visitors to Dylan Thomas's boathouse in Laugharne in 1983 were found largely not to have visited another attraction associated with a writer in the twelve months prior to their visit; fewer than three out of ten had in fact visited a similar attraction in the year before they were interviewed at Laugharne (Wales Tourist Board 1984a). Of visitors to Big Pit interviewed in the same year, most had not visited another industrial museum or other industrial attraction in the previous twelve

Table 4.7 Extent to which adult holiday tourists visiting the Isle of Man visit heritage sites on the island

Recency with which holiday tourists had visited sites:	Holiday tourists visiting IOM: Douglas Sea Front Survey 1988							
	Peel Castle %	Castle Rushen %	Manx Museum %	Nautical Museum %	Grove Museum %	Laxey Wheel %	Cregneash %	Odin's Raven %
Past week	21.7	13.3	12.4	8.5	9.1	30.4	10.0	11.5
Past month	0.3	0.0	0.3	0.3	0.0	0.3	0.0	0.0
Past year	2.4	4.8	3.3	0.9	1.5	5.1	2.1	1.5
Earlier	17.5	17.2	17.0	11.2	8.8	19.0	13.7	7.3
Never visited	58.1	64.8	67.0	79.1	80.7	45.2	74.2	79.8

N = 336

Source: unpublished survey undertaken by author for Manx National Heritage
Note: N = sample size

Table 4.8 Number of specified heritage sites visited in the previous seven days by adult holiday tourists visiting Manx heritage sites

| Number of sites visited (including site at which interviewed): | Holiday tourists visiting sites: Site Survey 1990 | | |
| | Peel Castle | Castle Rushen | Cregneash |
	%	%	%
1 (Had visited site of interview only)	25.0	15.1	20.2
2	26.6	41.1	23.0
3	25.0	29.2	21.9
4	10.9	9.7	18.5
5	7.1	3.2	11.2
6	3.3	1.6	3.4
7	1.6	0.0	0.6
8 (All sites specified visited)	0.5	0.0	1.1
N =	184	185	178

Source: unpublished survey undertaken by author for Manx National Heritage
Note: N = sample size

months, although four out of ten had, a larger minority than at Laugharne (Wales Tourist Board 1984b). No difference was found between tourists and day-trippers in this regard. Of the holiday tourists at the attractions surveyed on the Isle of Man in 1990, most had already in the week prior to being interviewed visited at least one other of the eight major heritage attractions on the island; few had, however, visited more than three other sites (Table 4.8). The 1988 site survey provides information on other visits which is site-specific. As would be expected from Table 4.7, Laxey Wheel was found to be the major attraction among the others visited, with the island's castles ranked a clear second (Table 4.9). The site-specific rates shown in Table 4.9 not only remind us of the differing popularity of sites to visitors at others, but also that certain heritage attractions in a destination area may not be visited by the large majority of those holiday tourists who choose to visit heritage sites as part of their holiday. This provides the opportunity to seek to encourage visits to these less visited sites as a means of varying the effective destination content of attractions for repeat holiday-makers.

The second kind of repeat visiting to types of sites is that to attractions outside of the tourist's destination area, either in his or her leisure time or on another holiday. The Manx database shows substantial visiting of other heritage attractions by tourists visiting the island's heritage sites (Table 4.10). Castles and museums would seem

Table 4.9 Extent to which adult holiday tourists visiting heritage sites on the Isle of Man had visited other heritage sites on the island

Recency with which holiday tourists had visited sites:	Holiday tourists visiting sites: Site Survey 1988						
	Peel Castle %	Castle Rushen %	Manx Museum %	Nautical Museum %	Grove Museum %	Laxey Wheel %	Cregneash %	Odin's Raven %
Past week	35.8	30.3	15.2	9.9	6.8	52.1	22.6	17.8
Past month	1.8	1.6	0.8	0.8	0.5	1.7	1.2	1.2
Past year	5.2	5.1	3.4	2.2	1.5	4.9	4.1	3.3
Earlier	14.5	15.7	12.9	9.3	5.5	16.2	11.7	7.4
Never visited	42.7	47.3	67.7	77.9	85.6	25.1	60.3	70.3

N = 1,714

Source: unpublished survey undertaken by author for Manx National Heritage
Note: N = sample size

Table 4.10 Extent to which adult holiday tourists visiting heritage sites on the Isle of Man had visited heritage sites elsewhere in the previous twelve months

| Site type visited elsewhere: | Holiday tourists visiting sites having visited a heritage site elsewhere in the previous twelve months: Site Survey 1990 | | |
	Peel Castle %	Castle Rushen %	Cregneash %
Cathedral	67.4	51.4	64.0
Castle	74.5	61.1	80.9
Abbey	41.3	20.0	32.6
Stately home	53.8	58.4	68.5
Museum	82.1	51.9	76.4
N =	184	185	178

Source: unpublished survey undertaken by author for Manx National Heritage
Note: N = sample size

particularly popular. However, the tourist visitors to the island's two castles are not more likely than those to Cregneash to have visited castles elsewhere, nor are those to Cregneash more likely to have visited a museum elsewhere. It seems that tourists inter-mix attraction types in their visiting. The Manx survey evidence would further suggest that tourist visitors to heritage attractions are in fact drawn largely from a population who visit heritage sites as a leisure activity or other holiday activity, indicating a possible link between tourist behaviour and leisure behaviour contrary to that suggested by other evidence (Prentice 1992b; Light and Prentice forthcoming). This 'discrepancy' may in part derive from the general recreational context in which visits to heritage attractions take place as a leisure activity; if households engage in a range of leisure activities, of which visits to attractions are one, it is likely to be impossible to predict heritage visits when on holiday from the range of leisure activites pursued, particularly for those tourists for whom heritage attractions are a low priority when on holiday. However, many tourists interviewed at heritage attractions will give such visits as a leisure activity. In view of this ambiguity, links of this kind would seem worthy of study as part of an agenda for heritage tourism research.

The link between leisure activities and tourist activities suggested by the leisure visits to heritage attractions made by the tourist visitors to the Manx heritage sites is particularly strong for non-manual tourists visiting the Manx attractions (Table 4.11), and among these tourists,

Table 4.11 Effect of social class on the extent to which adult holiday tourists visiting heritage sites on the Isle of Man had visited heritage sites elsewhere in the previous twelve months

Site type visited elsewhere:	Professional/ higher managerial	Intermediate managerial	Non-manual super-visory/ clerical	Skilled manual	Semi- and unskilled manual
	%	%	%	%	%
Cathedral	67.2	66.7	57.1	41.7	48.7
Castle	75.2	77.8	64.9	66.7	53.8
Abbey	38.4	38.9	27.3	13.1	17.9
Stately home	65.6	66.2	55.8	56.0	48.7
Museum	83.2	75.3	63.6	46.4	59.0
N =	125	198	77	84	39

Holiday tourists visiting sites having visited a heritage site elsewhere in the previous twelve months: Site Survey 1990

Source: unpublished survey undertaken by author for Manx National Heritage
Note: N = sample size

those from professional or managerial households. These social class differences are consistent across attraction types, but most marked for visits to museums. These differences would concur with the general parameters of demand discussed in Chapter 1. However, we should be careful not to exaggerate the extent of these differences as heritage attraction visiting by tourists as a leisure or other holiday activity is quite common across all social groups. This would suggest the wide social class appeal of heritage attractions as a leisure attraction to those tourists who also visit them when on holiday.

CONCLUSIONS

The present chapter has found a degree of homogeneity in the aggregate outcome of the general decision-making processes of tourists in terms of visiting heritage attractions. This does not, however, mean that tourist decision-making in terms of images, reasons for visiting and repeat behaviour is the same for all tourists. Tourists do differ in these respects but would seem to do so with some consistency. Most notably, sightseeing and general interest would seem to predominate as reasons for visiting attractions, with a particular interest in castles, historic sites or culture a less common motive. Although more highly educated tourists would seem to be more likely to visit attractions out of particular interests, the extent of this effect should not be exaggerated. In that the dominant market segment for heritage would seem to be the general interest consumer, presentations of heritage need to be based at least in part on this awareness. What might be termed 'heritage specialists' in terms of their particular interests would appear to be a secondary market segment in terms of their proportion among tourists visiting attractions.

However, many of these general interest consumers also visit heritage attractions other than on the holiday on which they were interviewed: such visits may be either a leisure activity or an activity undertaken on other holidays taken within the same year as the holiday for which they were surveyed. This gives a further dimension to the issue of who is a heritage tourist or enthusiast, for frequent consumers would generally be considered to be enthusiasts even if their enthusiasm is rather uninformed. Tourist visitors to heritage attractions would appear to be substantially drawn from households who otherwise visit such attractions, although the range of the attractions they visit would seem quite broad, further implying a general rather than particular interest in any one site or type of site. Manual worker tourists interviewed at attractions would seem disproportionately to regard heritage consumption in the form of attraction visiting as a holiday activity, but this difference should not be overemphasised.

Tourists visiting heritage attractions may be thought to have 'shopping lists' of attractions, selecting the most preferred first, and then on subsequent holidays visiting others. In this way the content of a holiday may be varied if the destination area is not. Again, this would concur with a substantially general interest market among the consumers of heritage.

Those tourists visiting attractions would seem from the Manx surveys to have different images of heritage attractions than tourists generally. Visitors it would seem perceive visits to attractions as less of a holiday activity than do tourists generally, and instead, more as a frequent leisure experience. This would concur with the reported behaviour of tourists prior to the holiday on which they were surveyed. Similarly, while tourists in general may see castles and museums as offering insufficient for children, the same is not true for those tourists actually visiting attractions.

5 Tourist trip making and visits to heritage attractions

SPECIFICNESS OF VISITS

Little has been known about how specific tourists are in their intentions to visit attractions when they set out for their day's activities. The 1985 survey of visitors to Welsh attractions (Public Attitudes Surveys Research 1986) mentioned in the previous chapter is a notable exception, including as it did a question on when the visit was planned: finding that only for less than four out of ten tourists had their visit either been planned on the day of their visit or had been decided on impulse when passing the attraction. Visits were found to have been largely planned on the day prior to the visit being made or earlier. However, planned visits which never in fact materialised are less easy to measure. The previous chapter has also shown that visits to heritage attractions are frequently part of a day out, at least for tourists on the Isle of Man. Exceptions can be found, for example, at Castle Rushen in 1991 this reason was less frequently given than at other attractions (Table 4.2). The inclusion of a visit to a heritage attraction as one aspect only of a day's excursion may imply that for at least some tourists the heritage attraction may not be the primary attraction to be visited, nor may these tourists have a specific intention to visit the attraction when setting out on their day's excursion. For example, when setting out, such itineraries may emphasise places to be visited, rather than attractions at those places or *en route*. The importance of a 'day out in the country' as a reason for trip making has also been found for visitors (tourists and day-trippers) to heritage attractions in Wales (Thomas 1989a). However, how such day out itineraries are planned has received little attention. This is an important oversight, for in designing promotional campaigns, for example, information of this kind is essential if promotional investment is to be effective.

The Manx database provides some limited insight into the issue of specificness of intentions by tourists in planning their days' out. A question to this effect was asked in both the surveys of 1991 at Castle Rushen. However, it would clearly be inadvisable to assume that these findings necessarily reflect a wider situation, particularly in view of the lower rating of a day out as a reason for visiting the castle in 1991 than in the other surveys, and generalisation must await investigation elsewhere. It should also be remembered that in 1991 the presentation of Castle Rushen had recently been upgraded, and so tourists may have been attracted to it specifically to see the new presentation. Despite these provisos the findings on specificness of visits are still of interest. Despite a majority of tourists claiming to have come to Castletown specifically to see the castle, substantial minorities had not, namely 47 per cent of the tourists interviewed in the Interpretation Survey and a third of those interviewed in the Marketing Survey. For these large minorities of tourists visiting the castle either a vague or incomplete image of Castletown may be assumed, illustrating the importance of non-specific or general factors in attracting tourists to attractions when on holiday.

It might be thought that the specificness of tourists' intentions to visit attractions would depend on factors such as social class, educational attainment or reasons given for visiting. The survey findings from Castle Rushen do not readily support such a conjecture. Neither the social class nor educational attainment of tourists were found to be determinants of the specificness of visiting intentions. Nor do the Manx surveys give consistent support for an argument that the reasons given by tourists for visiting an attraction may be associated with a specific intention to visit. Whereas the Marketing Survey found no such associations, the Interpretation Survey found quite unambiguous differences between general interest and particular interest tourists. Of those tourists interviewed as part of the Interpretation Survey, whereas only 47 per cent and 34 per cent respectively of those for whom the enjoyment of sightseeing or for whom their visit was part of a day out claimed to have visited Castletown with a specific intention to visit the castle, 64 per cent and 92 per cent respectively of those visiting out of a particular interest in castles or in Manx culture and history claimed to have come specifically to visit the castle. These are substantial differences, and of the kind which might be expected. However, the disparity between the 1991 surveys implies some caution in generalisation. Clearly, the inter-relationships of reasons given for visits and the specificness of tourist trip making warrants further investigation and needs to form part of a research agenda for heritage tourism.

LENGTH OF STAY AT ATTRACTIONS

Surveys undertaken at state monuments in Wales in 1986 reported that the most common length of stay by visitors at the attractions was between half an hour and one hour at Easter and between one hour and one and a half hours in the summer (Prentice 1989a). These attractions were largely castles, for which substantial variation in lengths of stay between castles were recorded which could not readily be explained by the extent of the sites nor the type of presentation to visitors. An exception was possibly Caernarfon Castle where the large site and extensive presentation could be advanced as the reasons why visitors generally stayed over ninety minutes at the attraction. On the whole it was concluded that visitors tended to stay at the Welsh attractions for shorter periods than at similar Irish attractions for which data were available for comparison. The length of stay by tourists was not separately analysed in these Welsh sudies, but would seem from the known visitor mix at those North Wales attractions which attract largely holiday-makers to have been substantially shorter than the average (mean) of four hours and twelve minutes, for example, reported as the length of stay by tourists at Beamish Museum (Johnson and Thomas 1990a), which may be taken as an example of a highly 'developed' historical or nostalgia theme park (Chapter 2). At Beamish, little difference was in fact found between the average length of stay of tourists and day-trippers, although the generality of this fact to other 'developed' attractions is uncertain. At Big Pit, for example, three-quarters of visitors have been found to stay between two and three hours (Public Attitudes Surveys Research 1986); but, although quite extensive, as a former coal mine this is an attraction concerned with primary production rather than a nostalgia park. In 1983 the length of stay at Big Pit does not appear to have been generally quite as long, but even then, just over half of its visitors surveyed had stayed at the site for between two and three hours (Wales Tourist Board 1984b). More generally at Welsh attractions visitors were found in 1985 by the same survey as at Big Pit in that year to spend between half an hour and an hour at attractions, a length of visit comparable to the 1986 surveys, some of which were at the same sites it should be noted, however. In some contrast, at Dylan Thomas's boathouse only one in six visitors were found in 1983 to have stayed under an hour at the attraction, with the tourists among them the most likely to stay longer (Wales Tourist Board 1984a). Considered collectively, these studies imply some considerable diversity in lengths of stays between different types of heritage attractions, and within similar

Table 5.1 Length of stays at heritage sites on the Isle of Man by adult holiday tourists

	Holiday tourists visiting sites:			
		Castle Rushen	Castle Rushen	
	Site Survey 1988	Site Survey 1990	Marketing Survey 1991	Interpretation Survey 1991
Length of stay:	%	%	%	%
Under 30 mins		5.9	0.7	0.5
30 mins–1 hr	41.5 }	53.5	11.6	8.9
1–2 hrs	51.6	40.0	70.5	79.2
Over 2 hrs	6.9	0.5	17.1	11.5
N=	1,939	547	146	192

Source: unpublished surveys undertaken by author for Manx National Heritage
Note: N = sample size

types, implying a further element of heterogeneity in the consumption of heritage.

The several types of attraction on the Isle of Man provide an invaluable opportunity to investigate the possible effects of attraction type, and the extent of presentation or 'interpretation' provided, on the length of tourist stay at the attractions. As reference to Table 5.1 shows, considerable variation can be found in the lengths of stays by tourists at the Manx attractions, but with almost all tourists staying between half an hour and two hours. Castle Rushen in 1991 was found to be a clear exception (Table 5.2), with seven out of ten tourists staying at the attraction for between one and two hours, compared to half or four out of ten tourists surveyed in 1988 and 1990. As the surveys of 1991 measure the length of tourist stay after the refurbishment of the castle, it may be inferred that the investment in contemporary presentational media at the castle has resulted in increasing the length of tourist stay at the attraction, as with Beamish, suggesting the importance of substantial investment in contemporary presentational media in enhancing tourist stay at attractions. As a more general point, the Manx surveys reveal the dangers inherent in using snapshot views gained from surveys of aspects of tourist trip making, such as length of stay at attractions. In 1990 the average length of stay at attractions was generally shorter than in 1988, a likely function of the weather prevalent during the survey periods at these largely open air attractions. The wider issue of the potentially varied promotion of alternative opportunities between years is one which should also be noted although its measurement is less easy to measure as changing between survey years. Some replication of surveys is implied in an agenda for heritage tourism, therefore, with reference to these possible determinants.

Further reference to Table 5.2 indicates quite substantial variation between the Manx attractions in the length of tourist stays at them, confirming the heterogeneity of visit durations noted earlier for the Welsh attractions. Only in part may this heterogeneity between the Manx attractions be explained by the the extent of what is on offer at the eight attractions. The Manx Museum, for example, has extensive galleries, and in 1988 this was reflected in comparatively lengthy tourist stays. Similarly, Cregneash as a *clachan* (village) with cottages open to visitors has comparatively much to see, and in 1988 at least had above average lengths of visits by tourists. Yet in 1988 Castle Rushen and Laxey Wheel did not have similarly extensive displays, but were equally characterised by lengthy stays by tourists. Other factors than the presentation of the attractions would therefore appear to be important in determining the length of tourist stays at attractions, for example, the ambience of a site or the views obtained from it. As a general point it should be noted that few tourists visiting the Manx attractions stayed over two hours at any of them, confirming the findings noted earlier for Wales, and suggesting that heritage attractions of the kind found on the island are only part of a day's activities for most tourists. As such, investment in the presentation of attractions of this kind may only result, in terms of enhanced lengths of stay at attractions, of an increase from one to two hours, as other activities create demands on the time available to holiday-makers. Attractions such as Beamish, presenting a replication of town and country living on a single site, should therefore be regarded as the exception rather than the goal to be pursued by most heritage attraction operators seeking to present an already existing monument and the like, rather than seeking to create one largely or totally from a 'green' field site.

It might be expected that those tourists more formally educated might stay longer at heritage attractions of the kind found on the Isle of Man, as they tend to visit out of more particular interests (Chapter 4). The Manx evidence is ambiguous, however. Although not statistically valid at 0.05, the 1990 Site Survey found that of tourists educated to 23 years of age or above, 57 per cent spent upwards of an hour at the attractions surveyed, compared to under 40 per cent of the lesser

Table 5.2 Length of stays at different heritage sites on the Isle of Man by adult holiday tourists

					Holiday tourists visiting sites:							
	Peel Castle		Castle Rushen		Manx Museum	Nautical Museum	Grove Museum	Laxey Wheel	Cregneash		Odin's Raven	
Length of stay:	1988	1990	1988	1990	1988	1988	1988	1988	1988	1990	1988	
	%	%	%	%	%	%	%	%	%	%	%	
Under 1 hr	41.3	68.5	21.6	59.5	18.7	72.3	53.8	33.5	24.7	52.3	98.0	
1–2 hrs	52.8	30.4	64.1	40.0	69.7	27.1	45.6	59.1	67.9	44.9	1.5	
Over 2 hrs	5.9	1.1	14.4	0.5	11.6	0.6	0.5	7.4	7.5	2.8	0.5	
N=	254	184	306	185	267	177	195	230	308	178	202	

Source: unpublished surveys undertaken by author for Manx National Heritage
Notes: see Table 5.1 for 1991 profile of Castle Rushen
      N = sample size

educated tourists. This feature was not replicated in 1991 at Castle Rushen, where the presentation of the castle had been changed. In view of the lack of adequate statistical validity of the 1990 finding the issue of how far, and at what types of attractions, educational levels may affect the lengths of stays by tourists at attractions will need to be resolved by future research. One problem needing to be overcome in future research designs will be that of ensuring adequate representation of the more highly educated in samples of tourists, implying the need for quota rather than random sampling as the basis for some research applications. Nor can the Manx database unambiguously sustain the more immediate argument that those tourists visiting an attraction out of more specific interests either in castles and other historic places or in Manx culture and history on the whole stay longer at the attractions. The 1988 Site Survey found some support for such an argument, but not that of 1990. Whereas in 1988 tourists visiting the attractions as part of a day out were likely to have stayed for shorter periods at the attractions than those visiting out of particular interests in castles or culture, the same was not true in 1990. Even in 1988 these differences were not substantial, with 53 per cent of tourists visiting the attractions citing a day out as a reason for visiting, staying over an hour, compared to two-thirds of both tourists citing a particular interest in castle and historic places and of those citing a particular interest in Manx culture and history. The ambiguity of these findings suggests the need for extreme caution in thinking that the reasons for visiting heritage attractions on the part of holiday-makers may consistently affect their length of stay at attractions: other factors are clearly of importance too, which may include time budgets and access to other attractions.

Despite the limitations in the extent of our present knowledge of the determinants of length of stay at heritage attractions, this knowledge is much greater than that concerning the length of stay such visits induce in the surrounding town or countryside. Yet knowledge of such induced stays is important if the economic impact of tourist attractions is to be properly understood, for tourists' spending on food and drink in a locality will likely increase as their length of stay increases. The Manx database provides some limited insight into this issue, but many more surveys are necessary from elsewhere before general conclusions may be drawn. In effect, we are seeking a delimitation by type of tourists and by type of attraction of the spatial extents of day trips made by tourists visiting heritage attractions. The Marketing Survey at Castle Rushen in 1991 included questioning on the extent to which tourists visiting the castle would recommend a friend visiting the island to plan to spend a whole day for a visit to Castletown, the town in which the castle is situated. Just over half the tourists asked agreed with this recommendation, although fewer than one in twelve strongly agreed. Few tourists, however, disagreed, although nearly a third were undecided. This recommendation could in part at least be expected to derive from experience of the castle and of its immediate surroundings. However, it was not explored further in the survey. As induced stays of this kind are important in the promotional and developmental strategies of tourist attractions, the inclusion of such linkages in an agenda for heritage tourism is clearly implied. That is, we should not just ask about length of stays at attractions, but also those made in the vicinities of attractions. Surveys in Wales in the 1980s already mentioned (Thomas 1989a) identified visits to nearby shops and towns as frequent activities of visitors to heritage attractions, further suggesting that the investigation of localised linkages and the time spent on such activities by tourists visiting heritage attractions is worthy of future research attention.

MARKET AREAS OF HERITAGE ATTRACTIONS

The market areas of heritage attractions have been found to be quite localised in terms of where visitors come from on their day of visit (Prentice 1989a). Upwards of half of the visitors to heritage attractions, mainly major castles, surveyed in Wales in 1986 were found to have travelled twenty miles or less to the attractions. The situation for tourists would seem more localised still, for at both Easter and in the summer it was those Welsh attractions which were located in the main holiday areas which were found to have the most localised market areas. This is confirmed by a similar survey of 1985: on average tourists visiting state monuments in Wales were found to have travelled only half the distance day-trippers had come (Public Attitudes Surveys Research 1986). A pertinent question is the extent to which these localised market areas of major castles in Wales result from the preferences of tourists not to travel far from the locality of their accommodation or from the absence in many areas of major castles as competing heritage attractions.

Trip distances on the Isle of Man are constrained by the size of the island, which is less than fifty kilometres in length in its longest dimension, north-east to south-west. This might be thought to imply that attractions throughout the island should be readily accessible to tourists and that the market areas of attractions would show only limited variations. This is not in fact the case. Reference to Table 5.3

Table 5.3 Area of origin on day of visit of adult holiday tourists visiting heritage sites on the Isle of Man

Origin of trip on day of visit:	Peel Castle 1988 %	Castle Rushen 1988 %	Castle Rushen Marketing Survey 1991 %	Holiday tourists visiting sites:					
				Manx Museum 1988 %	Nautical Museum 1988 %	Grove Museum 1988 %	Laxey Wheel 1988 %	Cregneash 1988 %	Odin's Raven 1988 %
Douglas/Onchan	55.0	55.4	63.0	70.6	46.9	42.6	56.5	34.4	51.0
Castletown	3.1	7.5	0.7	2.3	7.9	1.5	6.5	2.6	2.5
Port St Mary	3.5	3.0	5.5	1.1	6.8	3.6	3.0	5.2	1.0
Port Erin	13.7	21.0	19.9	8.0	20.9	14.9	7.0	35.4	18.8
Ramsey	8.2	1.6	}	5.0	2.8	13.3	6.5	5.5	5.4
Peel	9.0	5.2	10.9	4.6	5.1	4.1	8.7	2.6	10.9
Elsewhere on IOM	7.5	6.3	10.9	8.4	9.6	20.0	11.8	14.3	10.4
N=	256	305	146	262	177	195	230	308	202

Source: unpublished surveys undertaken by author for Manx National Heritage
Note: N = sample size

shows that the island is not a spatially uniform market for holiday-maker tourists visiting heritage attractions. Although the Douglas/Onchan area has a clear dominance in the origins of tourists visiting heritage attractions, other places of origin are of particular importance for tourists visiting certain of the attractions. Port Erin is of note in this regard, in 1988 supplying slightly more tourists to the nearby attraction of Cregneash than did more distant Douglas (Figure 2.2). More generally, Port Erin was an important secondary market for all of the Manx attractions, with Ramsey also of importance for tourists visiting the Grove Museum, which is situated on the outskirts of the town. Moreover, further reference to Table 5.3 shows that the Douglas/Onchan area varies quite substantially in its importance as a source of holiday tourists: for example, at the Manx Museum, sited in Douglas, seven out of ten of all holiday tourists in 1988 were from the Douglas/Onchan area, but fewer than half at the Nautical Museum in Castletown, the Grove Museum in Ramsey and (as already noted) at Cregneash. The importance of accessibility is unclear: both Laxey Wheel and Castle Rushen may be reached from Douglas by the island's vintage railway and tramway system (Figure 2.2), and these attractions disproportionately attract tourists from Douglas. But equally, the Nautical Museum is also accessible from Douglas by vintage railway, being in the same town as Castle Rushen, but is not so popular with tourists from Douglas. Similarly, tourists without cars on the island are reliant largely on bus services or coach tours to reach Peel, but tourists from Douglas are still found in sizeable proportion at Peel Castle, which is sited across the harbour a lengthy walk from where the coach and bus services set down and collect passengers. It would not seem, therefore, that accessibility can fully explain the pattern of market areas found on the island; comparative accessibility needs to be considered along with promotional activities and the preferences of tourists. The multiple determination of market areas where attractions can be assumed to be in competition for tourists should form a further part of a research agenda for heritage tourism. The Welsh survey findings already reported may generalise trip making in areas where major attractions are generally twenty miles or more apart, but not explain the situation within smaller areas with competing attractions.

The localisation of markets needs also to be considered in terms of the preferences of tourists, which may be inferred at least in part from the index of actual visiting patterns compared to the distribution of tourists throughout an area. Reference to Table 5.4 shows, for the Isle of Man, that the Douglas/Onchan area is overwhelmingly the most

Table 5.4 Area of accommodation of holiday tourists on the Isle of Man

| | Holiday tourists visiting IOM Passenger Survey 1988 | |
	July %	*August* %
Douglas/Onchan	86	88
Port Erin/South	9	8
Ramsey/North	2	1
Other IOM	3	2

Source: Isle of Man Passenger Surveys undertaken by Economic Adviser's Office, Douglas: Isle of Man Government

important tourist centre in the summer months. However, reference to Tables 5.3 and 5.4 together would suggest that although Douglas/Onchan as an area is a dominant supplier of tourists to the Manx heritage attractions, it could be expected to be a much greater supplier than it actually is, for in 1988 no attraction received either an equal or greater market share of Douglas/Onchan based tourists known to have been present on the island. This facet of the distortion of the localisation of spatial markets is illustrated in Table 5.5, in which the percentage distribution of tourists by area of origin (standardised by the IOM Passenger Survey) by attraction is divided by the percentage distribution of tourists by accommodation location, the latter as indicated in Table 5.4. Localities supplying the same proportion of tourists to an attraction as the proportion of the island's total tourists accommodated would have an index of 1.00, indicating parity of supply. Localities supplying fewer tourists to an attraction than expected from their accommodation market share have indices of under 1.00, and those supplying more than expected numbers of tourists have indices exceeding 1.00. Without exception, despite their dominance at the island's heritage attractions, tourists staying in the Douglas/Onchan area would seem to be under-represented at the island's heritage attractions. In contrast, those staying in Ramsey or the North of the island are on average almost eight times over-represented at the attractions, and those staying in Port Erin or the South of the island, three times over-represented. This is a clear indication that the island's tourism accommodation sector is spatially differentiated by the preferences of tourists for heritage attractions, and suggests an extension of the spatial localisation of tourism noted from accommodation studies elsewhere (Pearce 1987).

However, localism may also be seen within the profiles presented in

Table 5.5 Areas of the Isle of Man over-supplying and under-supplying adult holiday tourists to Manx heritage sites

Percentage distribution of holiday tourists visiting sites as a proportion of the known percentage distribution of tourists by accommodation location:

Tourists staying in:	Peel Castle 1988	Castle Rushen 1988	Manx Museum 1988	Nautical Museum 1988	Grove Museum 1988	Laxey Wheel 1988	Cregneash 1988	Odin's Raven 1988
Douglas/Onchan	0.64	0.64	0.82	0.54	0.49	0.65	0.40	0.59
Port Erin/South	2.35	3.79	1.50	4.46	2.41	1.84	5.16	2.65
Ramsey/North	8.63	2.62	5.13	4.14	17.87	10.15	9.53	6.63
Other IOM	4.24	2.62	3.08	2.71	3.50	4.70	1.95	5.97

Source: unpublished survey undertaken by author for Manx National Heritage

Table 5.5. The area of Port Erin/South is unambiguously important as a locality supplying tourists to Cregneash, the Nautical Museum and Castle Rushen (all southern attractions) and Ramsey/North for the Grove Museum (a northern attraction). Ramsey/North is also disproportionately important as a suplier of tourists to Laxey Wheel, the two Peel attractions, but also to the extreme southern attraction of Cregneash. Our conclusion must be that local markets exist, but may be distorted by tourists' preferences for type of heritage attraction. As part of the agenda of heritage tourism spatial markets clearly need to be defined in terms wider than accommodation mixes alone, but equally a degree of preference to visit a local attraction as convenient among other demands on tourists' time needs to be acknowledged, and with it the implicit indication that, because of tourists' perceptions of distance, attraction preferences may be substituted over even comparatively small distances within a destination area.

MODE OF TRAVEL

A repeated finding of studies of visitors to heritage attractions in England and Wales is the dependence of visitors on private transport, mainly cars, to reach attractions (Wales Tourist Board 1984a & b; Prentice 1989a). This dependence is the case at both urban and rural attractions, the former often being located in towns served by frequent public transport offering an alternative to the private car, the latter less often so well served. It may well be that this dependence results from day-trippers using their cars for days out from home, and tourists having arrived at their destination area by car using their car for trips out while on holiday. The same cannot be expected to be the case in those parts of Europe which are generally reached by tourists via air or sea travel. At the latter destination areas tourists wishing to visit heritage attractions may either have to rent cars or use public transport, unless they transport their cars with them. As such, it would seem inadequate to generalise uncritically from mainly British mainland studies of visitors to heritage attractions in terms of modes of transport used by tourists elsewhere in Europe. Regional differences may instead be supposed.

The Isle of Man is an example of a European destination to which tourists cannot drive: its island location means that air or sea travel is needed to reach it. The Irish Sea passenger ships carry some cars as well as passengers, but many summer holiday makers do not bring their cars with them to the island. In particular, the IOM Passenger Survey shows that in August most tourists staying in paid accommodation do not bring their cars with them to the island, 70 and 62 per cent respectively in 1988 and 1990 having been recorded as not having a car with them for their holiday. In July the proportion of tourists without cars on the island is less, but still substantial: 57 per cent in 1988 and 49 per cent in 1990. For tourists in Douglas the proportion without cars would seem even greater, adding to the differences already noted between Douglas-based and other tourists on the island: the Douglas Sea Front Survey of 1988 recorded almost exactly three-quarters of tourists interviewed as lacking a car on the island. However, the island's public transport system counters most tourists' perceptions of inaccessibility without a car, principally of being restricted to Douglas. The Douglas Sea Front Survey of 1988 recorded almost exactly three-quarters of the tourists interviewed disagreeing with the statement, 'Without cars holiday makers are restricted to Douglas'. Of tourists interviewed at Castle Rushen for the Marketing Survey of 1991 and who had not arrived by public transport, almost all, or 92 per cent to be precise, were aware that the castle could have been reached from Douglas or Port Erin (the major tourist centres) by the island's vintage steam railway. As such, it would be inappropriate to infer from the dominance of car-borne trips noted from past studies that in the absence of private transport that tourists on the island necessarily perceive restrictions on their ability to reach at least some heritage attractions in their destination area outside of the town in which they are staying. However, the absence of a private car places part of the decision-making to visit a heritage attraction outside of the control of the tourist, and involves the services offered by public transport operators, notably in the form of scheduled routes and coach excursions. On the Isle of Man scheduled bus and rail services are a public sector responsibility. However, as in many tourist destinations decision-making for public transport may not be within the control or influence of tourism planners, tourist boards seeking to promote heritage tourism can experience the added difficulty of ensuring access by public transport to such sites. Because of the official linkages between the island's scheduled transport services and the tourism promotion agency, the Manx findings on tourist perceptions of accessibility may not be readily comparable to other like island destinations within Europe.

Tourists' perceptions of accessibility and inaccessibility may diverge from that suggested by their behaviour. In particular, although tourists might not perceive their trip making to heritage attractions to be constrained by inadequate transport, their trip making behaviour may suggest otherwise if the users of public transport are under-represented among tourists visiting the attractions. In the Manx case, in 1988, 61 per cent of tourists interviewed at the attractions had arrived by car, a proportion more than twice as great as would have been expected from the proportion of tourists found by the Douglas Sea Front Survey to have access to a car on the island, and between twice and 40 per cent greater than the Passenger Survey proportions for those bringing their car with them. Our interpretation must be that either tourists with cars on the island are disproportionately inclined to visit the island's heritage attractions, as may be the case with higher social class groups disproportionately bringing their cars with them, or accessibility is in practice affecting trip making, irrespective of the generalised perceptions of tourists. Issues of accessibility of this kind clearly warrant inclusion in research agendas elsewhere for heritage tourism.

Site-specific factors are clearly also of importance within the general dominance of car-borne visits. This is the case at the Manx attractions (Table 5.6). Some other modes of transport have particular local importance, notably walking to the Manx Museum which is sited within Douglas. At Castle Rushen and Laxey, both served by rail and bus, public transport is of disproportionate importance, a finding confirmed for the castle from the Marketing Survey of 1991 which found that a third of tourists had arrived at the castle by train or bus as their main form of transport. These variations would further suggest that although tourists on the island tend not to perceive themselves as constrained without private transport, in practice they are, at least in terms of restricting the range of heritage attractions which are feasible to visit within the general leisure context of a day out from, in the case of most holiday-makers, Douglas. Table 5.6 confirms this surmise in a second way. It suggests the extent to which private coach operators on the island include heritage attractions within their tours: whereas at Odin's Raven one in ten holiday-makers were found in 1988 to have arrived by coach, the proportion at nearby Peel Castle was much less. Accessibility of attractions to tourists is therefore an important, if not straightforward, issue in the development of heritage tourism.

LINKAGE BETWEEN VISITS TO HERITAGE ATTRACTIONS AND OTHER HOLIDAY ACTIVITIES

Linkages between visits to heritage attractions and other holiday activities can be considered both for the day of visit and for the period of the tourist's holiday. Previous studies of visitors' trip making on their day of visit to castles and abbeys in Wales have shown substantial

Table 5.6 Means of transport to heritage sites on the Isle of Man by adult holiday tourists

Main means of travel to site:	Peel Castle 1988 %	Castle Rushen 1988 %	Manx Museum 1988 %	Nautical Museum 1988 %	Grove Museum 1988 %	Laxey Wheel 1988 %	Cregneash 1988 %	Odin's Raven 1988 %
				Holiday tourists visiting sites:				
Foot	4.7	6.6	59.6	5.1	5.1	0.0	11.0	5.0
Bus	15.6	10.8	3.0	7.3	5.6	3.9	4.2	24.8
Coach trip	3.9	4.6	0.4	2.3	3.6	7.0	4.2	10.9
Car/van	74.2	54.1	33.0	65.0	75.9	52.2	78.2	57.9
Train/tram	0.0	22.3	3.4	17.5	9.2	35.2	1.0	0.0
Other	1.6	1.6	0.6	2.8	0.6	1.7	1.4	1.4
N=	256	305	267	177	195	230	308	202

Source: unpublished survey undertaken by author for Manx National Heritage
Note: N = sample size

linkages with eating out, visits to shops, towns and drives in the countryside (Thomas 1989a). These studies in Wales have confirmed the general recreational context of visits to heritage attractions, with only one in five visitors intending to visit another castle or abbey on their day of visit to the attraction at which they were interviewed. These Welsh findings were presented for visitors rather than for tourists alone, almost all of whom had arrived at the attractions by private car and who could thus be expected to use their car to link their visit to other activities. Such a profile of including a visit to a heritage attraction within a general day out would seem usual. Visitors to British cathedrals in the late 1970s were found generally to combine a visit to a cathedral with one to a shopping centre (Cathedral Tourism Advisory Group 1979). Durham and Norwich cathedrals and St Pauls provided some exceptions; a visit to the city's castle was common at Durham and Norwich, and at St Pauls to other historic sites, museums and galleries. At these three cathedrals the proximity of other heritage attractions probably explains these visiting patterns. Tourist visitors to churches have been reported as frequently combining their visit with one to a neighbouring stately home or castle, or a visit to a picturesque village or to attractive countryside (Hanna and Hall 1984). As such it would seem probable that many visits to churches are occasioned by the church being in the vicinity of a principal attraction. The 1983 survey of visitors to Laugharne found that the most popular other activity on the day of visit was a visit to a beach or other coastal location, reported by 44 per cent of those tourists intending to visit somewhere else (Wales Tourist Board 1984a). At Big Pit in 1983 four-fifths of visitors were found not to be visiting another attraction on their day of visit; of those who were visiting another attraction, castles, another primary production monument and national park landscape topped the list (Wales Tourist Board 1984b).

The Manx database confirms the general applicability of the Welsh findings to tourists on the Isle of Man visiting heritage attractions. Eating out, visits to shops, towns and to the countryside predominate as other activities pursued (Table 5.7). As such, the general recreational context of visits to heritage attractions can be said unambiguously to pertain to these tourists. Only a quarter of the tourists interviewed at the Manx attractions in 1988 had visited, or intended to visit, another historic site on the day of their visit, and similarly only one in six had visited or intended to visit another museum. For most of the tourists interviewed, therefore, it would be inappropriate to think of them as seeking to cram as many visits to heritage attractions as possible into their holiday days' out, adding further to the discussion

Table 5.7 Visits made or intended to another attraction on the day of visit to Manx heritage sites by adult holiday tourists

Other attractions visited/intended to be visited later:	Peel Castle 1988 %	Castle Rushen 1988 %	Manx Museum 1988 %	Nautical Museum 1988 %	Grove Museum 1988 %	Laxey Wheel 1988 %	Cregneash 1988 %	Odin's Raven 1988 %	All sites 1988 %
				Holiday tourists visiting sites:					
Restaurant/cafe/pub	64.1	73.2	72.4	81.4	64.6	65.2	71.8	83.2	71.6
Shops	52.3	51.0	73.9	74.0	55.4	31.7	52.3	66.8	56.4
Nearby town	55.5	55.9	28.4	52.5	56.9	58.3	60.4	86.1	56.0
Surrounding countryside drive/walk	39.5	45.1	29.1	44.1	48.7	44.8	79.5	91.1	52.6
A beach	35.5	30.1	29.1	30.5	23.6	39.6	29.9	26.2	30.7
(Another) historic site	17.2	14.4	11.2	54.8	19.5	10.4	19.2	65.8	24.2
Tourist railway/tramway	3.5	32.0	20.9	22.0	18.5	48.3	7.5	3.0	19.5
National glen	19.5	14.7	9.3	12.4	21.5	25.2	15.3	18.8	16.8
(Another) museum	21.5	29.4	3.0	16.9	19.0	10.9	12.0	17.8	16.4
Gardens	5.5	9.2	23.9	7.3	16.9	24.8	5.2	1.0	11.7
N=	256	306	268	177	195	230	308	202	1,942

Source: unpublished survey undertaken by author for Manx National Heritage
Notes: Only the ten most frequently nominated types of other attractions are tabulated
N = sample size

of Chapters 3 and 4 as to the generalistic nature of much heritage consumption. For most tourists, visiting a heritage attraction as part of their holiday is one activity only among many activities which may be pursued. With the latter in mind it is perhaps not unsurprising that three out of ten of the tourists interviewed at the Manx attractions in 1988 had visited, or intended to visit, a beach on the same day as their visit to the heritage attraction, indicating an unambiguous link at least for a significant minority of the island's holiday-makers between beach and heritage tourism. This linkage concurs with the argument made by Prentice (1992b) that many beach tourists also make visits to heritage attractions, and that visits to heritage attractions have a wide popularity among tourists pursuing other activities as their principal entertainment while on holiday.

The Manx database also illustrates variations between sites in the linkages found to other activities. In particular, the activities undertaken on their day of visit by tourists to the two Peel attractions differ substantially between the sites. Those tourists interviewed at Odin's Raven were much more likely on their day of visit in 1988 than those at Peel Castle to visit another historic site, surrounding countryside and the town, suggesting the more common integration of Odin's Raven into composite tours than for those tourists visiting the nearby castle. Tourists visiting Laxey Wheel can be expected to have visited the tramway as many of them will have ridden on it to get to the attraction, but the frequent linkage to a beach as another activity would imply that a substantial minority of these tourists are beach tourists (and, via the tramway, from Douglas on a day away from sitting on the town's beach). The proximity of Laxey Glen is also reflected in the activity pattern reported, which together with the tramway may suggest the general attraction of Laxey as a day out for beach tourists staying in Douglas. Differences may also be seen in the activity patterns of tourists visiting the two Castletown attractions, Castle Rushen and the Nautical Museum. Tourist visitors to the latter are much more likely to have visited or to be intending to visit another historic site on their day of visit than those interviewed at the castle, and to have or intend to visit shops. Differences of this kind imply important segmentations between tourists visiting the different heritage attractions on the island, and linkages to other activities may usefully form part of a research agenda for visitor segmentation within the wider research agenda for heritage tourism.

Linkages between visits to heritage attractions and other activities pursued over the holiday period may be explored also from the Manx database. Of those tourists interviewed at the attractions in 1988 just under three-quarters, or 73 per cent to be precise, agreed that they would probably visit another castle/historic site/museum (the term used dependent on the type of attraction at which the tourist was interviewed) on the island 'soon'. However, some of these respondents may in the event not have visited any other heritage attractions, and so this response needs to be interpreted as an indicator of background intentions rather than as likely demand. Peel Castle and the Manx Museum were the two attractions thought most frequently as likely to be visited by the tourists interviewed at the other attractions in 1988 (Table 5.8), followed by Castle Rushen, Cregneash and Laxey Wheel. A clear hierarchy of preferences may be discerned from these intentions, with the Grove and Nautical Museums thought least frequently as likely to be visited during the remainder of the tourist's holiday.

Table 5.8 may also be read to infer some information on the general disposition of tourists visiting the Manx attractions to visit heritage sites generally. For example, tourists interviewed at the Manx Museum in 1988 were consistently less likely than on average for all the attractions to give intentions to visit other attractions. Although consistent, this effect is not strong; however, it concurs with those findings for the general statement of propensity to visit another museum 'soon', for at the Manx Museum a disproportionate minority disagreed with this statement. Taking these two findings together it would seem that the Manx Museum attracts perhaps a greater proportion of tourists with less enthusiasm for heritage than may be the case at the other Manx attractions. Such a conclusion would concur with the Manx Museum's accessibility to Douglas beach tourists as a wet weather attraction. This is further indication of the pertinence of tourist segmentations between the Manx attractions.

Further indication of segmentations between the tourists visiting the Manx attractions may also be inferred from Table 5.8 in terms of the preferences for attraction types implied. For example, tourists interviewed at Laxey Wheel showed a below average disposition to visit the island's museums, Cregneash included. Conversely, tourists interviewed at the Grove and Nautical Museums showed a greater than average disposition to visit other museum attractions on the island. Location is also of some importance, too; most notably at the two Peel sites, Odin's Raven and Peel Castle, with greater than average dispositions to visit the other attraction. However, the extent of these differences should not be exaggerated. While Table 5.8 does reveal unambiguous differences by site in intentions to visit other attractions, it also reveals a picture of the interrelatedness of visiting by tourists across attraction types within the broad historical theme.

Table 5.8 Disposition of adult holiday tourists visiting Manx heritage sites to visit other heritage attractions on the island during their holiday

Intending to visit site on present holiday:	Peel Castle 1988 %	Castle Rushen 1988 %	Manx Museum 1988 %	Holiday tourists visiting sites: Nautical Museum 1988 %	Grove Museum 1988 %	Laxey Wheel 1988 %	Cregneash 1988 %	Odin's Raven 1988 %	All sites 1988 %
Peel Castle	–	38.6	30.2	38.4	32.3	39.6	26.9	52.5	35.9
Castle Rushen	42.6	–	23.5	27.7	35.9	34.3	31.8	28.2	31.8
Manx Museum	40.6	28.1	–	42.9	44.6	27.4	31.3	40.1	35.0
Nautical Museum	21.1	36.7	18.7	–	29.2	16.1	25.4	17.8	23.7
Grove Museum	19.1	16.3	19.0	25.4	–	15.2	25.3	16.3	19.5
Laxey Wheel	36.7	30.1	27.2	36.2	21.0	–	27.6	31.3	29.8
Cregneash	33.6	29.4	26.1	33.9	38.5	21.3	–	31.7	30.3
Odin's Raven	36.3	25.8	18.3	33.3	33.3	27.4	24.0	–	27.6
N=	256	306	268	177	195	230	308	201	1,941

Source: unpublished survey undertaken by author for Manx National Heritage
Note: N = sample size

This is a similar conclusion to that reached in Chapter 4 about the substitution of attractions, resultant of a general rather than a particular interest in heritage and history by most tourists. In this sense the overall visiting patterns shown in Table 5.8 suggests a homogeneity in tourists' consumption of heritage 'products' which encompasses heterogeneous heritage product–types, in a form of undifferentiated consumption, in which context specific segmentations of tourists need to be seen.

THE POTENTIAL MARKET SIZE FOR TRIPS TO HERITAGE ATTRACTIONS BY TOURISTS

The potential market size for heritage attraction visits by holiday tourists may be presumed to vary by destination area within Europe, and by the differing reasons for holidaying. However, as visits to heritage attractions would appear to be a popular part of even pool and beach-based holidays (Prentice 1992b) some minimum consistency may be apparent in the market size as more studies are undertaken to ascertain market size. Heritage tourism market size, for all its theoretical importance to heritage development and promotion, is a highly neglected part of tourism econometrics and equivalent predictive sciences. Combined with the broad parameters of demand reviewed in Chapter 1, the Manx database may hopefully be used to prompt interest in this issue, and by so doing to place the issue of heritage tourism market size squarely into a research agenda for heritage tourism.

Of the tourists interviewed on Douglas Sea Front in 1988, just over half, 54 per cent, agreed that they would probably visit a castle or museum on the island 'soon', a period which we may equate with their holiday. However, of these, the proportion strongly agreeing was negligible, and this should be taken as a restraint on enthusiastic equation of the potential summer market for heritage attractions on the island as about half of all summer holiday-makers visiting. This interpretation would concur with the earlier conclusion in this chapter that for most holiday-makers on the Isle of Man a visit to a heritage attraction is only one of a range of activities which may be pursued, and thus be liable to be substituted by another activity as a holiday evolves. At best estimates of market size derived in this way can be interpreted as dispositions to visit, rather than as intentions to visit. Despite what might be expected from the discussion in Chapter 1, the social class of tourists was found not to have an affect on their propensity to say that a heritage site was likely to be visited 'soon'. In view also of the social class profile actually pertaining in visits (Chapter 3), further caution is implied in interpreting this disposition as an intention to visit. The earlier discussion of access to heritage attractions may be returned to here, for whether or not tourists had the use of a car on the island was associated with their stated propensity to visit a heritage attraction: nearly four out of ten tourists without cars on the island thought that it would be unlikely that they would visit a site, compared to slightly fewer than three out of ten tourists with cars.

The Douglas Sea Front Survey also enables the comparative attractiveness of the island's heritage attractions to be investigated. Notable variations in the tourists' dispositions to visit the island's heritage attractions were found. The Manx Museum topped the list, with 23 per cent of tourists stating an intention to visit this attraction. Laxey Wheel and Peel Castle formed a second tier, with between one in six and one in seven tourists interviewed stating an intention to visit these attractions. Castle Rushen, the Grove Museum and Cregneash gained visiting intentions from about one in ten holiday-makers interviewed, and the Nautical Museum and Odin's Raven from between one in twelve and one in fourteen tourists. As noted above, these 'intentions' should properly be regarded as dispositions to visit. These Manx findings clearly illustrate that the potential market size for heritage attractions is highly site specific, despite the effective substitution of attractions within the broad theme of historical or heritage attractions.

Some of the tourists interviewed in Douglas in 1988 had already visited some attractions in the week prior to their interview. As already discussed in Chapter 4, Laxey Wheel predominated among these visits already made, with three out of ten tourists already having visited the attraction in the week prior to their interview. A comparison between the findings discussed in Chapter 4 and those concerning intentions is illustrative for the Manx Museum provides a notable exception in its rankings for actual compared to intended visits. It is also only one of two attractions where intentions to visit exceeded actual visits. The proportion of tourists stating that they intended to visit this museum was double that which had done so: a substantial disparity. This would suggest that this museum is regarded by many Douglas holiday-makers as a significant place to visit, but of insufficient priority to warrant a visit early on in a holiday, or perhaps not at all in the event of other attractions and activities taking energies and time. The Manx Museum may be regarded by some tourists as a wet weather insurance, which might be deferred until a subsequent holiday. Once again, important segmentations are implied between potential as well as actual 'heritage' tourists.

Rankings of attractions such are apparent on the Isle of Man demonstrate that the overall size of the market for heritage attractions, even in a comparatively small area, is insufficient for projecting the market size for any one attraction within that area, even for different major attractions. Some attractions, such as Laxey Wheel, are visited early in a holiday; others may have to compete for tourists not just with other attractions but with fine weather permitting beach activities. Hierarchies of visiting preferences such as identified on the Isle of Man clearly need to be identified before market size can be estimated for any particular attraction, and thus before the comparative share of the total market likely to be gained by an attraction can be estimated. These hierarchies of preference also have obvious implications both for the promotion of individual attractions and for the overall promotion of the destination area. The hierarchy of preferences identified within the general market for heritage attractions on the Isle of Man also has important implications for the 'shopping list' of visits suggested in Chapter 4, as the intentions to visit expressed may in some cases be realised on subsequent holidays. These hierarchies of preference are also important in understanding the opportunities to encourage the substitution of trips by tourists and, thus, the spreading of tourist impacts across a destination area. For these several reasons the preference hierarchies implied in Chapter 4 and in the present discussion unambiguously warrant inclusion in a research agenda for heritage tourism.

CONCLUSIONS

Visits by many tourists to heritage attractions are made within a general recreational context of their visit being one part only of their day's enjoyment. This concurs with the predominance of general interest tourists at heritage attractions found in Chapter 4. Within this broad recreational context, variations in the activities undertaken by tourists on their day of visit are apparent, suggesting both a degree of site-specific segmentation among heritage tourists and the impact of localised differences in opportunities for visiting other attractions. Hierarchies of preferences among intentions to visit attractions may be identified, adding further to the implicit 'shopping list' of activities which may structure tourists' activities when on holiday. This is confirmed by the impression that most tourists pre-plan their visit to an attraction, at least during their holiday if not before, although a substantial minority would seem not to. As a holiday progresses this 'shopping list' of activities, as a disposition rather than a commitment to do something, changes as some activities are substituted for others. In effect, the market size for heritage can only be defined at a site-specific level if such estimates are to have any relevance to tourism development.

Localised market areas can be identified even for attractions on an island as small as the Isle of Man. However, these market areas may also suggest spatial segmentations between tourists in terms of their preferences overall for heritage consumption, as well as affect their propensity to visit individual attractions. Tourists staying in resorts which superficially may seem much alike may collectively in their behaviour and intentions demonstrate different preferences for visiting heritage attractions. Access to attractions is a further factor to be considered. Even on the Isle of Man, a destination area to which few summer tourists bring their cars, access to a car has important implications for visits to attractions. Although tourists may not in general perceive the inaccessibility of attractions, their behaviour may demonstrate otherwise. This has important implications for the promotion of heritage consumption.

The length of tourist stays at heritage attractions would seem generally to range between half an hour and two hours, but exceptions abound and variation between attractions of different types and of the same type is extensive. Those attributes affecting this length of stay would not seem easily identified. Reasons expressed for visiting attractions would seem to be ambiguous as determinants of a tourist's likely length of stay at an attraction, perhaps somewhat surprisingly. However, investment in enhanced promotion of attractions, as evidenced by the presentational refurbishment of Castle Rushen, can pay off in terms of enhancing tourists' stays at attractions. This effect should not be thought of as unlimited, for tourists may budget time on the basis of general experience of heritage attraction visiting, and be unable to greatly exceed such budgets without disrupting their days' intended activities. The issue of time spent in the vicinity of attractions is of importance here, and surprisingly little is known of the time spent by tourists in surrounding towns as a result of being attracted to a heritage attraction, and even less about the substitution of time spent at attractions for that spent in their vicinity.

6 The promotion of heritage attractions to tourists

PROMOTIONAL MEDIA AND THE DETERMINATION OF TOURIST TRIP MAKING TO HERITAGE ATTRACTIONS

In order to maximise the effectiveness of promotional expenditures the operators of heritage attractions need not only to know the characteristics of those tourists already visiting or likely to visit their attractions, but also which of the many promotional media tourists visiting heritage attractions tend to use in their decision to visit. Central to many promotional campaigns is advertising. Advertising can have at least five objectives: to communicate information, to highlight specific features, to build a brand image, to reinforce behaviour and to influence intermediaries, such as travel agents, in the decision-making process (Cannon 1986). Advertising is generally directed to the early stages of the consumer's decision-making process, namely to convert unawareness of a destination or attraction into awareness, to convert awareness into knowledge about the destination or attraction, and to increase liking or preference (Ashworth and Voogd 1990a). However, it also has a role in the subsequent stages of gaining the consumer's conviction that the destination or attraction is appropriate, and of finally converting this conviction into a holiday booking or visit to an attraction (Prentice 1989c). It is important that the effectiveness of advertising and of other forms of promotion is appraised and not simply assumed. In particular, media should not be assumed to be equally effective in influencing the behaviour of tourists. For example, advertising on local television is unlikely to be effective in encouraging tourists to visit attractions if few tourists in the locality watch television when on holiday. For those attractions heavily dependent on tourists among their visitors, therefore, television may be a most inapproporiate medium through which to promote visits. As such, evaluation of promotional campaigns, and their elements, is essential. Such evaluations may have any of four objectives (Prentice 1989c):

- to test the overall awareness of the potential tourist of the destination area or attraction which is the subject of the promotional campaign;
- to test by recall how the promotional campaign has informed the potential tourist;
- to test how past behaviour has been reinforced; and
- to test how the campaign has affected bookings or visitor numbers.

However, how these indicators are applied needs to depend upon the particular objectives of the campaign. For example, if habitual holiday-makers to an alternative destination are being targeted in the campaign, these should form the basis of the assessment; but if people with passive wants are the object of the campaign, new buyers or visitors should be the object of the assessment (O'Shaughnessy 1984).

The increased awareness during the 1980s on the part of heritage attraction operators of the importance of promoting their attractions did not bring with it a comparable emphasis on the assessment of the effectiveness of this advertising. Such studies as have been undertaken among tourists and others visiting heritage attractions have usually reported only the immediate influences on visitors' decision-making, rather than have sought to determine either at what stage in the decision-making process such media are important or to identify those influences which may be determining those recognised by the visitors themselves. Although some tourist boards monitor their promotional campaigns in the manner outlined above, such assessment does not feature prominently as an interest of many heritage attraction operators concerning their individual attractions. This lack of sophistication is important, for as Thomas (1989b) has commented, as many visitors to heritage attractions report the importance of 'local' knowledge or 'social' sources of information, such as personal recommendation, the immediate impact of promotional media may appear slight. However, what is unknown is the extent to which local knowledge and personal recommendation and the like in turn depend on promotional media. Nor is it adequately known how tourists may differ from other visitors in their sources of information. The topic of tourist use of media, and of the background determinants of this use, should properly form part of a research agenda for heritage tourism.

Studies of the sources of information reported as important by visitors to heritage attractions have generally identified personal and social sources of information as the most commonly used. For example, visitors to Scottish folk festivals surveyed in 1990 reported word of mouth and having been before as their main sources of information, these sources being reported by 51 per cent and 44 per cent of visitors respectively (Scottish Tourist Board 1991b). Similarly, visitors to Stan Hywet Hall in Ohio are reported as frequently having relied on the recommendations of their friends as both a source of information about this attraction and as their prompt to visit (Achmatowicz-Otok and Goggins 1990). In Wales, having 'always known' about a heritage attraction was found in 1985 to be the most frequently quoted source of information about attractions by their tourist and day-tripper visitors alike (Public Attitudes Surveys Research 1986). Information from friends and relatives was rated as the second most frequent source by both groups. Although tourists were found to rely more frequently than day-trippers on information from tourist information centres, tourist guides, or (as would be expected) leaflets in hotels, these sources of information were comparatively unimportant for both groups, personal and social sources predominating. Contrary to what might be expected, tourists interviewed at Dylan Thomas's boathouse at Laugharne were notably *more* likely than day-trippers to give friends and relatives as a source of information: for tourists this source topped the list, with a quarter mentioning it (Wales Tourist Board 1984a). A similar pattern was found in 1983 at Big Pit, except that at this attraction, recommendation by friends and relatives was noted by 37 per cent of tourists interviewed (Wales Tourist Board 1984b). At both of the attractions surveyed in 1983, media advertising was in fact more important as a reported source of information by day-trippers than by tourists. The immediate relevance in promoting heritage attractions to tourists of personal recommendation and personal knowledge forms the context in which the effectiveness of particular advertising media need to be assessed.

PROMOTIONAL MEDIA USED PRIOR TO ARRIVAL AT A DESTINATION AREA BY TOURISTS VISITING HERITAGE ATTRACTIONS

Tourists visiting a heritage attraction in a destination area will either have found out about the attraction prior to the start of their holiday or once having begun their holiday. For a destination area like the Isle of Man, which attracts substantial repeat visiting, the determinants of attraction awareness may lie in past holidaying, and be difficult to define. This is a further facet of the 'shopping list' approach to attraction visiting over a number of holidays noted in Chapter 4.

It should not be assumed that for a destination area such as the Isle of Man that awareness of attractions prior to a holiday is generally invariant, one year with another. The Site Survey of 1988 found that 44 per cent of tourists visiting the Manx heritage attractions claimed to have been aware of the attraction being visited prior to their holiday beginning, but in 1990 the corresponding proportion at the three attractions surveyed was 59 per cent. Clearly, fewer attractions were surveyed in 1990 than in 1988, but at all the three sites surveyed in 1990 the proportion of tourists claiming knowledge of the attraction prior to their holiday was greater, most notably at Cregneash and Peel Castle. In part this may be explained by the greater proportion of new tourists visiting the island in 1988 than in 1990, and although this is not a complete explanation it emphasises the need for heritage attraction operators to be aware of comparative trends in repeat and first visiting to a destination area in designing their promotional strategies.

Despite the extent of repeat visiting to the Isle of Man it would be wrong to assume that all prior knowledge of attractions results from past holidaying, for such attractions as Laxey Wheel, Cregneash, Peel Castle and Castle Rushen feature prominently and frequently in Manx tourism advertising. At Laxey Wheel in 1988 nine out of ten tourists interviewed at the attraction claimed to have known of it prior to their holiday, as did half of the tourists interviewed at the two castles. However, at other attractions the extent of admitted prior knowledge of the site was less. Most notably, prior kowledge of Cregneash was similar to that for the island's smaller museums, and well below average, despite its prominence in advertising material. The example of Cregneash serves as a reminder that the exposure of attractions in promotional media need not effect awareness nor visiting. The large number of tourists arriving on the island without prior knowledge of its major heritage attractions also illustrates the opportunity to influence tourist decision-making during holidays, and suggests for many tourists who may visit heritage attractions that the content of their holiday is largely undecided prior to its commencement, and is decided as the holiday progresses. This interpretation would concur with our previous discussions of the general recreational context of many heritage attraction visits and the general rather than particular interest of many visitors in the attractions visited (Chapters 4 and 5). The extent to which these findings on when the planning of visits takes place are replicable elsewhere in Europe is an important component of a research agenda for heritage tourism, for they have unambiguous importance for the design of promotional strategies, both by the operators of heritage attractions and by the promoters of destination areas.

The Manx database suggests that the determinants of the awareness of attractions prior to a holiday may not be readily defined. For example, although in 1988 tourists from professional and higher managerial households were generally found to have been more aware prior to their holiday of the island's heritage attractions visited than were tourists from other backgrounds, this effect was not found in 1990, when social class in general was not found to be a predictor of prior knowledge of attractions. Reasons for visiting heritage attractions would seem also to have equal ambiguity as determinants of prior awareness. Whereas in 1988 those tourists found to be visiting attractions out of a particular interest in Manx culture or with a particular interest in historic places tended to have been more aware of the attractions prior to their holiday than tourists visiting the attractions for other reasons, the same conclusion cannot be drawn for tourists surveyed in 1990. Indeed, although statistically significant at 0.05, the sizes of the effects identified for 1988 were not substantial, with the probability that a tourist had known of an attraction prior to his or her holiday being increased by only about a fifth through particular interests in Manx culture or historic places. It may be that as fewer tourists in 1990 were new to holidaying on the island than had been the case in 1988, that those determinants important in creating awareness of attractions among new tourists were masked in the survey data. If so, this would emphasize the need in future heritage tourism research designs to separately investigate the determinants of the awareness of tourists new to a destination area and those repeat visiting. A general point to be made from these Manx findings for a research agenda for heritage tourism is that the absence of a specific awareness of a holiday destination in the minds of many tourists may be pervasive across socio-economic groups and across groups of tourists with different interests. The need for research elsewhere in Europe to investigate the generality of this preliminary conclusion is vital if the process of decision-making in heritage tourism is to be fully understood.

The importance of tourism advertising to tourist awareness of heritage attractions prior to a holiday may be explored only in a quite limited way from the Manx Passenger Survey. In particular, this Survey provides no information on how the promotion of particular attractions feature in this awareness. As with many passenger surveys,

Table 6.1 Main perceived influence on decision to holiday on the Isle of Man by holiday tourists staying in paid accommodation

| | Holiday tourists visiting IOM: | | | |
| | Passenger Survey 1988 | | Passenger Survey 1990 | |
Influence	*July* %	*August* %	*July* %	*August* %
Advertising media	3	3	7	10
Previous visit	54	54	48	44
Recommendation of travel agent	0	0	1	2
Recommendation of friends or relatives	16	18	12	11
Particular 'event' being held	2	2	7	2
Other	24	23	25	32

Source: *Isle of Man Passenger Surveys* undertaken by Economic Adviser's Office, Douglas: Isle of Man Government

that for the Isle of Man is concerned primarily with the generalised impact of media on how tourists' decisions to holiday on the island are made, and not by specific reference to the attractions the island has to offer. The Passenger Survey provides support for an argument that advertising in general is unimportant in the destination choice of many tourists to the island, at least in terms of what the tourists themselves consider to be of importance in influencing their decision-making. In 1988, for example, tourists staying in paid accommodation on the island generally considered advertising to have been unimportant in their holiday choice, only 3 per cent of tourists in this year in either July or August considering advertising to have been important in their choice. In 1990 the proportion was slightly higher, with 7 and 10 per cent respectively in July and August considering advertising to have been important (Table 6.1). In contrast, for these summer months the Passenger Survey shows the importance of previous visits in the decision to holiday, this influence being important for roughly half of the summer holiday tourists staying in paid accommodation interviewed. The island's built heritage attractions were so infrequently given as reasons for visiting the island that not only were they not separately tabulated in the Passenger Survey, they were not even exampled as those residual reasons grouped as 'other' in Table 6.1. However, the size of this residual category, 'other', would imply some diversity in individual decision-making, otherwise some recurrent reasons could easily be abstracted from it; some of these diverse reasons may include the island's built heritage attractions, although their frequency is unlikely to be great. In 1988, in particular, the recommendation of friends and relatives formed a reason of second order importance to that of having visited the island previously. In 1988, the last year in which the Passenger Survey included this question, upwards of six out of ten summer holiday tourists staying in paid accommodation on the island had not obtained an official (or other) brochure, despite the official promotion of this brochure. However, in terms of accommodation rather than destination area choice, advertising media may be shown to be of greater recognised importance to holiday-makers visiting the island. In 1988 – the question was not asked in 1990 – about half the tourists staying in paid accommodation in both July and August gave advertisements as the principal reason for their choice of accommodation, with roughly a fifth and tenth respectively indicating a previous stay or friends and relatives as their principal reason for choosing their accommodation. Thus, from the Manx database it would appear that advertising media are more frequently recognised by tourists as important in specific decision-making about a holiday, once the destination area has been chosen, rather than in the initial selection of the destination area. As such, how far the somewhat trivial recognised importance of advertising in gaining tourists to the destination area of the Isle of Man can be generalised to its heritage attractions is ambiguous, but the overall context of personal and social sources of information in general decision-making about a holiday prior to arrival at the destination area would seem worthy of inclusion in an agenda for heritage tourism research. The Manx findings may imply, at least for some destination areas, the immediate irrelevance of destination advertising to many potential heritage tourists on their main holidays.

PROMOTIONAL MEDIA USED AFTER ARRIVAL AT A DESTINATION AREA BY TOURISTS VISITING HERITAGE ATTRACTIONS

On arrival at a destination area the decision-making process leading to a tourist visiting a heritage attraction has been largely unknown in terms of the sources of information used. As noted at the outset of this chapter, past work has tended not to differentiate between visitors on the basis of when the information was gained. Similarly, as also noted above, this past work has emphasised the immediate importance of informal sources of information, such as personal knowledge or being told by friends and relatives; with formal sources, such as advertisements and guide books, rated as of immediate secondary importance in terms of tourists' reported uses of these media as information sources.

However, for tourists visiting the Manx heritage attractions more of a dual pattern of information sources may be identified than has been found elsewhere to generally pertain to visitors (Table 6.2). On the one hand, friends and relatives, and on the other, brochures produced by the island's Tourist Department, predominate among the sources of information about the attractions given by the tourists interviewed while visiting them. Guidebooks, tourist information centres and holiday brochures form a second order of sources. Notably, local or personal knowledge is only a third order source of information, a situation in particular quite different to that described for the Welsh attractions surveyed in 1985 (Public Attitudes Surveys Research 1986).

Although the sources of information about the attractions listed in Table 6.2 might be comprehensive, they do not indicate which source of information might be most important to a tourist, tourists being able in the 1988 Site Survey to indicate as many sources as they considered appropriate. In contrast, the 1990 Site Survey sought to force a choice as to which source of information was considered most important by the tourists visiting the attractions, and the results are set out in Table 6.3. For the three attractions surveyed in 1990 the importance of informal information takes on a clear secondary importance when compared to guide books, brochures and advertisements, at least as the most important sources used. This provides some support for conventional promotional strategies which rely on these media, and may suggest that other sources of information, sometimes more frequently given, may be of secondary or background importance. However, some caution is implied by the fact that the information sources given in 1990 may reflect a different promotional context to that of 1988. With this proviso in mind, a comparison of Tables 6.2 and 6.3 would suggest that tourists' use of information sources to make decisions to visit heritage attractions may be ranked into primary and secondary, perhaps reinforcing, sources. The confirmation of this ranking would seem a topic worthy of inclusion in a future research agenda for heritage tourism.

Further reference to Tables 6.2 and 6.3 indicates substantial variations in the recognised importance of information sources between attractions, and to some extent between years. Personal knowledge, recommendation by friends and relatives, and television, were of

Table 6.2 Main sources of information about heritage attractions of adult holiday tourists visiting heritage attractions on the Isle of Man

Main sources of information:	Holiday tourists visiting sites:								
	Peel Castle 1988 %	Castle Rushen 1988 %	Manx Museum 1988 %	Nautical Museum 1988 %	Grove Museum 1988 %	Laxey Wheel 1988 %	Cregneash 1988 %	Odin's Raven 1988 %	All sites 1988 %
Local knowledge	14.5	22.9	10.8	8.5	6.2	25.2	9.1	18.8	14.8
Friend/relative	34.8	19.6	29.9	28.2	25.6	50.9	38.3	19.3	31.1
Map	23.8	17.0	11.6	16.9	19.0	3.0	20.1	3.5	14.8
Tourist information centre	16.8	20.6	22.0	21.5	19.0	24.3	17.9	16.3	19.8
Guidebook	22.7	18.6	15.3	20.9	20.0	19.6	18.8	29.2	20.3
Tourist Board brochure	36.3	28.1	17.2	23.2	21.5	24.3	27.3	35.1	26.7
Television	3.5	0.3	1.1	1.2	1.0	25.2	8.8	4.5	5.7
Holiday brochure	21.5	14.4	7.5	16.9	13.3	26.5	12.0	35.6	17.8
Saw site when passing	12.5	19.6	13.1	24.9	21.5	4.8	8.4	24.3	15.4
Saw signposts	1.6	2.3	14.2	19.2	13.8	0.9	8.8	10.9	8.3
Brochure at holiday accommodation	8.2	9.2	3.0	6.8	9.7	2.6	11.4	10.9	7.8
N =	256	306	268	177	195	230	308	202	1,942

Source: unpublished survey undertaken by author for Manx National Heritage
Notes: More than one source could be given
N = sample size

Table 6.3 Single main source of information about heritage attractions of adult holiday tourists visiting heritage attractions on the Isle of Man

| | Holiday tourists visiting sites: | | | |
Main source of information	Peel Castle 1990 %	Castle Rushen 1990 %	Cregneash 1990 %	All sites 1990 %
Local knowledge	5.5	11.0	14.6	10.3
Advertisement/handbill/ brochure	24.0	4.9	29.2	19.3
Told about it	17.5	6.0	16.9	13.4
Guide book	14.8	44.5	19.1	26.2
Passing by/sign posts	4.9	9.3	9.6	7.9
Previous visit to island	25.7	24.2	5.6	18.6
Other	7.6	0.1	5.0	4.3
N=	183	182	178	543

Source: unpublished survey undertaken by author for Manx National Heritage
Note: N = sample size

particular importance as sources of information at Laxey Wheel, for example. In contrast, the Nautical Museum would appear to be disproportionately seen when passing or from signposting, suggesting its secondary role as an attraction in Castletown to Castle Rushen. In 1990, guide book entries were much more important at Castle Rushen than at the other two attractions surveyed. These differences would not only imply the need for site-specific analyses, but also the need to look widely at the range of possible sources of information: general profiles may not pertain at all attractions, nor at attractions of a like type or 'importance', and are subject to change dependent on the promotional strategies employed by a range of agencies and operators.

The analysis so far has treated tourists visiting the attractions as a single group, undifferentiated by prior knowledge of an attraction, as has been the tradition of most heritage attraction market research to date. The vital dimension of *when* information is important and needs to be added into the analysis. As Table 6.3 indicates, previous visits to a destination area can be important sources of information at some attractions. It is likely that the comparative importance of sources of information to tourists will vary by whether or not the tourist was aware of the attraction before the holiday began. Such an assumption does not solely apply to seeing a site in passing, nor to seeing signposts, but also to media which could reasonably be seen before or during a holiday. The issue of when media are important is important

Table 6.4 Effect of awareness of heritage attraction prior to arrival on Isle of Man for holiday on the main sources of information about the attraction used by adult holiday tourists visiting heritage attractions on the Isle of Man

Main sources of information	Tourists claiming to have known of attraction prior to arrival on island 1988 %	Tourists claiming not to have known of attraction prior to arrival on island 1988 %
Local knowledge	27.4	3.2
Friend/relative	35.5	27.7
Map	12.4	16.8
Television	11.9	0.8
Holiday brochure	20.8	15.6
Saw site when passing	10.6	19.4
Saw signposts	6.4	9.9
Brochures at holiday accommodation	6.3	9.1
N =	848	1,071

Source: unpublished survey undertaken by author for Manx National Heritage
Notes: More than one source could be given
    N = sample size

for promotional planning, for heritage attraction operators seeking to influence the choices made by tourists after their arrival at a destination area not only need to include those types of media most used by tourists, but also to know in the design of promotional messages the extent to which tourists may already be aware of the attraction.

Reference to Table 6.4 shows that not all of the major sources of information used by tourists visiting the Manx heritage attractions in 1988, when the full range of sources were recorded, differed in their importance to those tourists previously aware of an attraction and those not. Some sources of information transcend the divide of awareness prior to arrival on the island and that of subsequent to arrival. Such sources would appear to act equally as reinforcers of awareness and creators of awareness of an attraction among tourist visitors. Notable among such sources are friends and relatives, holiday brochures and maps. As such, we must presumably include social networks between households of tourists when on holiday as pertinent sources of recommendation of heritage attractions, as well as friends and relatives at home who may previously have visited a destination area. However, local knowledge and television were sources of information disproportionately associated with awareness of an attraction prior to a holiday, compared to awareness when on holiday.

'Local knowledge' may be thought of as a proxy for knowledge gained on a previous holiday, the determinants of which are clearly unknown. As might be expected, sources more important to tourists unaware prior to their holiday of an attraction include the casual sources of information such as seeing a site when passing or seeing signposts, although these media also reinforce the awareness of some preinformed tourists too. It is fair to conclude for tourists aware prior to their holiday of an attraction that friends and relatives, personal knowledge and holiday brochures are of importance, but for those only aware subsequent to the beginning of their holiday that personal knowledge and holiday brochures are varyingly replaced by more casual information sources. The apparent hierarchy of information sources by stage of awareness of a heritage attraction implied by Table 6.4 warrants further research elsewhere, for it has unambiguous implications for investment in differing kinds of promotional media. In particular, it may imply the need for heritage attraction operators to recruit accommodation managers as informal promoters by recommendation of heritage attractions.

The use of information sources listed in Table 6.2 was pervasive across all social classes of tourist interviewed at the Manx attractions in 1988. Only one source had unambiguous social class associations. Tourists from professional and managerial households when compared to others were found to disproportionately have used guidebooks as a source of information. This was particularly so for tourists from professional households who had been unaware of an attraction prior to their holiday; approximately a third of tourists in this group claiming to have used a guidebook, compared to fewer than a fifth of other tourists similarly unaware of an attraction prior to their holiday beginning. However, the general lack of association between sources of information used and the social class of tourists on the island means, if the Manx findings are replicated elsewhere in Europe, that media types cannot readily be used to target specific social classes of tourists to expand the market for heritage attractions across the social spectrum.

THE ROLE OF PROMOTIONAL LEAFLETS IN ENCOURAGING TOURISTS TO VISIT HERITAGE ATTRACTIONS

If only because of its frequency of use by heritage attraction operators one form of promotional media requires particular discussion, namely that of handbills and leaflets. Most heritage attraction operators produce either handbills or leaflets for display in racks at tourist information centres, at other attractions or in accommodation enterprises. Indeed, one innovation of the past decade was to combine the leaflets of local attractions into composite booklets known as 'bedroom browsers' for guests to read in hotel and guesthouse bedrooms. The Manx database for 1990 and 1991 provides some insight into the significance of particular handbills and leaflets, for tourists interviewed visiting the attractions were asked if they had seen particular leaflets, the interviewers producing copies as a means of prompting recall and of avoiding error in tourists recalling which, if any, leaflet they had seen. As the extent to which tourists visiting Manx heritage attractions recalled having seen specific leaflets can be assumed in part to depend both on their distribution and design, many more case studies are needed before generalisations may be made. The present discussion is intended to encourage such studies.

The 1991 surveys at Castle Rushen each included questioning about tourists' recognition of two leaflets produced by separate Manx departments of government to promote the island's heritage attractions, both leaflets being widely available in tourist displays throughout the island, and particularly in hotels and guesthouse displays, throughout the survey period. One leaflet will be called after its content, 'Discover the Story of Mann', and was produced by Manx National Heritage; the other, 'Visitors Sightseeing', was produced by the Department of Tourism and Transport. Despite the widespread availablity of these leaflets six out of ten tourists surveyed, visiting Castle Rushen in 1991, did not recognise having seen the 'Visitors Sightseeing' leaflet, and nearly half, or 48 per cent to be precise, did not recognise having seen the 'Discover the Story of Mann' leaflet. Of all the tourists interviewed at Castle Rushen in 1991, slightly fewer than three out of ten, 28 per cent to be exact, had used the 'Visitors Sightseeing' leaflet and slightly fewer than four out of ten, 39 per cent, had used the equivalent, 'Discover the Story of Mann'. Where a leaflet was recognised it generally had been used as a source of information by the tourists concerned. Most users of both leaflets were in fact the same people, suggesting that one leaflet was not being used as a substitute for the other. Eight out of ten of the tourists who recognised having seen the 'Visitors Sightseeing' leaflet also recognised having seen the 'Discover the Story of Mann' leaflet. Similarly, fewer than one in twenty tourists interviewed at Castle Rushen who had used the 'Visitors Sightseeing' leaflet had not seen the other leaflet. This duplication of readership and users might imply that tourists have preferences for and against leaflet use, and that those tourists unprepared to read one leaflet on heritage attractions despite being prepared to visit such an attraction are likely to be unprepared to read or use another in planning their holiday activities. This inference needs also to be tested on non-visitors to heritage attractions among tourists, for an alternative interpretation may be that the reinforcement of leaflet messages by other leaflets is important in effecting visits to heritage attractions from the tourist readers of these leaflets. If the latter is the case redundancy in leaflet distribution cannot be equated with duplication in distribution, whereas if the former case applies, redundancy is implied. As such, the issue of reinforcement as against substitution in leaflet use is an important element of a research agenda for heritage tourism.

The determinants of whether or not a tourist uses a leaflet to plan a visit to a heritage attraction as part of his or her holiday are of unambiguous interest in developing effective promotional campaigns based upon leaflets as a principal form of media. The Manx database may be used to investigate these possible determinants, which may be assumed to include social class or educational attainment. Any conclusions would seem as yet to be ambiguous. In 1990 Manx National Heritage had linked a 'Story of Mann' leaflet to a promotional ticket, or 'passport', giving access to all major eight heritage attractions on the island. Two-thirds of the tourists interviewed at the three attractions surveyed in 1990 did not recognise having seen this ticket/leaflet package, a proportion reaching four out of every five tourists interviewed at Castle Rushen in 1990. Awareness of the ticket/ leaflet package was highest amongst tourists educated above the age of eighteen, and the few purchasers of the ticket/leaflet package were generally from this more educated group of tourists. The extent to which educational attainment affected the awareness of this ticket/ leaflet package, if not the purchase of it in large numbers, is indicated by the respective proportions recognising the package when it was presented to the tourists when interviewed. Whereas only 27 per cent of tourists educated to eighteen years of age or younger claimed to recognise this ticket/leaflet package, 46 per cent of those tourists formally educated to more than eighteen years of age claimed to recognise having seen it. However, this effect was not replicated for leaflet recognition at Castle Rushen in 1991, nor in either year for the social class background of tourists. Some caution in generalising the effect of educational attainment found in 1990 is therefore called for. It may be that the combined ticket/leaflet of 1990 was considered by tourists to be akin to the 'heritage clubs' run by major operators of attractions, such as English Heritage, Cadw, Historic Scotland or the National Trusts. These memberships are known to be markedly skewed socially to non-manual households (Prentice 1989a), and thus the response noted in 1990 may not be a true response solely to leaflet awareness.

Nor would the specificness of a trip to visit an attraction seem an unambiguous determinant of whether a tourist was more likely or not to have seen a leaflet. It might be thought that those tourists coming specifically to see an attraction might have been more likely to have seen a promotional leaflet for the attraction, for, after all, this is the objective of producing leaflets. When tourists are divided in terms of whether or not their visit to Castletown in 1991 was made specifically to visit Castle Rushen at most only a weak effect can be found in support of this supposition. A greater proportion of tourists setting out specifically to visit the castle were found to have seen the 'Discover the Story of Mann' leaflet than those not coming specifically to the town to see the castle, but the size of the effect was not great. Whereas 56 per cent of tourists coming to the town specifically to see the castle claimed to have seen the leaflet, 46 per cent of the other tourists also said that they had seen the leaflet. Although a like affect could be found for the 'Visitors' Sightseeing' leaflet, its size was even less. The effectiveness of leaflets in prompting specific visits to this castle would seem questionable, therefore. However, the generalisation of this affect must await studies elsewhere.

The general conclusion to this discussion into the possible determinants of whether or not tourists visiting heritage attractions have read promotional leaflets must be that from the Manx survey data these determinants are far from clear, but warrant further inclusion in a research agenda for heritage tourism. It may be that the more educated or more prepared tourist is more likely to make use of promotional leaflets, but such inferences are far from unambiguous. It is interesting also to note that the recognition of specific leaflets may be more extensive than their reported use as main sources of information. The reported use of leaflets at Castle Rushen in 1991 is greater from the general frequencies recorded in Tables 6.2 and 6.3 for earlier years at the Manx attractions. Either leaflet design or distribution may have improved by 1991, or a wider role of leaflets may have been identified, namely that of providing background rather than immediate information. As such, leaflets may be seen as one of many diffuse stimuli prompting visits by tourists to heritage attractions. If the latter is in fact the case leaflet distribution cannot solely be deemed successful or unsuccessful from the sources of information reported to be important by tourists. The investigation of this wider effect warrants inclusion in a research agenda for heritage tourism.

CONCLUSIONS

The importance of personal and social sources of information for tourists visiting heritage attractions frequently found by attraction surveys would seem to require some qualification from the Manx findings. The Isle of Man surveys suggest that not only may formal media, such as brochures, also be of general importance as sources of tourist information about attractions, they would seem more important than social sources when tourists are required to nominate the single most important information source regarding their visit. The Manx surveys have also served to raise the issue of *when* in the decision-making process media types are important. Large numbers of tourists would appear to choose their destination area without recourse to formal media; many arrive, it would seem, at their destination area unaware in any detail of its heritage attractions even if they have a general propensity to visit such attractions. If replicated generally throughout Europe, this would suggest a need on the part of attraction operators not to neglect the promotion of tourist awareness of their attractions *within* the destination areas in which they are located; that is, to target holiday-makers once they have arrived, rather than to rely on destination area brochures designed to attract tourists to the area also to promote specific visits once the tourist has arrived. The importance of knowing when in the decision-making process different sources of information are of importance is illustrated by the Manx surveys. Whereas informal sources of information would seem to predominate among tourists unaware of attractions prior to their holiday, social and personal sources of information and brochures would seem to be of importance to those tourists aware of the attractions prior to their holiday.

The users of leaflets would seem to be a discrete group among heritage tourists, with a clear dichotomy between users and non-users apparent: some tourists read leaflets, others ignore them, and there would appear to be little middle position. Clearly, the non-readers of leaflets need to be reached by other media. Findings of this kind imply the need for greater research into the effectiveness of promotional media within heritage tourism. Moreover, this need is only part of the wider need to assess the effectiveness of promotional campaigns in the manner outlined at the outset of this chapter. In this, heritage tourism has lagged behind other areas of tourism, making the challenge for the present decade all the greater.

7 The retailing role of heritage attractions

TOURIST SPENDING AND A DEFICIENCY OF DATA

Tourist boards Europe-wide collect data on tourist spending. However, this data is usually collected under categories inappropriate to the particular study of heritage attractions as the recipients of tourist spending. The inappropriateness to a study of heritage tourism of the expenditure categories used in the Isle of Man Passenger Survey is no exception to this general picture. Headings have included travel to and from the island, travel within the island, accommodation, alcoholic drinks, meals and snacks, gifts and presents, cigarettes and tobacco, and entertainment and facilities. Expenditure at heritage attractions on the island, and in the vicinity of these attractions during a visit, may be categorised under several of these headings, and cannot be assumed to be encompassed in the final category, that of entertainment and facilities. Of equal importance, this latter category encompasses many other attractions than heritage sites, and heritage attractions cannot be separately identified.

The data collected by tourist boards on the expenditure by tourists is deficient in a further respect for the study of heritage tourism, for other than broad categories of tourist, such as business tourist or holiday tourist, tourists are subdivided, if at all, into groups determined by their accommodation type, rather than by their interests or activities when on holiday. In the absence of data collected by official tourist expenditure surveys in the form needed for the present discussion, inference has to be made from the official sources which are available, although these are not fully appropriate, and from specific surveys undertaken at heritage attractions. The omission of classification by tourist type defined in terms of activities in official surveys is surprising for heritage tourism is one form of tourism increasingly used to 'spread the load' of impacts of tourism spatially and by season, especially the economic impacts of tourism. Without even a basic understanding of the expenditure patterns of heritage tourists such strategies can neither be adequately justified nor appraised. At best they are founded on wishful thinking that heritage tourists are at worse much the same as tourists generally in their expenditure, or, at best, more likely to spend locally than tourists in general.

The deficiencies of exisiting data not only mean that we are unable to compare the economic impact of heritage tourists, say, with beach tourists, but, as most attraction surveys which have questioned tourists on their spending have focused on on-site expenditure alone, we are also unable as yet to say much about the wider impact of spending induced in the vicinity of attractions by the visit. This is despite the known linkage of visits to heritage attractions with activities such as eating and drinking (Chapter 5), and the assumption that at least some of this expenditure is in the vicinity of an attraction if not actually within its site. The Countryside Commission represents an exception to this on-site emphasis in surveys of what visitors spend when consuming heritage by visiting attractions. The Commission estimates for 1990 in England, that 40 per cent of visitor spending on visits to the countryside was spent on food and drink (Countryside Commission 1991a). Entrance fees, in contrast, are estimated at 14 per cent of visitor expenditure, impulse purchases at 10 per cent and spending on crafts and souvenirs, 5 per cent. The location of this spending within the countryside in terms of attractions and their vicinity is less apparent from such figures. The more general emphasis in surveys on on-site expenditure may be assumed to have arisen from the financing of many of these surveys by site operators interested in souvenir and food sales development at their own sites, rather than with the more general economic impact of their sites.

Edwards (1989) has summarised past studies of visitor spending at heritage attractions with the overall conclusion that these sums are generally quite small, but that at attractions in Wales in 1986 holiday-makers were found to spend more at the sites than day-trippers, although the differential was not substantial. Set with the dual context of tourists and other visitors frequently having a general rather than a particular interest in heritage and that of the general recreational context of many visits (Chapters 4 and 5) the generally low sums expended at attractions in addition to the entrance fees paid are not unexpected. Other studies confirm this. In the late 1970s, visitors to cathedrals were much more likely to buy postcards than guidebooks or other souvenirs (Cathedral Tourism Advisory Group 1979). Lower priced souvenirs also predominated among those reported purchased at Stan Hywet Hall in Ohio (Achmatowicz-Otok and Goggins 1990). The greater propensity of tourists compared to day-trippers to buy refreshments and postcards is also confirmed by the 1983 survey of visitors to Laugharne, with 38 per cent of tourists buying refreshments at the site compared to 27 per cent of day-trippers, and 32 per cent of tourists buying postcards compared to 22 per cent of day-trippers (Wales Tourist Board 1984a). The Big Pit survey of the same year also confirms this difference, although the extent of the difference found was not so great (Wales Tourist Board 1984b). The latter survey reported that only one in five visitor groups made no purchase at all at the site. However, studies of this kind do not show how many jobs are dependent on retailing at attractions, compared, say, to those dependent on admissions income. Data on employment directly created by visits to heritage attractions tend both to be from other sources and not to differentiate between sources of income. For example, in 1989 it is estimated that historic houses in Scotland employed 419 people, only 19 per cent of whom were employed full time throughout the year, that castles employed 634 people of whom 18 per cent were employed full time throughout the year, and that museums and galleries employed 1,185 people, 64 per cent of them on a full-time basis throughout the year (Scottish Tourist Board 1990a). The importance of retailing to this employment is less easy to identify, either in aggregate or in terms of part-time or seasonal employment, for example.

One exception to the general emphasis on on-site expenditure in studies at specific sites may be found in a recent study of visitors to Scottish folk festivals in 1990 (Scottish Tourist Board 1991b). In total, tourists were found to spend per day 26 per cent more than day-trippers visiting these festivals. However, both groups spent notably more per day than tourists generally do on a daily basis in Scotland. Certain studies take such expenditure analyses further, to estimate the employment impacts of visitor spending inside and outside attractions. One recent study of this kind, an exception to the general focus on on-site spending only, concerned the economic impact of Beamish (Johnson and Thomas 1990a). This study assessed the impact of spending by day-trippers and tourists both inside and outside the site. The Beamish study confirmed the Welsh findings summarised by Edwards (1989) that tourists were more likely to spend within the site than were day-trippers, although once again the magnitude of the difference was not substantial with seven out of ten tourist groups spending on shopping items within the site compared to six out of ten day-tripper groups. The direction of difference was replicated for expenditure on eating and drinking within the Beamish site. However, when compared to day-trippers, tourists were also more likely to have spent outside the site on eating and drinking, shopping and admission fees to other sites. For example, over half of the tourist groups surveyed at Beamish had spent money on admission fees to other attractions on their day of visit to Beamish, compared to about one in thirty day visitor groups. Only a quarter of tourist groups had spent nothing on food and drink outside of the site on their day of visit, compared to eight out of ten day visitor groups. The economic impact of this expenditure was calculated in terms of employment as that not only created directly in local shops and restaurants and in the attraction itself, but also in terms of those jobs created in supply industries within North East England, less those lost through the diversion of consumer spending from elsewhere (Johnson and Thomas 1990b). As such, the employment impact was calculated in terms not only of tourists' spending but also of day-trippers. The net job creation represented by Beamish inside and outside its site in North East England was estimated at 114 jobs, the proportion of these represented by tourists' spending not being reported. A second study of wider impacts of this kind concerns Scottish salmon fishing (Mackay Consultants 1989). Not only does this study confirm the higher spending of tourists when compared to day-trippers among the sportsmen fishing the Scottish rivers, it has estimated that this activity is responsible directly or indirectly for at least 1,512 full-time or equivalent jobs in Scotland.

The food and shopping impacts of tourist and day-tripper expenditure outside of heritage attractions would appear from the location of shops serving 'tourists' to be quite localised around the attraction or pedestrian flows within a historic town (Pearce 1987; Ashworth and Tunbridge 1990). In particular, souvenir and like shops have been found in cities to cluster around principal attractions, historic waterfronts or pedestrian flows between attractions and car parks, and the like. A degree of functional specialism may be supposed in large cities, but similar concentrations of souvenir shops and the like can be found in some of the smaller towns of Europe too. For example, of the comparison and specialist goods shops in the English towns of Glastonbury, Tewkesbury and Hexham in 1991, most gift shops clustered in each town around the principal heritage attraction, the abbey (Figure 7.1). A similar pattern can be identified for 1991 in Chepstow and Richmond around the castles in these towns (Figure 7.2). In other towns a more dualistic pattern may be found, with the principal heritage attraction attracting some of a town's gift shops but

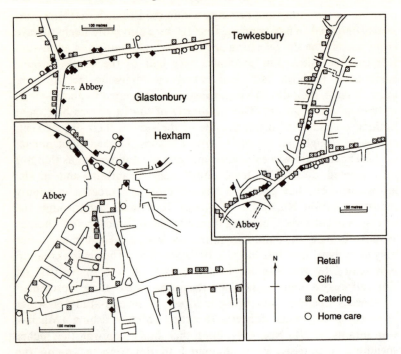

Figure 7.1 Locational clustering of gift shops around abbey attractions in heritage towns

with a further cluster elsewhere in the town (Figure 7.3). Although such clustering very close to attractions may not be found in all English towns it is a familiar enough pattern to suggest that tourists and other visitors rarely stray far from the main attractions in any volume, and that the direct retailing impact of tourists is spatially concentrated and not generally spread across the shopping centres of such towns.

The general conclusion to this survey of past research and of the spatial retailing structures of towns is to imply the pertinence of research not only into the economic impact of heritage tourism but also of historic sites as key features of historic towns providing 'out of conurbation' shopping centres for comparison goods, part of the leisure shopping aspect of heritage demand noted in Chapter 1.

TOURIST SPENDING ON THE ISLE OF MAN

As noted above, the Manx Passenger Survey does not differentiate between holiday tourists pursuing a heritage based holiday or other

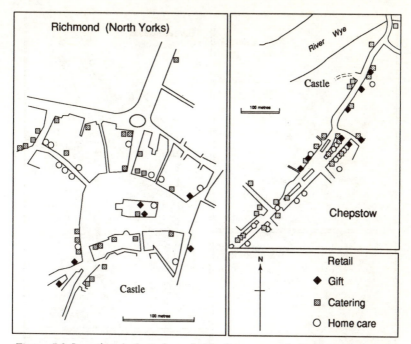

Figure 7.2 Locational clustering of gift shops around castle attractions in heritage towns

types of holiday, nor does it allow figures to be abstracted either on expenditure at heritage attractions or in their vicinity as part of a visit. As reference to Table 7.1 indicates, very little of the expenditure of tourists holidaying on the island is spent on entertainments and facilities, of which of course heritage attractions are only in turn one part. Meals, snacks and gift purchases, some of which may be associated with visits, in total amount to around one-fifth of tourist expenditure on the island, but are associated with many other activities than heritage attraction visits. This distribution of expenditure may be compared with 18 per cent reportedly spent on shopping by British holiday-makers to Wales, and 22 per cent on eating and drinking (Survey Research Associates, 1988). Table 7.1 clearly shows that the main beneficiaries of tourist spending on the island, at least in terms of primary impact, are the accommodation industry, ferries and airlines. To set a perspective, in contrast, heritage attractions are one part only of a sector equivalent in tourist expenditure to one half of that spent by tourists on alcoholic drinks while holidaying on the island. It is within this context of a comparatively minor sector of

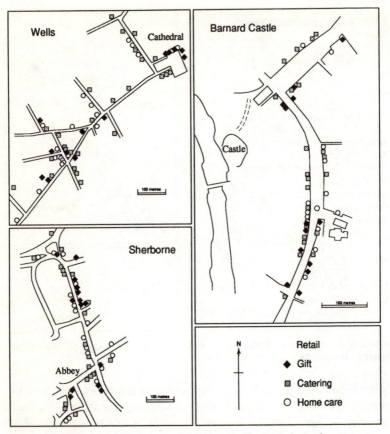

Figure 7.3 'Dualistic' locational clustering of gift shops in heritage towns

spending, but one at least diverting some other expenditure into their vicinity, that heritage attractions need to be appraised for their economic impact. The Manx case is unlikely to be substantially different from other north European seaside destinations in this regard, but a spatially differentiated expenditure analysis across Europe generalised by destination area type must await data disaggregated in an adequate way from other destination areas.

TOURIST SPENDING AT MANX HERITAGE ATTRACTIONS

Other than paying for admission to those attractions where an admission charge is levied (all of the island's major heritage attractions surveyed, except at the Manx Museum, where admission is free) the

Table 7.1 Expenditure distribution per head by holiday tourists to the Isle of Man

| | Holiday tourists visiting IOM, staying in paid accommodation: | | | |
| | Passenger Survey 1988 | | Passenger Survey 1990 | |
	July %	August %	July %	August %
Travel to/from island	26.7	25.5	26.5	24.7
Accommodation	36.2	34.6	34.9	36.7
Travel within island	5.9	4.8	3.8	4.4
Alcoholic drink	6.5	8.9	7.6	6.6
Meals/snacks	12.5	12.4	15.1	16.5
Gifts/presents	7.2	8.8	7.7	6.6
Tobacco/cigarettes	1.0	1.0	1.0	0.5
Entertainments/facilities	3.9	4.0	3.4	4.0
	£	£	£	£
N=	212.96	194.42	253.41	259.96

Source: *Isle of Man Passenger Surveys* undertaken by Economic Adviser's Office, Douglas, Isle of Man
Notes: Excludes tourists on package holidays
     N = sample size

major opportunities for tourists to spend at the Manx heritage attractions are on souvenirs, guidebooks and, at certain attractions, refreshments. The 1988 Site Survey established that 27 per cent of the tourists interviewed at the seven heritage attractions where a guidebook was available claimed to be unaware of it, and that a further 43 per cent of tourists had otherwise not purchased the guidebook. At certain attractions the proportion of tourists not spending on a guidebook was substantially greater than average, notably at Laxey Wheel and Castle Rushen. The 1990 Site Survey confirmed this general pattern of most tourist groups not buying a site guidebook, but found this lack of purchasing to be more extensive than recorded two years previously. At Cregneash in 1990 only a fifth of tourist groups had bought the site guidebook, and of these tourists, two-thirds had bought the guidebook not on the visit during which they were interviewed but either on a previous visit or elsewhere. Similarly, at Castle Rushen in 1990 only 14 per cent of the tourist groups interviewed had bought the guidebook, all but two of whom had bought this booklet prior to the visit on which they were interviewed. At Peel Castle in 1990 no tourist was found to have purchased a guidebook on their visit to the castle. Similar variation in the proportion of tourists purchasing literature of this kind has been found at attractions in Wales, with rates varying from 63 per cent of all visitors buying a guide leaflet at Big Pit to 22 per cent at Conwy Castle (Public Attitudes Surveys Research 1986). Big Pit was a clear exception in this regard and at the nine attractions surveyed in Wales in 1985 purchasing rates for guide literature varied between a quarter and a third of all visitors surveyed. Low rates of purchase of this kind have clear implications for the operators of heritage attractions. They may provide opportunities for booklet redesign and vigorous promotion, but equally they may reflect the unwillingness of many customers to spend on guidebooks. Such low rates of sales also have implications for how attractions are presented to tourists (Chapter 9), for strategies reliant on guidebooks which need to be purchased by tourists visiting an attraction may be ineffective through lack of purchase by their intended consumers. Traditionally, guidebooks have formed a major part of presentational strategies to interpret what a tourist sees at attractions: from the Manx findings such traditional strategies would appear to have been ineffective.

The 1988 Manx Site Survey would suggest that the failure to buy a site guidebook is prevalent across all social classes, effectively denying the otherwise plausible assumption that as the higher social groups tend both to be more used to dealing with written information and to be more affluent they might be more likely to buy a guidebook. Nor would it seem that those tourist groups buying a guidebook can readily be predicted from the reasons tourists give for visiting heritage attractions, for the 1988 Site Survey showed that, at these attractions, these reasons were unrelated to guidebook purchases by tourists. The one reason for visiting which might be thought to be an exception, namely education, is in fact no exception to this general case: tourists visiting for educational reasons in 1988 were no more likely to purchase a site guidebook than those visiting for other reasons. One attribute of a tourist's visit to a heritage attraction was, however, found to assist in predicting guidebook purchase at the Manx attractions surveyed in 1988. This was the attribute of length of visit. Tourists staying longer at the attractions being more likely than shorter stayers to have bought the site guidebook. If length of stay is interpreted as a surrogate measure, however imperfect, of interest in a site, this would imply that the traditional form of site retailing and interpretation, guidebook sales, has been most effective in the case of the more interested consumers of heritage among tourists visiting attractions, but has been disproportionately inappropriate for the more casual tourist visitors to attractions.

The loss of revenue to attraction operators through the failure of tourists to buy guidebooks, and the potential ineffectiveness of those presentational strategies largely reliant on guidebooks to interpret to visitors what a site means, raises questions as to the preparedness of tourists to pay for guidebooks. At best answers to the hypothetical questions needed to investigate preparedness of this kind should be regarded as guidelines, for in reality the purchasing behaviour of tourists may be different from what is stated in prospect. One means of compelling the purchase of a guidebook or other information leaflet is to include this sum in the entrance fee paid by visitors, and to give out the guidebook 'free' to visitors as they pay to enter an attraction. Such a strategy implies increases in the entrance fees charged, which may discourage visiting. The 1988 Site Survey on the Isle of Man included the statement, 'I would be willing to pay 25p more if a short guide booklet were included in the entrance fee'. Just over seven out of ten tourists agreed with this statement, although few strongly agreed. However, at two of the seven Manx attractions where entrance fees were levied disagreement was more substantial. At Laxey Wheel 44 per cent of tourists interviewed disagreed with the statement, and at Odin's Raven slightly fewer than half the tourists interviewed. In contrast, at Cregneash, Peel Castle and Castle Rushen, eight out of ten tourists agreed with the inclusive strategy. The reasons for these differences are unclear, but have obvious importance not only for retail development at the Manx attractions but more generally. Differences can be more readily explained, however, in terms of the reasons given by tourists for visiting the attractions suggesting a form of segmentation or division of tourists by the benefits gained by visiting. Tourists visiting the attractions out of a particular interest in historic places or with a particular interest in Manx culture were more likely to agree with the inclusive package than those tourists not giving these reasons. Whereas eight out of ten tourists indicating a particular interest in historic places and a similar proportion of those indicating a particular interest in Manx culture said that they would have been prepared to pay an additional 25p more for a short guide booklet if included in the admission fee, only about two-thirds of other tourists similarly agreed. In contrast, tourists for whom their visit was part of a day out in the countryside were more likely to disagree with the idea of the inclusive package, although the size of the effect was not substantial. If length of stay is again interpreted as a proxy for interest in a site, those tourists more interested in a site were to a greater degree in favour of the inclusive arrangement than their less interested counterparts, although once again the size of the effect was not substantial, with in excess of eight out of ten tourists staying over an hour at an attraction stating agreement with the idea, but fewer than seven out of ten of those staying under an hour. Although the extent of these individual differences should not be over-emphasized, collectively they might suggest the pertinence of allowing tourists to segment themselves into two groups: one, the larger group, buying a small guide booklet inclusive of their admission fee, and the other group buying their admission alone.

An alternative strategy to encourage guidebook sales is to change the product on offer, to redesign the guidebook and vigorously promote sales through display and recommendation. With the presentational enhancement of Castle Rushen in 1991, the Marketing Survey of that year included a statement to this effect, namely, 'If a full colour souvenir guide to this castle had been available for between £5–£10 I would likely have bought one'. Again this is a hypothetical statement, and the responses need to be interpreted accordingly. The price of the proposed guidebook was set at an expensive sum to indicate the quality of the guidebook intended. Fewer than one in five, or 18 per cent to be exact, of tourists agreed with this statement, with most, seven out of ten, disagreeing. The market opportunity would not, from this one case study, seem great, at least at attractions visited by largely domestic tourists. This finding concurs with that for 1990 concerning Manx National Heritage's major book on the major Manx heritage attractions, '100 Years of Heritage', which celebrated the one hundredth anniversary of the Manx Museum in 1986 (Harrison 1986). Fewer than one in thirty tourist groups interviewed at the three Manx attractions surveyed in 1990 had bought this book, and none had bought their copy on the visit on which they were interviewed.

The previous discussion about including a cheap form of guidebook in with an enhanced admission fee to attractions identified the importance of a particular interest in historic places or in Manx culture, and of length of stay at an attraction, in predicting a tourist's propensity to purchase this cheaper alternative, although the sizes of the individual effects were not found to be substantial. For 1991 and the much more expensive guidebook proposed at Castle Rushen a similar affect was found for a declared interest in castles as a reason for visiting, although not for an interest in Manx culture (this difference possibly resultant of tourists not seeing this attraction as particularly Manx, representing as it does the subjection of the island to English authority). However, tourists visiting the castle as part of a day out were also more likely than those not giving this reason for visiting to agree that they might have purchased the proposed guidebook: the opposite of what the previous conclusion would have implied. Unlike for the cheaper guidebook, length of stay at Castle Rushen in 1991 as a proxy for interest in the site was not found to be a predictor of a tourist's declared propensity to purchase the proposed guidebook. The reasons for these differences are unclear, but may result from the hypothetical nature of the questions asked. As such, any general conclusions should be extremely tentative, and the current profile of purchasers and non-purchasers of expensive guidebooks at other attractions in Europe needs to be included in a research agenda in order that possible determinants can be identified. One obvious determinant, that of social class, would seem equally as unpromising as some of the other possible determinants considered from the Manx surveys: at Castle Rushen in 1991 the social class of a tourist was irrelevant as a predictor of declared preparedness to purchase the expensive guidebook proposed. The generality of the Manx findings on guidebook purchase need to be tested elsewhere, but from the Manx evidence it would seem that most heritage tourists, or at least those of domestic rather than international origin, want at most a cheap guidebook or do not want one at all. Retailing and inter-pretative strategies need to be designed with this in mind.

Souvenir sales are a further source of actual or potential income to heritage attraction operators. The 1988 Site Survey at the Manx attractions showed that only a quarter of the tourist groups surveyed at these attractions had made a souvenir purchase at the sites, and that only a further quarter had any intention of doing so. With approx-imately half of an attraction's tourist visitors neither purchasing a souvenir nor having any intention of doing so the retail market for heritage attractions of the Manx type would seem substantially less than that of the total number of tourists visiting. The generality of the Manx case is as yet unknown. The extent of purchasing by tourists at the Manx attractions would seem, for example, substantially less than at Beamish, where, as already noted, seven out of ten tourists were found to have bought souvenirs and gifts on site (Johnson and Thomas 1990a). It needs also to be noted that the 1988 Site Survey found substantial variations between the Manx attractions in terms of purchasing by tourists, suggesting the importance of site-specific factors. Purchasing by tourists was greatest at Cregneash and at Castle Rushen, and least at Odin's Raven, Peel Castle, Laxey Wheel and the Nautical Museum. As, in particular, in 1988 the major souvenir shop was at the Manx Museum, the array of souvenirs available cannot readily be advanced as a reason for this variation between the attractions.

Propensity to purchase souvenirs was found to be greatest among those tourists giving a particular interest in historic places or in Manx culture as important reasons for their visit, and among those tourists staying longer at the attractions, the latter which again we may regard perhaps as a proxy for interest in the attractions. As such, the determinants of souvenir purchasing would appear to mirror those concerning the purchase of a cheap guidebook inclusive with the admission fee, discussed earlier in this chapter. As a determinant of souvenir purchase, length of stay at an attraction was quite substantial in its importance: for example, tourists staying at an attraction for over two hours were found to be more than twice as likely to have bought souvenirs than those staying under an hour. Interest in historic places or in Manx culture was also, however, of unambiguous importance in purchasing: around half as many more tourists stating that a particular interest in historic places or in Manx culture was important in their decision to visit had bought souvenirs at the attractions than had those tourists visiting not giving these reasons. Together, these findings would suggest that souvenir sales to holiday tourists at heritage attractions like those on the Isle of Man are disproportionately to the more specialist or interested consumers of heritage and their children, suggesting an implicit limit to the extent to which souvenir purchases might be developed, at least for attractions generally visited for under two hours. The determinants of souvenir purchasing by tourists need to form part of a research strategy for heritage tourism, and to include among them such possible determinants as site ambience and tourists' emotional reactions to sites, as well as the more usual socio-economic and behavioural determinants: in this way site-specific variations might be explained.

One strategy to encourage souvenir sales is to manage visitor flows at attractions, so to pass through or by the souvenir selling area. The new presentation of Castle Rushen in 1991 was so designed, and in consequence, slightly more than nine out of ten tourist groups interviewed in 1991 for the Marketing Survey were found to have visited the souvenir shop at the castle. Of these, slightly fewer than half, or 47 per cent to be precise, had purchased an item, or items, at the shop. However, when compared to 1988 when the souvenir sales area was not integral to the visitor flow nor when such an extensive range of items was available, the overall proportion of tourist groups buying an item at the castle had in fact decreased, a result which might be thought surprising. What is unknown for 1988 at the castle is how much on average each group buying an item spent, but as the product range available in 1991 had been extended into more expensive items rather than had been replaced, the apparent drop in spending by tourists cannot be readily explained by the changed product range. This finding might suggest that tourists do not in fact generally buy souvenirs on impulse, but instead at least intuitively budget some expenditure to include or to exclude such purchases as part of their visit to an attraction, and that as a consequence directing tourist flows through souvenir areas may not of itself enhance sales. If this is so, other factors may be more important in determining souvenir sales to tourists. However, it should be borne in mind that although the proportion of tourists prepared to spend on souvenirs at an attraction may not be elastic in response to retail strategies, overall sales may be enhanced by increasing the total number of tourists visiting an attraction, and, as such, retailing at heritage attractions depends on the promotion and development of attractions in non-retailing ways.

The adequacy of the range of souvenirs available at attractions may be thought to be one determinant of sales, not measured as the range of souvenirs available for purchase, but in terms of tourists' perceptions. The Manx evidence would suggest that this factor should be discounted somewhat. The 1988 Site Survey at the Manx attractions included the following statement to investigate this perceptual effect, 'There is an excellent range of souvenir items available for sale at this site'. Those tourists who had seen the souvenirs available at the attractions divided into roughly equal proportions in terms of disagreeing or agreeing with this statement, suggesting that in 1988 the range of souvenirs available was not adequate for all tourists. This in itself might be thought to limit spending, but no relationship may be found at either a site or aggregate level between the perceptions of tourists in this regard and whether or not purchases were made. Site-specific variations in perceptions may be identified from the 1988 survey, with tourists at the Grove Museum, Laxey Wheel, Castle Rushen and Odin's Raven substantially more likely to agree than to disagree with the excellence of the souvenir range, but those at the Nautical Museum and Peel Castle much more likely to disagree than to agree. As these variations bear no relationship to the variations in the actual frequency of purchases made at the attractions, the interpretation of these variations is unclear. The divergence between perceptual and behavioural indicators would lend implicit support to the suggestion of an implicit budgeting of some expenditure for souvenir purchase prior to a visit rather than to impulse purchases when at an attraction.

The amount spent by a tourist on souvenirs at any particular attraction is of importance to attraction operators in the planning of the content of souvenir ranges. At Castle Rushen in 1991 the range of souvenirs started with pencils and the like, priced at under £1 each, and extended upwards in price to include jewellery. Despite the range of souvenirs available, three-quarters of tourist groups buying an item, or items, spent under £3 on their purchases from the shop. The presence of more expensive items available for purchase meant that the distribution of spending was slightly bimodal, with one in ten of the tourist groups having spent over £7 in the souvenir shop. Other than the few high spenders being, in all but one case, from non-manual households, social class as a proxy for disposable income was not a determinant of the amount most tourists were likely to spend in the castle's souvenir shop. Length of stay at the castle had only a slight effect on the amount spent by a tourist, but one confirming the relationship noted earlier, namely that those tourists staying longer tend to be more likely to spend. The substantial bias in souvenir spending towards small items is likely to continue to be found in studies elsewhere, if only because a visit to a heritage attraction is often one visit among other activities when on holiday, many of which offer opportunities to buy gifts and souvenirs.

Food and drink sales via a buttery or cafeteria are a further form of on-site sales for the operators of heritage attractions. Sales of this kind may also be used to extend the length of stay of tourists and to enhance their satisfaction with their visit. At those sites where a café or buttery was available, the 1988 Site Survey asked about the extent to which this facility had enhanced the tourists' enjoyment of their visit. At Cregneash seven out of ten tourists agreed that their visit had been made more enjoyable because of the café facility, and likewise two-thirds at Castle Rushen. At other attractions, tourists were asked a hypothetical question about how such a facility, had one been available, might have enhanced their visit. The latter findings were more varied, and, perhaps surprisingly, were unrelated to the proximity of the attractions to exisiting refreshment facilities in the vicinity. The extent to which tourists expect café facilities to be available at heritage attractions may usefully form part of an agenda for heritage tourism, as although this expectation is unknown the provision of such facilities is increasingly common at attractions. Similarly, the extent to which refreshment sales may affect other sales at attractions is also worthy of research.

TOURIST SPENDING IN THE VICINITY OF MANX HERITAGE ATTRACTIONS

Earlier in this chapter the propensity of tourists visiting Beamish in north eastern England to spend on admission fees to other attractions, and on eating, drinking and shopping outside of the site on their day of visit was noted (Johnson and Thomas 1990a). The Beamish study does not specify the spatial proximity of this other spending, but from the location of shops serving tourists visiting heritage towns noted earlier, we may assume that much induced spending is in general very localised to the vicinity of heritage attractions, at least for those sited in towns (which in fact Beamish is not). What is generally as yet unknown is the extent of this localised spending, and how far it results from tourists visiting the heritage attractions of towns or from tourists visiting the towns specifically for shopping. This is an important topic to include in a research agenda for heritage tourism, for without such knowledge the impact of heritage attractions on their local economy can only be guessed at.

The 1991 Marketing Survey at Castle Rushen included questioning of tourists visiting the castle on the expenditure by their personal group in the town of Castletown, outside of the castle. As many tourists would not have completed their visit to Castletown when leaving the castle, they were also asked to estimate how much money they would likely spend during their visit. The latter has some obvious limitations, but at least recorded expectations of spending on meals and alcoholic drinks in the castle's vicinity. The survey did not, however, record spending by tourists visiting Castletown but not visiting the castle.

Of the tourist groups interviewed inside the castle in 1991, slightly fewer than one in five had either spent nothing in Castletown outside of the castle or expected to spend nothing in the town. As such, the castle would appear to be acting as an enhancement of the retailing economy of the town in which it is sited. However, the size of the expenditures made or expected were not large, with three-quarters of all tourist groups expecting to spend under £10 in the town, and with few groups expecting to spend or having spent over £15. The extent of localised spending by most tourists would not seem to be great, particularly when it is remembered that in 1991 Castle Rushen did not have a buttery and so that all expenditure on refreshments by tourists visiting the castle would, if spent in Castletown, have been spent outside of the castle walls. These figures would also concur with the general pattern of tourist spending on the island noted earlier in the chapter. An average (mean) figure of each tourist group spending a little over £5 in the town in association with their visit to the castle implies some caution in enthusiastic associations of heritage attractions with retailing, and in consequence with economic development. The 1991 survey gives some support to the idea that the general interest tourist, rather than the tourist particularly interested in heritage, was most likely to spend outside of the castle, with half as many general interest tourists not spending in Castletown than other tourists, 14 per cent compared to 31 per cent. This would concur with the visit to the castle being one part only of a day out. This would imply a degree of segmentation between tourist visitors to heritage attractions in terms of their spending location: if the Castle Rushen findings are more generally applicable it would seem that heritage specialists tend to spend more within attractions whereas more general interest tourists tend to spend more in the vicinity of attractions. Perhaps of wider significance, the generality or otherwise of the Manx findings has to await further research elsewhere in Europe, but in the meantime some caution is implied in assessing the wider economic spin-off from visits by holiday tourists to heritage attractions.

CONCLUSIONS

At present, assessments of the retailing importance, and wider economic importance in employment creation, of heritage attractions are limited by the way in which official data on tourists' spending are collated. Tourists visiting heritage attractions are generally not an identifiable group in such statistics; and nor is their spending at heritage attractions or in their vicinity. Specific data need therefore to be collected, and this requirement should form part of an agenda for heritage tourism.

The market size for souvenirs and refreshments at heritage attractions cannot be equated with the volume of tourists visiting such attractions, although it would seem that tourists are more likely than day-trippers to spend not just inside an attraction but outside too. Guidebooks would seem a particularly unpopular purchase, and in consequence interpretative strategies to explain to visitors the significance of an attraction are likely to be unsuccessful if reliant on visitors purchasing site guidebooks. Souvenir sales would appear to vary by site in the proportion of tourists buying them, but generally purchases are of small items. This is to be expected for the visit is frequently part of a day out with plenty of other opportunities to buy souvenirs (Chapters 4 and 5). Tourists may also have implicit budgets to spend on souvenirs and extending a product range into more expensive items may not effect a marked change in expenditure patterns by tourists.

Within the largely general interest day out context in which attraction retailing has to compete for sales with other retailers, what might for the present at least be termed the more specialist or interested consumers of heritage would seem more likely to make purchases at heritage attractions, although the extent of this effect should not be exaggerated. Tourists with a particular historical or cultural interest in an attraction, or staying longer at a site, are more likely to make purchases inside the site. Equally, general interest tourists are more likely to spend in the vicinity of the attraction, as part of their general day out. In general, spending in the vicinity of the one Manx attraction surveyed would not seem substantial; rather most tourists expect to spend outside an attraction, but they do not expect to spend very much. This perhaps accounts for the tight clustering of gift shops and the like frequently found around attractions: as the market is not substantial a site to maximise market share is essential to such retailers.

8 Tourist disposition towards conservation and commitment to heritage

TOURISM AND THE NEED FOR CONSERVATION

At one and the same time tourism provides a means by which the conservation of historic sites may be afforded but also a mechanism making conservation an imperative. The term 'conservation' is used intentionally here for rarely is the exact physical form of a building or townscape *preserved* as it is, more commonly its essential features are *conserved*, and conservation may involve new buildings in an area which harmonise with the old (National Commission for European Architectural Heritage Year 1975). Scheduled ancient monuments are perhaps an exception to this, with preservation paramount. However, the partial rebuilding of monuments is not unknown, and as such the distinction is a matter of emphasis rather than of principle. Indeed, in terms of landscape conservation, in an era of food surpluses within the European Community, the opportunity arises not only to retain landscapes but also to recreate them in images of what is considered treasured, in terms not only of wildlife and amenity, but also of appearance. With incomes from food and fibre production depressed farmers' organisations are increasingly emphasing the importance of landscape quality as a product for which they should be paid. The Environmentally Sensitive Areas of Britain established this policy in the 1980s (Prentice 1992a), a policy which the Countryside Steward-ship scheme in England and the Tir Cymen scheme in Wales are now in effect spreading much more widely. The 1990s are likely to be an era of explicit environmental 'enhancement' (National Parks Review Panel 1991). In effect, conservation takes on a new dimension in the 1990s: the creation of a landscape in our own image, a new landscape vernacular so to speak based upon landscape elements remembered from a past system of less intensive agriculture. Indeed, the Countryside Commission has called for a 'new map of England' to be created in this fashion, 'Setting out our objectives for the beauty of the

countryside in the next century – a new map of England, so to speak'
(Countryside Commission 1991b: 4). Significantly, this is presented as
a *conservation* initiative, 'to retain the best from the past'. In effect, we
are entering an era when as a society we can create our heritages in
landscape terms all around us.

The impact of tourists can be substantial in terms of environmental
change. At destination areas tourism may effect a physical transformation through hotel and infrastructure development. The expansion of
tourism in a destination area usually replaces one market segment or
type of tourist with another, with tourists previously attracted to a
destination area by the historic or landscape resources being replaced,
for example, by tourists attracted by poolside activities and night-
clubs: the island of Mallorca is a case in point. Even at destinations
which promote heritage as their principal attraction, conservation may
not be assured. Tourists, themselves, may be one source of damage to
sites and buildings, their feet literally wearing away the historic
attraction they are visiting (Cathedral Tourism Advisory Group 1979;
Fowler 1990b). Nor can medieval stone built cathedrals easily with-
stand the fluctuations in humidity and temperature caused by large
volumes of tourists breathing. Indeed, this increased humidity is
thought to combine with dust in the atmosphere which contains
sulphur to form sulphuric acid: to create a form of internal acid rain
within such buildings. The demands of tourists may also alter the way
an attraction is presented. In the extreme case, a 'heritage' attraction
may be contrived quite differently from the contemporary site itself.
As Light has commented about the presentation of heritage attractions:

> In contrast to earlier thinking which emphasised interpretation as
> secondary to the resource, at many modern heritage sites the
> interpretation itself may be the sole basis of the attraction.
>
> (Light 1991: 9)

Walsh-Heron and Stevens have made a similar point:

> Increasingly, especially at heritage properties, the role of interpre-
> tation is becoming the attraction. The techniques and the media
> used to bring a place to life can very often be the motivator that
> attracts.
>
> (Walsh-Heron and Stevens 1990: 101)

The Jorvik Viking Centre at York is substantially a case in point.
Although the buildings and alley layout of the reconstruction of
Viking Coppergate have been based on archaeological finds, and the

sequential visit ends in a conventional museum display, the attraction is principally the 'time tunnel' ride taking visitors 'back in time' and through the reconstructed alley stage set or 'three-dimensional archaeological interpretation of the immensely detailed archaeological evidence' (Addyman and Gaynor 1984: 11). The ride given to visitors in the time capsule vehicle is fully programmed and does not allow the visitor the initiative to stop the sequence, or repeat parts of it, to answer questions as the ride progresses. Further, the attraction is housed in a modern city centre development and the visitor finally emerges back into the street in similar fashion to leaving the illusions of a film suddenly behind when leaving a cinema.

Other than in providing resources from which heritage attractions may be conserved (English Heritage 1988), the past literature on the impact of tourists on the built artefacts of the historic past of Europe has tended to either be hostile to tourist development or to urge constraint. Extreme responses have included the construction of replica attractions in the vicinity of real attractions, with tourists directed to the replicas (Edwards 1989). Techniques of visitor management may otherwise emphasise alternative attractions to visit, so to 'spread the load' across a greater number of sites, or at some attractions to constrain visitor flows. For example, cathedrals have responded to visitor pressures by roping off areas, covering surfaces, providing overshoes, providing replica monuments for brass rubbers, and enhanced 'policing' through staffing (Cathedral Tourism Advisory Group 1979). At the most popular attractions visitor numbers have sometimes resulted in a somewhat sterile site experience, 'We have reached the position where so many people try to see Stonehenge that very few see it properly' (Chippindale 1990: 31). The particular problems of visitor pressure at Stonehenge have resulted in substantive proposals to redesign the site around the stones to enable visitors to see them in their topographic perspective and to spread the visitor load over a wider area around the stones. Proposals have included the clearance of modern intrusions from the environs of the stones, giving public access to a wider area around the stones, and the location of a new visitor centre away from the monument and out of sight from it (Chippindale and Fowler 1990). English Heritage's scheme announced in 1989 is currently priced at £10 million, and includes the setting up of an independent Stonehenge Trust to manage the site, which currently is in part owned by the state and partly by the National Trust. The intended visitor centre is to be sited one kilometre away at Larkhill, and it is intended that non-disabled visitors should walk to the stones through a landscape rich in archaeological remains.

With the intended visitor centre to be built at Larkhill the intention is that the walking tourist will see the stones in topographical context, the stones gradually disappearing below the horizon as the tourist descends to cross a shallow valley, to reappear as he or she climbs up out of this valley. The intention is to increase the average visitor stay at Stonehenge from twenty minutes to two hours.

Solutions of the expense proposed for Stonehenge are clearly unaffordable at many heritage attractions. Part of a less expensive strategy of constraint is to use the concerns of visitors, tourists included, for the conservation of historic sites to effect a change in visitors' behaviours, or to develop sympathetic attitudes to the cause of conservation among visitors. Such strategies have been part of countryside management practices for some years (Aldridge 1975; Pennyfather 1975). In particular, strategies of this kind have been advanced as a means of reducing vandalism (Harrison 1976).

TOURIST PERCEPTIONS OF THE FUNCTIONS OF HISTORIC SITES AS HERITAGE ATTRACTIONS

The extent to which tourists see the functions of historic sites, museums and like attractions as conservational resources has important implications for using visitor attitudes as a basis for the conservation of sites. The Manx database provides some insight into this issue. Reference to Table 8.1 shows the perceptions held by tourists of the functions of sites being visited on the island, and in the case of tourists interviewed in the area of Douglas Sea Front, tourists' views of the functions generally of historic and like sites. One aspect of these findings results from survey differences: in 1990 higher frequencies for functions ascribed at the attractions were recorded than two years earlier, consequent of prompting. More than a single function could be ascribed to the sites by the tourists interviewed. Among those functions commonly ascribed to sites by tourists visiting them, conservation clearly ranks as important, being rated second to education as the most commonly perceived function in both 1988 and 1990. This is not the case, however, for tourists in general on the island, for whom education, information, the pleasure of viewing and a diversity of 'other' reasons are given as functions either of historic monuments or of museums. A substantial minority of the tourists interviewed on Douglas Sea Front in 1988 were found to have no perception of heritage attraction functions, and generally tourists interviewed in Douglas were less able to name multiple functions than were those tourists interviewed at the attractions. The information

Table 8.1 Main functions perceived of heritage sites by adult holiday tourists to the Isle of Man

| | Holiday tourists visting sites: | | Holiday tourists visiting IOM: | |
	Site Survey 1988 %	Site Survey 1990 %	Douglas Sea Front 1988 Historic monuments %	Museums %
Pleasure of viewing	23.7	63.3	12.9	17.3
Education	48.0	73.5	14.9	27.2
Conservation	35.8	68.2	6.4	5.8
Information	33.8	44.4	11.1	19.9
Unspecific visits/ days out	5.0	2.9	5.0	2.6
Tourism	–	22.3	7.9	1.5
Other	12.4	1.1	31.0	27.5
Don't know	1.1	0.0	24.0	18.7
N =	1,942	547	342	342

Source: unpublished surveys undertaken by author for Manx National Heritage
Notes: More than one function could be given
        N = sample size

presented in Table 8.1 would imply not only substantial differences in the perception of the functions of heritage attractions between tourists visiting them and the generality of tourists from whom they are drawn, but also that conservation in particular is mostly seen as a function by site visitors. As such, the Manx findings would imply sympathy among tourists visiting heritage attractions for their conservation, but not equivalent sympathy among holiday-makers generally. For the immediate needs of site conservation the sympathy towards site conservation among visiting tourists is an asset for managers seeking to promote conservation: it is the wider need for support for conservation among the population more generally which seems less assured, and needs to be developed. Site-based strategies of promoting heritage conservation are clearly inappropriate for reaching this wider audience where the message needs to be heard.

Reference to Table 8.2 shows that we should not assume that tourists visiting heritage attractions have a uniform view of the functions of such sites by the type of heritage attraction. The Manx surveys reveal substantial variations between attractions in the functions ascribed to them by their tourist visitors. Certain attractions on the island are seen more frequently in conservational terms than others by their tourist visitors, notably Cregneash in both 1988 and 1990, and in 1988 both the Grove Museum and Odin's Raven. The frequency

Table 8.2 Main functions perceived of different heritage sites by adult holiday tourists visiting heritage attractions on the Isle of Man

	Peel Castle 1988 %	Peel Castle 1990 %	Castle Rushen 1988 %	Castle Rushen 1990 %	Manx Museum 1988 %	Nautical Museum 1988 %	Grove Museum 1988 %	Laxey Wheel 1988 %	Cregneash 1988 %	Cregneash 1990 %	Odin's Raven 1988 %
Pleasure of viewing	37.9	54.9	12.4	74.1	22.8	23.7	19.0	34.3	27.9	60.7	10.4
Education	75.8	73.4	48.0	69.2	34.3	42.9	31.8	33.5	57.8	78.1	52.5
Conservation	39.5	48.9	36.6	73.5	13.8	26.6	45.1	17.4	49.7	82.6	58.4
Information	13.7	65.8	10.5	23.2	67.5	49.7	14.4	33.9	33.4	44.4	55.0
Unspecific visits/days out	4.7	1.1	7.5	4.3	0.7	6.2	1.5	13.5	2.3	3.4	4.0
Tourism/ other	5.5	44.0	36.9	10.3	0.7	0.0	24.6	23.5	0.3	15.8	4.5
Don't know	0.4	0.0	1.3	0.0	0.4	0.0	1.0	5.7	0.0	0.0	0.5
N=	256	184	306	185	268	177	195	230	308	178	202

Source: unpublished surveys undertaken by author for Manx National Heritage
Notes: More than one function could be given
N = sample size

with which a conservational function is ascribed to Odin's Raven might be thought surprising as the boat which is displayed is a late twentieth-century replica. Similarly, the omission of the island's other museums from those sites most frequently rated with a conservational function may be thought surprising, as in 1988 both displayed conserved artefacts. Instead, these two museums were perceived as informational; in the case of the Manx Museum by two-thirds of its tourist visitors. Nor can we presume that tourists disproportionately see museums as having educational functions: in 1988 these functions were more frequently ascribed to Peel Castle, Castle Rushen, Cregneash and Odin's Raven. The determinants of site-specific perceived functions warrant research if variations of this kind are to be understood. In particular, tourists need to be asked *why* they ascribe the functions they suggest for sites.

The perceptions of the functions of museums and monuments among the holiday-maker tourists interviewed on Douglas Sea Front were found to be held consistently across social classes, and were irrespective of propensity to visit and views on the attractiveness of such places for visiting. This general picture was the case with only two exceptions. First, non-manual, and especially professional and higher managerial, tourists were more likely to ascribe informational functions to museums than were other tourists, with holiday tourists from professional and higher managerial households being twice as likely to give this function than holiday tourists from manual worker households. Second, holiday tourists disagreeing that museums were boring places to visit were twice as likely than those agreeing to ascribe educational functions to museums. However, neither of these determinants were replicated for the functions ascribed to monuments. For tourists generally, therefore, the Manx survey data would suggest that the determinants of how heritage attractions are perceived in terms of function are far from straightforward.

For tourists visiting attractions, however, the determinants of how functions are perceived would appear easier to identify, particularly for educational roles, and both the 1988 and 1990 Site Surveys at the Manx attractions suggest direction as to future research. However, the conservational function of the attractions was somewhat of an exception to the general pattern. In both years the conservational functions of attractions were more likely to be given by tourist visitors with a declared particular interest in castles and historic places, compared to those tourists not visiting for this reason. However, the size of this difference was not substantial, with in 1990, for example, just over seven out of ten tourists visiting out of a particular interest ascribing a conservational function to the attraction, compared to 63 per cent of other tourists. However, the Manx surveys give greater guidance as to the determinants of perceived educational functions: tourists giving this function were more likely to be from non-manual households than from manual households, to be educated to twenty-three years of age or above, to be visiting out of a particular interest in Manx culture or with a particular interest in historic sites, or to be visiting out of an educational reason. For example, in 1990 three-quarters of non-manual tourists visiting the attractions ascribed an educational function to the site visited, compared to six out of ten manuals; and, similarly, eight out of ten tourists visiting out of a particular interest in Manx culture ascribed an educational function to the site visited, compared to seven out of ten other tourists. In contrast, tourist visitors were less likely to ascribe an educational function to an attraction if they were visiting out of an enjoyment of sightseeing. Although the strengths of the individual determinants of tourists' perceptions of the educational functions are not great from the Manx surveys, the overall picture is one of tourists visiting out of a particular interest being more likely than general interest tourists to ascribe an educational role to an attraction. In turn, this would imply a greater opportunity at attractions to develop conservational awareness among particular interest tourists who are disproportionately disposed to an educational role at sites, that is, among those tourists most likely already more exposed to conservational issues, rather than their more general interest counter-parts. Such a conclusion would imply some caution in any enthusiastic equation of visits by tourists to heritage attractions with the enhancement of conservational awareness through education at attractions, irrespective of background determinants. Because of its importance to heritage conservation, this issue warrants inclusion in an agenda for heritage tourism.

COMMITMENT OF HERITAGE TOURISTS TO HISTORY AND HERITAGE

So far in this book enthusiasm for heritage or history has tended to be somewhat blurred together as an enthusiasm for the same things, which clearly history and its derivative, heritage, are not. Similarly, so far in this book 'enthusiasm' has been defined somewhat loosely, implicitly or explicitly, to include frequent visiting heritage attractions, longer lengths of stays at attractions and specialist reasons for visiting, however imprecisely the latter can in practice readily be defined. As such, it would be more satisfactory if both the issues of history versus heritage consumption and of the characteristics of 'enthusiasts' could be clarified. The Manx database may be used to help answer the question as to how committed to learning about history tourists visiting heritage attractions might be. A visitor stereotype frequently talked of by the conservators of monuments is the historian wishing to see sites conserved as uninterpreted ruins for private study; the ruins retained in the manner in which they entered conservation. The 1990 Site Survey at the Manx attractions included the opinion statement, 'History is an exciting subject', which for the present will be interpreted as an indicator of the extent to which tourists saw themselves as enthused with history. More than nine out of ten tourists interviewed at the Manx attractions in 1990 agreed to varying extents with this statement, three out of ten strongly agreeing with it. The latter group might in consequence be thought of as the history enthusiasts among the tourists. Notable site variations were found, with two out of five tourists at Cregneash strongly agreeing that history was exciting, but only one in five at Castle Rushen. If the interpretation of this indicator is correct, this would suggest that, of the Manx attractions surveyed in 1990, Cregneash would seem disproportionately attractive to history enthusiasts, and Castle Rushen, the least attractive. More generally it should be remembered that the conservators' stereotype of the history enthusiast is really a stereotype of a minority group among tourists if the present definition in terms of the extent to which history is thought exciting is accepted.

To define enthusiasm for history in terms of those tourists strongly agreeing that it was an exciting subject would appear to have some utility as a summary measure of reasons for visiting attractions, for those tourists giving the reasons of education, a particular interest in historic sites or in Manx culture, as their reasons for visiting the attractions were more likely than those not giving these reasons to strongly agree that history was exciting. In contrast, those tourists for whom a general interest in sightseeing or for whom a day out were important reasons in their decision to visit were less likely than those not giving these reasons to strongly agree with the excitement of history. The differences recorded were quite substantial. For example, twice as many, in total nearly half, of those tourists not giving sightseeing as a reason for visiting, compared to those giving this reason, strongly agreed that history was exciting. Of those tourists giving an interest in Manx culture, 46 per cent strongly agreed that history was exciting, compared to only 26 per cent of those tourists not giving this reason. Those tourists strongly agreeing that history was exciting were also disproportionately educated, and a clear educational gradient was apparent in the likelihood of a tourist strongly agreeing with the statement. At the extremes, twice as many tourists educated to twenty-three years of age or above compared to those educated to sixteen years or younger strongly agreed that history was exciting, amounting to nearly half of the more educated group. The Manx findings would clearly suggest the utility to future research in heritage tourism of the perceived excitement of history as an indicator of enthusiasm for history among tourist visitors.

The issue of the commitment of tourists to history or heritage can also be investigated by reference to the memberships of historical and heritage bodies reported by tourists visiting heritage attractions. This may form an alternative definition of enthusiasm. However, it should also be borne in mind that joining a historical or heritage organisation may have social as well as conservational implications, membership of such organisations being known to be socially skewed to the higher social class groups (Prentice 1989a). The 1990 Site Survey at the Manx attractions included questioning about membership of nine types of heritage organisation, namely, National Trusts off the island, conservation societies, historical societies, archaeological societies, geographical societies, English Heritage's club, the clubs of Cadw and what is now known as Historic Scotland, Friends of the Manx Museum and Friends of the Manx National Trust. Membership of these organisations was not found to be extensive among the tourists visiting the Manx heritage attractions in 1990. Heritage, rather than historical or geographical memberships predominated, with a quarter of the tourists interviewed claiming membership of a National Trust, although mostly of a Trust off the island. One in seven tourists claimed membership of a conservation society, but fewer than one in thirty claimed to be members of a historical society, and likewise of an archaeological or geographical society. This membership pattern serves to emphasise the importance of *heritage* rather than *history* or *historical geography* to those holiday-maker tourists visiting heritage attractions who are sufficiently enthusiastic to join formally organised societies promoting heritage or history. This would imply some caution in interpreting the earlier findings about tourists' excitement for *history* in the literal sense of an excitement for history rather than for heritage.

The tourists interviewed at the Manx attractions in 1990 were divided into two groups, those who were a member of at least one heritage or history organisation, and those who were members of none. Those tourists who were members of at least one organisation may be thought of as the more committed heritage enthusiasts among the tourists. Of the tourists interviewed in 1990, 37 per cent could in this manner be classified as committed heritage enthusiasts. However, site specific variations between the numbers of heritage enthusiasts so defined were found: both Cregneash and Peel Castle were found to attract one and a half times as many enthusiasts in proportion to their tourist numbers than was Castle Rushen. These differences would imply further segmentation among the tourists visiting the Manx heritage attractions.

The socially skewed nature of heritage society membership is shown by the Manx findings. Approximately half of the tourists from professional and managerial households claimed to be a member of at least one heritage or historical organisation, compared to fewer than three out of ten tourists from clerical and supervisory households, and one in ten tourists from manual households. A similar gradient in membership was also demonstrated in terms of the formal education of tourists. At the extremes, just over six out of ten tourists educated to twenty-three years of age or above claimed to be a member of at least one heritage organisation compared to fewer than one in five tourists educated only to sixteen years of age or less.

Membership of a heritage or historical organisation may also be shown from the Manx database to be associated with a particular, rather than a general, interest in visiting attractions. However, the extent of this effect should not be exaggerated. Holiday tourists visiting the Manx attractions in 1990 who were members of a heritage organisation were more likely than other tourists to have come to the attractions out of a particular interest in historic sites or in Manx culture, and less likely to have come out of an interest in sightseeing. For example, whereas 64 per cent of holiday tourists who were members of a heritage organisation had come out of a particular interest in historic places, 54 per cent of non-members gave this reason; and, likewise, three out of ten and 23 per cent of members and non-members coming out of an interest in Manx culture. Although the individual sizes of these differences are not great, together they may suggest the utility of membership as an indicator of a committed enthusiast for heritage. Equally, it would be wrong to *equate* membership with differing reasons for visiting attractions.

The potential utility of membership as an indicator of heritage enthusiasm is further suggested by its association with the functions of sites as perceived by their tourist visitors. Those heritage organisation members among the tourists interviewed at the Manx attractions in 1990 were more likely to give education and conservation as functions than were non-members, and less likely to give pleasure of viewing as a function. Once again the sizes of the differences individually were not great, with, for example, three-quarters of members citing conservation as a function compared to 64 per cent of non-members. However, the collective pattern of differences would again suggest the utility of membership as an indicator of enthusiasm and commitment to heritage.

The two indicators of enthusiasm or commitment to heritage used here, namely seeing history as exciting and being a member of a heritage organisation, may be measuring different aspects of enthusiasm or commitment and, in consequence, may not fully replicate one another among tourists. Equally, if one indicator does not at least partly predict the other among the sample of tourists interviewed they might be thought of limited use. An unambiguous association between the indicators can in fact be found from the Manx database, but this is far from perfect: whereas 52 per cent of heritage organisation members strongly agreed that history was exciting, 24 per cent of non-members did likewise. Combining these two indicators would suggest a fourfold classification of enthusiasm or commitment among tourists visiting heritage attractions as part of their holiday: namely, (a) heritage organisation members for whom history is a strongly felt excitement; (b) heritage organisation members for whom history is less strongly felt to be exciting; (c) non-members for whom history is a strongly felt excitement; and (d) non-members for whom history is less strongly felt to be exciting. The Manx database would further suggest as a basis for further research the following breakdown of holiday tourists visitors to heritage attractions into these four groups. Group (a) would appear to account for about one in seven tourists (say, 15 per cent) visiting the Manx attractions surveyed in 1990; group (b) approximately one fifth of tourist visitors (say, 20 per cent); group (c) approximately one in seven tourist visitors (say, 15 per cent); and group (d) approximately half of all tourist visitors (say, 50 per cent). If group (a) alone are thought of as committed to heritage, commitment to heritage is clearly a minority interest among those tourists visiting Manx heritage attractions. Even if group (c) is added to group (a), to overcome the potential social constraints to membership effectively demonstrated by few lower social class members of heritage organisations, much the same conclusion pertains. The general conclusion of a lack of commitment to heritage by most tourists visiting heritage attractions needs confirmation elsewhere, but concurs with a general interest perspective to the development and presentation of heritage attractions, irrespective of the preferences of many conservators noted earlier. If heritage attraction development and presentation are to be demand-led, that is, to respond to consumer preferences rather than necessarily to professionals' preferences, the general lack of enthusiastic commitment to history among tourists already visiting such attractions needs to be recognised. Such a recognition does not mean that historical accuracy is irrelevant, only that it has to be presented in a manner which the bulk of visitors demand.

Several overall conclusions may be drawn from the discussion so far in this chapter. First, the Manx surveys would suggest that those tourists who show a commitment to history or heritage through organisational memberships are largely committed to the latter, that is to heritage, rather than to the history from which heritage is to varying extents derived. This has unambiguous implications not only for site development and presentation as already noted, but also for the promotion of attractions. Second, there would appear to be quite marked differences in visitor profiles defined in terms of commitment among tourists visiting what are quite similar sites within a destination area as small as the Isle of Man. This confirms the existence of a further dimension of the heterogeneity of heritage attractions, one frequently alluded to throughout this book. In the Manx case, Cregneash would appear, compared to the two castles, to attract disproportionate numbers of tourists enthusiastic for history and committed to heritage. Castle Rushen, at least prior to its presentational refurbishment, would appear to attract disproportionately more less committed tourists. This would imply the need to base presentational developments on an understanding of local market segmentations among visiting tourists. The third conclusion which may be drawn is that despite the social bias to non-manual households and particularly to the higher non-manual groups among tourists visiting heritage attractions, most tourists visiting the Manx attractions would not appear to be overtly committed to heritage conservation, at least as implied by memberships and enthusiasm. At best the commitment of many tourists visitors to heritage conservation would seem supportive but passive. The generality of these findings must await research elsewhere in Europe, but their potential relevance to the conservation of heritage sites implies their need to be included as a priority in a research agenda for heritage tourism.

TOURISTS' PREPAREDNESS TO PAY FOR HERITAGE CONSERVATION

Past studies have shown that visitors to built heritage attractions expect to pay for their admission, whereas those visiting 'natural' landscapes are not, despite visitors to the latter attractions being aware of the need for active maintenance of supposedly 'natural' attractions (Prentice 1989b). Indeed, at the prices generally charged for admission to historic monuments in the 1980s, potential visitors were not found to be substantially deterred by prices charged. In particular, the social class bias found at heritage attractions in favour of higher social class visitors could not in the 1980s be explained by potential visitors from lower social class groups being deterred by admission prices at least at the majority of monuments for which data were collected (Prentice 1989b). That landscape can generally be enjoyed free of admission charge whereas monuments and museums frequently cannot be, may be one explanation of public acceptance of charging for admission at the latter but not at the former type of attractions. However, this is not a sufficient explanation, for visitors are prepared to pay for admission to see many waterfall or cave attractions, both of which are at least in origin if not in subsequent presentation 'natural' attractions. Similarly, when asked to justify why admission fees need to be charged at monuments, site upkeep is frequently the justification given (Prentice 1989b); yet, as noted above, upkeep is also recognised as required at certain 'natural' attractions where fees are not levied. To some extent therefore visitor *expectation* may be a factor in its own right in explaining acceptance or rejection of charging.

This general preparedness to pay for the conservation of built heritage sites through admission charges was confirmed by the Manx surveys, for tourists visiting the eight attractions surveyed in 1988 were found in substantial proportion to agree with the statement, 'Admission fees should be charged in order to pay for the upkeep of sites such as this'. In fact, nine out of ten tourists interviewed at the eight sites agreed with this statement, with nearly a quarter strongly agreeing. At the one attraction where no admission charge was levied, the Manx Museum, two-thirds of tourists were found to agree with the principle of charging to effect conservation. At one attraction over four out of ten of tourists interviewed strongly agreed with charging for conservation, namely at Laxey Wheel. Concurrence with charging for the upkeep of castles and museums was also found among those tourists interviewed in 1988 on Douglas Sea Front, with three-quarters of tourists asked agreeing with this principle for charging at both types of attraction. However, the strength of agreement noted among this general sample of tourists was less than at the attractions, with few tourists in Douglas strongly agreeing with this statement. This difference may result either from some deterrence effect from charging among the wider population of tourists on the island or from satisfaction on the part of visitors to the attractions with their visit. This difference apart, the general principle was clearly endorsed both by visitors to attractions and other tourists alike on the island.

Of the tourists interviewed at the attractions, agreement with charging for the conservation of sites was strongest among tourists expressing a particular historic interest as their reason for visiting, although the strength of the effect should not be exaggerated. Of those tourists giving this reason, 28 per cent strongly agreed with charging to upkeep attractions, compared to just under one in five tourists not giving this reason for visiting. The direction of this difference was the same for those tourists giving a particular interest in Manx culture as their reason for visiting, although its extent was less. A more general conclusion would be that preparedness to pay for conservation through admission fees was largely irrespective of reasons given for visiting, and, in fact, also irrespective of a tourist's social class. The survey of tourists in Douglas confirms this general conclusion. Indeed, among the latter tourists even the minority agreeing that museums were boring places were only slightly less inclined to agree that museums should charge admission fees, and the expressed propensity of tourists in Douglas to visit a castle or museum had no effect on perceptions of the legitimacy of charging for admission to pay for conservation.

The generality of the preparedness to pay for conservation through site admission fees cannot, however, be assumed to be boundless. The fact that only about one in twenty tourists interviewed at the Manx attractions in 1988 thought that the entrance fee charged was more than they had expected to pay might be taken to suggest that the agreement with the principle of charging resulted from the acceptable levels of the charges actually made. However, at one of the seven attractions where charges were made for admission a significant minority of tourists did consider the charge to have been too great compared to that which they had expected. This attraction was Laxey Wheel, where three out of ten tourists interviewed in 1988 thought the charge greater than expected. As this was the attraction at which tourists expressed the strongest agreement with the principle for charging to finance upkeep, and in fact had only a single tourist interviewed disagreeing with this principle, a link between the principle of charging for conservation and the perceived reasonableness of an admission price cannot be sustained from the Manx evidence.

CONCLUSIONS

From the analysis of organisational memberships of tourists visiting heritage attractions, tourists visiting such attractions would seem generally to be consuming *heritage* rather than *history*, or like academic subject matter. This has important implications for both the conservation and presentation of attractions, not least in how visiting tourists are to have the meaning of the attraction explained to them. The consumption of heritage, rather than history, might be thought to concur with the generalist interest of many tourists visiting attractions. This may in part be so; however, it needs also to be noted that membership is disproportionately associated with particular interests in attractions and the ascribing of educational and conservational roles to attractions. As such, membership may be indicative of an important segmentation between tourists visiting heritage attractions.

Membership of heritage and history organisations is strongly biased to non-manual households, and within them to professional and managerial households. As such, the equation of membership and enthusiasm for heritage is inappropriate for it fails to take into account the social meaning of joining a heritage organisation. In this chapter a segmentation has been attempted combining membership with self-rated excitement for history. The segmentation shows that the largest segment of tourist visitors are those who are neither members of heritage or history organisations nor are strongly excited by history. In short, this confirms the dominance of the general interest tourist among the visitor profile of tourists visiting many heritage attractions. The enthusiast among tourist visitors to attractions is in a clear minority, it is only the extent of this minority segment which is less unambiguously defined.

This chapter has confirmed that tourists generally expect to pay for admission to heritage attractions as a contribution to their upkeep, whether or not they visit such attractions, and irrespective of whether or not they ascribe conservational roles to such attractions. However, the promotion of heritage conservation through visits by tourists to heritage attractions is not likely to be successful in promoting a general concern for conservation as those tourists already visiting the attractions are more likely already to have conservation objectives in mind, especially the enthusiasts for heritage among them. A conservation message needs to be sold in a different manner if it is it to reach the wider public for whom conservation is not a frequently ascribed function to historic sites and museums.

9 Tourist assessment of heritage presentation

TOURIST RESPONSES TO PRESENTATIONAL MEDIA

Studies of the responses of visitors to the media used to present heritage attractions are few in number, especially when compared to the literature asserting implicitly or explicitly the merits of different media. Presentational media are used at heritage attractions to interpret the meaning or significance of the attractions to visitors, and as such the study of the responses of visitors to these media is properly the study of the effectiveness of interpretative (or interpretive) media. From its outset, interpretation of attractions has generally been considered to be an 'art', a view which still prevails. For example, 'In its widest sense then, interpretation is a means, indeed almost an art, of communicating. . .which enables a visitor to develop a better understanding of the resource' (Light 1987: 34) and 'Interpretation is the basic art of telling the story of the place, an object, or an event' (Walsh-Heron and Stevens 1990: 101). Tilden (1977: 70) talked of 're-creation of the past and kinship with it', and in his seminal text laid down certain principles of interpretation, including those of *provocation* and *revelation*: 'The chief aim of interpretation is not instruction, but provocation' (Tilden 1977: 9); and 'Interpretation is the revelation of a larger truth that lies behind any statement of fact' (Tilden 1977: 8).

This background in education and self-fulfilment, distinguishing between information and understanding, is pervasive today as the ideal to be strived for in the presentation of heritage attractions. For example, 'In the interpretation of a documentary historic site, a visitor should learn not only what events occurred in this place at a specific time in history, but *why* they occurred in just this particular place and nowhere else' (Alderson and Low 1986: 61).

However, other objectives to that of education and self-fulfilment may be identified for interpretation, and what has been termed Tilden's 'worthy and altruistic' objective for interpretation (Light

1991) cannot be assumed to be the only motive behind the interpretation of attractions to their visitors. Indeed, this objective may in some cases be seen as secondary or supplanted by more commercial objectives. This can be the case in the public as well as the private sectors. Describing the interpretative objectives of South Somerset District Council, its Tourism and Marketing Officer has commented:

> Interpretation is really central to our approach towards tourism development in the area. However, it would be wrong to assume that we are solely interested in interpretation, since at the end of the day we are judged not only on the style and quality of publications, but by the growth in the tourism sector of the local economy.
>
> (Wood 1991)

Light (1987) has listed seven additional objectives to that of education which may be found as motivations for interpretative provisions. These are: entertainment; visitor management; satisfying demand for countryside recreation; attraction promotion; influencing visitor attitudes; propaganda and public relations; and as a means of promoting economic development or regeneration. The objective of influencing visitors' views has already been discussed in conservation terms in Chapter 8. Similarly, the tendency for some attraction presentation to depart from the resource base and itself become the attraction was also noted in Chapter 8.

One legacy of interpretation being regarded as an 'art' is that systematic assessment of it has been limited; good practice has instead tended to be assumed rather than proven by formal assessment. Techniques for investigating the effectiveness of presentational media include studies of non-verbal communication as a means of feedback from visitor to guides providing verbal information (Risk 1989), the unobtrusive recording and subsequent analysis of visitors' conversations at attractions (McManus 1989), time lapse photography, (Vander Stoep 1989), the reports made by visitors on the media seen (Herbert 1989), and unobtrusively tracking visitors and recording their behaviour (Russell 1989). Some of these techniques might be thought less invasive of the visitor's privacy than others. However, the basic point to be made is that studies of the effectiveness of media types are few and far between, and as yet a science of interpretative effectiveness is at most just coming into being. For example, Shettel (1989) has commented that despite their prevalent educational objectives, evaluation of this kind has not been a common priority of museums. Miles *et al.* (1988) make a similar comment about the designers of educational exhibits. Uzzell *et al.* (1981) commented on the rudimentary nature of interpretative evaluation in forest visitor centres; Robinson (1989) that many visitor centres lacked a sense of place and thus could be assumed not to effect a sense of place in the visitor. The scarcity to date of such studies compels their priority for inclusion with a research agenda concerned with heritage attractions and the use of heritage as a resource for tourism. In particular, such an agenda needs to include not only the assessment of how tourists respond to presentational media but also to include an assessment of in what ways they benefit from it.

Studies in Wales in the 1980s showed that visitors to heritage attractions were strongly in favour of the provision of exhibitions of crafts, costumes and armour, but also favoured the partial reconstruction of ruined sites, re-roofing of rooms, and 'events' to portray images of past happenings (Herbert 1989). These studies used visitors' ratings of the different media found at sites as their primary indicator of the effectiveness of media provision, but did not assess in what ways the media rated were important to visitors in the latters' receipt of the interpretative messages which these media were presenting. This importance may be assessed in several ways, including visitor recall or recognition of the information provided by the presentational media at attractions, the increase in visitor sympathy towards conservational or other messages conveyed, or increases in the affection of visitors for a site and its meaning.

Light (1988) has reviewed the difficulties of assessing the impact of presentational media as a means of site interpretation, and his main points are worthy of report here. First, clear objectives are needed as to what a visitor is expected to have achieved on his or her visit; for example, to have left with a knowledge of the century in which an abbey was built. Second, decisions have to be made about the selection of questions. Is all the attraction's interpretation to be covered? What happens if a visitor has missed out part of the attraction? As an alternative, should visitors only be questioned on that part of the attraction they found most interesting? However, the latter strategy creates problems of comparability between respondents for it is impossible to know if the questions pertaining to one part of an attraction are of equal difficulty if recall is being assessed to those for other parts. Also, such a strategy may not in effect be comparing those parts of an attraction's interpretation found most interesting but rather for some visitors, those found the least uninteresting. Further, to allow visitors to select that part of the interpretation found most interesting implicitly assumes galleries or other multiple displays are being studied, from which sufficient information can be extracted to form an evaluation for each component part: it is not a practical technique at many monuments as these frequently lack large discrete displays of this kind. Prior knowledge needs also to be allowed for, as some visitors may arrive at an attraction knowledgeable about it, but others not. To ascribe on leaving the attraction the former visitors' knowledge to the presentation of heritage at the attraction would clearly be wrong.

Previous studies in Wales have also included a case assessment of the effectiveness of site interpretative media for higher educational visitors, in this case, undergraduates on a field visit (Prentice 1991). This study used both satisfaction measures developed through student recommendation of the site and multiple choice recognition tests to measure the recall of students leaving the site. These measures of interpretative effectiveness were applied to student visitors to Kidwelly Castle and related to the information to which they had been exposed, information to be found principally on panels displayed around the castle. The case study reported a wide range of accuracy, inaccuracy and ignorance in recall across ten different questions asked. For example, half of those questioned did not know either correctly or incorrectly the settlement function of the town of Kidwelly at the time of the castle's building, and a similar proportion did not know where the original town of Kidwelly was located. Both of these questions could be answered from the interpretation presented at the castle. In contrast, only a quarter of those asked did not know either correctly or incorrectly on whose orders the castle was first built. Generally, the most frequent response chosen by those students claiming to know an answer was that correct in terms of the interpretation provided at the castle, although this was not necessarily the case. As well as establishing the wide range in recall between students, the study also sought to investigate the determinants of recall. These determinants included the students' self-rated interest in Welsh history and in historical geography, and attention reportedly paid to the panels around the castle. A general conclusion from this case study of particular pertinence to the present discussion was that even when given a learning task, many students through lack of thorough attention to the media around the castle failed to recall correctly or at all much of the information presented around the castle. The principally leisure context of tourist visits to heritage attractions sets an even greater challenge for the designers of presentational media for a learning objective cannot be assumed to be to the fore, unlike on a university field excursion.

The published studies on the effectiveness of presentational media have not usually considered tourists as a separate group among visitors. Indeed, much of the discussion of recognition or recall has been within educational terms of reference. The absence of studies of tourists in this regard is surprising as tourists form a major market segment of heritage attraction customers, and a segment potentially least informed of the significance of attractions prior to their visit, having come some distance and frequently having travelled across national boundaries to countries whose history is unknown from school days. As such, the study of the effectiveness of the presentational media used to interpret the meaning of attractions to their visitors should form part of a research agenda for heritage attractions, and particularly so for heritage tourism. The Isle of Man is a useful case study in this regard for it mirrors the international dimension of tourist unfamiliarity with the history of their destination area, with most tourists to the island having been exposed not to Manx history at school, but, instead, to the history of England, Ireland or Scotland. In view of the importance of this topic to heritage attraction development throughout Europe, the present discussion of presentational effectiveness extends across two chapters of this book: in the present chapter tourist satisfaction with presentational media is discussed, and in the subsequent chapter, (Chapter 10), attention is paid to a discussion of recall and its determinants, both chapters relying heavily on the Manx surveys.

TOURIST SATISFACTION WITH ON-SITE PRESENTATIONAL MEDIA AT MANX HERITAGE ATTRACTIONS

The Manx database was developed with the primary objective to overcome the lack of research into tourist responses to interpretative media at heritage attractions. As such, it provides a useful source of data by which issues of effectiveness may be appraised. Indicators both of satisfaction and recall were developed, with the presentational refurbishment of Castle Rushen providing in particular the opportunity to study the effects of presentational change.

Reference to Table 9.1 would suggest that most holiday tourists visiting the eight Manx heritage attractions surveyed in 1988 were well satisfied with the presentation of the sites. This satisfaction was recorded across a range of attributes: information displayed, content of interest to children, and, for those who had bought and read the site guidebook, the content of the site guidebook. Guided tours, which at most attractions were unavailable, were more divisive of tourist opinion. These results would concur with a view that tourists generally

Table 9.1 Satisfaction of adult holiday tourists with the presentational media at Manx heritage sites

| | Holiday tourists visiting sites in 1988: | | | | | |
	Strongly agree %	Agree %	No strong feelings %	Disagree %	Strongly disagree %	N
'The information provided on the displays helped me to enjoy my visit'	18.6	75.2	2.8	3.3	0.2	1,916
'The guidebook I purchased provided exactly the kind of information necessary for me to enjoy my visit'	5.4	70.2	6.3	15.1	2.9	205
'A guided tour of the site would have increased / did increase my enjoyment'	5.3	37.6	9.6	44.8	2.7	1,939
'There was enough at the site to keep the children interested'	11.9	68.9	8.4	10.0	0.8	951

Source: unpublished survey undertaken by author for Manx National Heritage
Notes: Tourists who had not seen the displays are excluded from the statement on display content; tourists who had not bought a guidebook, and those who had bought a copy but not read it, are excluded from the statement on guidebooks; and tourists without child(ren) in their personal group are excluded from the statement on child interest
N = sample size

wish to feel unconstrained or unregimented on their visits to heritage attractions, and in particular to guide themselves around sites without feeling that they are being managed in their enjoyment. The one common feature of site presentation in 1988 were displays, although in reality these were a diverse group ranging from displays of information on wall panels to displays of artefacts. For the subsequent survey in 1990 these media were separated out. Because of the diversity inherent in the word 'display' the inter-site variations found in 1988 may in part at least result from tourists having appraised quite different displays. Agreement was strongest in 1988 that the displays had aided enjoyment at the Manx Museum and Castle Rushen (Table 9.2). The museum had extensive displays of artefacts and models in 1988, but Castle Rushen was largely interpreted to its visitors by wall plates, supplemented by a few models and a display of prison artefacts, mainly ledgers recording prisoners' crimes and sentences (the castle having been a gaol in the nineteenth century). The second order ranking of Cregneash shown in Table 9.2 is surprising, as the attraction had, and retains, several displays: however, the ranking may result from the cottages themselves at this *clachan* being the main object of enjoyment and not the interpretative displays.

Although analyses of the kind used in 1988 at the Manx attractions to ascertain satisfaction with presentational media provide a summary picture for attraction managers, satisfied customers being of undoubted importance to heritage attraction operators, their very summary nature constrains more detailed analysis, either by specific media or in terms of the determinants of satisfaction. As such, a research agenda for heritage tourism needs to look beyond summary satisfaction measures of this kind.

An assessment of satisfaction with staff roles was included as part of the 1991 marketing survey at Castle Rushen, and illustrates the kind of more detailed analysis of tourist satisfaction with presentational media required as part of a research agenda for heritage tourism. The new presentation of Castle Rushen in 1991 included the use of staff to act as non-intrusive guides, as sources of information, but not to act as organisers of visitors, nor to assume that all visitors wished to know a standard text of facts. Tourists interviewed leaving the castle were asked in 1991 as to their preferences for changes in staff roles across a series of dimensions, namely whether they wished staff to be more or less talkative, informative, intrusive, conspicuous, guiding or reserved, or whether for each of these dimensions they wished the staffs' manner to remain as they had experienced it. The dominant response was for the roles of staff to remain as found (Table 9.3). As such, the roles of

Table 9.2 Satisfaction of adult holiday tourists at different Manx heritage sites with the information provided on the displays at the sites

'The information provided on the displays helped me to enjoy my visit'	Holiday tourists visiting sites in 1988:							
	Peel Castle %	Castle Rushen %	Manx Museum %	Nautical Museum %	Grove Museum %	Laxey Wheel %	Cregneash %	Odin's Raven %
Strongly agree	4.3	30.5	31.1	18.2	18.0	12.6	21.5	5.0
Agree	74.0	65.9	12.5	79.0	80.4	74.9	76.9	90.1
No strong feelings	5.5	1.3	1.1	2.3	0.5	8.8	1.3	2.0
Disagree	15.7	2.3	0.4	0.0	1.0	2.8	0.3	3.0
Strongly disagree	0.4	0.0	0.0	0.6	0.0	0.9	0.0	0.0
N =	254	305	267	176	194	215	303	202

Source: unpublished survey undertaken by author for Manx National Heritage
Notes: Excludes tourists who had not seen the displays
   N = sample size

Table 9.3 Satisfaction of adult holiday tourists with staff roles at Castle Rushen

| | Holiday tourists visiting the castle in 1991 (Marketing Survey) stating a preference for or against change | | | |
	More %	The same %	Less %	N
Talkative	13.1	86.2	0.7	145
Informative	18.6	80.7	0.7	145
Intrusive	0.0	97.9	2.1	144
Conspicuous	19.4	79.2	1.4	144
Guiding	27.8	71.5	0.7	144
Reserved	0.0	85.6	13.0	144

Source: unpublished survey undertaken by author for Manx National Heritage
Note: N = sample size

the guides could be thought of as highly satisfactory in terms of the perceptions of tourists visiting the attraction. However, closer inspection of Table 9.3 would also imply some scope for change towards more guiding, conspicuous and informative staffing, if at the same time this could be achieved without causing dissatisfaction to the majority of tourists. It is the investigation of tourist satisfaction in less summary ways as illustrated in this example which is needed to form the basis of an enhanced understanding of the dimensions of tourist satisfaction with presentational media.

Although the sample sizes are small the findings for staffing roles at Castle Rushen in 1991 give some indication of the type of tourist wanting a more active role for staff than was the case at the castle in 1991. As such, some indication of the type of tourist who may need particularly to be identified in future staffing studies at heritage attractions can be given. In general it was those tourists who had come specifically to Castletown to see the castle who disproportionately preferred a more conspicuous, guiding, informative and talkative staff than was the case in 1991. Frequently the same was the case for the general interest but more educated tourist. As such, it would seem that an enhanced role for staff was wanted by the more general interest but educated tourist who had come specifically to see the castle out of a sightseeing interest. It is these tourists who could be expected to have included a disproportionate group of uninformed but at the same time questioning tourists within their number. This small segment of visitors may need to be especially identified in future research designs and specially catered for in presentational developments.

TOURIST SATISFACTION WITH OFF-SITE
PRESENTATIONAL MEDIA ON THE ISLE OF MAN

In 1990 Manx National Heritage introduced a central interpretative facility for the island at the Manx Museum. This facility, organised around the 'Story of Mann' film, was intended as a gateway medium to Manx heritage, setting the island's historic and other heritage sites within a narrative of the island's historical geography. So to encourage tourists to come to the museum to see the film it was not released on video for use on the ferries and in the island's hotels, although in July 1991 the Welsh television station *S4C* did broadcast the film to its Welsh audience on prime time Saturday night television. Other than this showing, during 1990 and 1991 all tourists to the island who had seen the 'Story of Mann' film would have had to have seen it at the Manx Museum. This unique interpretative development warrants some attention as to its effectiveness in introducing tourists to Manx culture.

Reference to Table 9.4 shows the difficulty in getting tourists to visit a central interpretative facility, even when that facility is within the holiday centre within which most tourists stay. In 1990 only about one in six tourists interviewed at the three heritage attractions surveyed had in fact seen the film, although in 1991 at Castle Rushen the situation had improved somewhat, but still to only about a third of tourists visiting the castle. Moreover, this improvement was unequal between types of tourist. Whereas in 1990 the likelihood that a tourist visiting an attraction had previously seen the 'Story of Mann' film did not depend either on socio-demographic characteristics or on reasons for visiting, in 1991 this was not fully the case at Castle Rushen. At the castle in 1991 tourists stating a particular interest in castles as a reason for visiting were more likely to have seen the film than other tourists; whereas 43 per cent of tourists giving this reason had previously seen the film, fewer than three out of ten other tourists had done so. Likewise, 44 per cent of tourists giving an educational reason for visiting had previously seen the film, compared to 34 per cent of other tourists. Although the individual sizes of these differences are not great, together they would suggest that the more committed consumers of heritage had by 1991 become disproportionately more aware of the film as an introduction to Manx heritage than other tourists. As the questions on membership and enthusiasm were not asked in 1991, the 1990 classification of commitment to heritage cannot be used to further test this hypothesis. Having seen the film may also have encouraged some visits to be made by tourists to the

Table 9.4 Satisfaction of adult holiday tourists with the 'Story of Mann' film at the Manx Museum

| | Holiday tourists visiting the sites: | | | |
| | Peel Castle | Castle Rushen Interpretation Survey | | Cregneash |
	1990 %	1990 %	1991 %	1990 %
Watched 'Story of Mann' film	12.5	17.8	34.4	21.5
N =	184	185	192	177
Tourists having watched the film who would recommend a friend to watch it if visiting the island	95.7	100.0	—	100.0
N =	23	33	—	38
Of those tourists who would recommend the film, the stage in a holiday they would recommend it to be watched:				
• on arrival	78.3	31.3	—	53.8
• any time during stay	21.7	68.8	—	41.0
• ideally prior to arrival	0.0	0.0	—	5.1
N =	22	32	—	38

Source: unpublished surveys undertaken by author for Manx National Heritage
Note: N = sample size

castle, for in 1991 whereas four out of ten tourists who had come specifically to Castletown to see the castle had seen the film, only three out of ten of the other tourists had seen it. A more general conclusion would seem to be that we should not expect a central 'gateway' facility to attract all tourists, for as it becomes known it may disproportionately attract those tourists more inclined towards visiting heritage attractions. As such, the appropriate baseline from which to measure the success of such developments may not be the full population of tourists either at a destination area or visiting the attractions a central interpretative facility is intended to introduce. In particular, it would seem inappropriate to expect such a facility to first attract casual tourist visitors to major heritage sites. Equally, a central interpretative facility may become an attraction in its own right. With these points in mind, one research question for heritage tourism becomes the identification of the size of the effective market among tourists for such facilities. Central interpretative facilities may be justified, therefore, not for reaching all potential visitors to heritage attractions among holiday tourists, but for enhancing the experience of existing heritage consumers for whom enhanced presentations elsewhere are likely to be increasingly familiar and to be expected at destination areas too.

Of those tourists interviewed at the Manx heritage attractions who had seen the 'Story of Mann' film, almost all were sufficiently satisfied to be prepared to recommend a friend to see it, if visiting the island, with six out of ten tourists recommending that the film be watched on arrival or before if possible. Not only is this an unambiguous endorsement in terms of customer satisfaction, more generally it illustrates the potential contribution to customer satisfaction of gateway facilities of this kind, if tourists can be encouraged to visit them early on in their holiday.

TOURISTS' ATTENTION TO ON-SITE PRESENTATIONAL MEDIA ON THE ISLE OF MAN

Rarely do two neighbouring heritage attractions make use of exactly the same range of presentational media conveying similar messages. This makes comparison between the different uses of the same medium difficult by surveys at attractions, unless matched pairs of attractions can be found. However, more generally, comparisons between attractions enable packages of media to be evaluated as more likely to gain and hold the attention of visitors, and the tourists among them, and individual media may be suggested as more or less effective even if this cannot be unambiguously demonstrated. Such unambiguous demonstration has to await generalisation from many studies, a database at present uncollected. The Manx heritage attractions well demonstrate the diversity in media to be found at attractions, but with the presentational refurbishment of Castle Rushen in 1991 also enables an assessment of how presentational change may affect tourists' responses to an attraction. Clearly, the case of Castle Rushen is only one site, and generalisation from it cannot be made until further research at other European attractions which are subject to substantial changes in presentation has been undertaken. However, 'before and after' studies of the effectiveness of presentational changes are extremely rare to date, and so the Castle Rushen study is presented

Table 9.5 Presentational media provided at attractions seen or heard by adult holiday tourists visiting different Manx heritage sites

	Holiday tourists visiting the sites having seen or heard presentational media:			
	Peel Castle		*Castle Rushen Interpretation Survey*	*Cregneash*
	1990	*1990*	*1991*	*1990*
	%	*%*	*%*	*%*
Guidebook(s)	10.9	33.0	—	68.9
Guide leaflet	89.1	87.0	—	81.9
Guided walk leaflet	0.5	—	—	19.1
Directional signs	—	100.0	100.0	—
Tape player for personal tour	—	—	—	8.0
Introductory film/ video	—	—	97.4	81.4
Exhibition panels introducing site	—	—	99.5	96.0
Information panels around site	98.4	100.0	98.4/ 99.0	—
Model(s)/ costumed figures(s)	—	97.8	100.0	—
Print(s), photograph(s), painting(s)	—	60.5	—	79.5
Map(s)/ plan(s)	—	48.9	—	75.9
Other displayed item(s)	—	87.6	—	93.8
Furnished room(s)	—	63.2	100.0	98.9
Person(s) in period dress	—	—	—	74.0
Demonstration of crafts	—	—	—	50.3
Music	—	—	100.0	—
'Voices' of costumed figures	—	—	100.0	—
Live animals	—	—	—	99.4
Reconstructed wooden buildings	—	—	92.7	—
N =	184	185	192	177

Source: unpublished surveys undertaken by author for Manx National Heritage
Note: In 1991 at Castle Rushen the panels were of two different types and respondents were asked questions about each
    N = sample size

as a model from which other studies elsewhere will hopefully flow as a research agenda for heritage tourism develops in Europe.

Reference to Table 9.5 shows the awareness of tourists visiting the Manx attractions surveyed in both 1990 and 1991 of the presentational media at the attractions. It should be remembered in reading this table that the presentation of Castle Rushen was quite different in 1991 than in 1990. The main media of which the tourist visitors were aware at the attractions were furnished rooms, models including costumed figures, introductory exhibitions, information panels around the sites, directional signs, live animals, music and the 'voices' of costumed figures (life-sized models of persons of the historic period presented). This array of media of which tourists were most aware at the attractions emphasises the importance of a multi-media presentation at attractions, stimulating a range of senses, and would suggest that the traditional way of presenting historic monuments by means of a site guidebook and wall plates or panels naming towers and rooms is insufficient for contemporary heritage attraction visitors, or more strictly, for the tourists among them. However, the earlier warning needs to be repeated, for these can only at best be tentative general conclusions. As few of these media are available at all of the Manx attractions, the site-specific effectiveness of any one medium cannot be ruled out as the cause of the high awareness of tourists of any one medium, and the table may not be recording the general effectiveness in gaining tourists' attention of all the media noted, but rather the skilful use of a medium at any of the sites. Such generalisations may only safely be made after research has been undertaken elsewhere, and when our limited body of present knowledge is extended. At the Manx attractions certain media can be seen to have had low impacts, most notably guided walk leaflets, tape players at the one attraction where they were available, and, at two sites, guidebooks. These media are, in particular, subject to stocking and display policies and practice, and it may have been that not all tourists were able to see these media. The same is not true, however, for prints or maps at the attractions, which although more frequently reported as seen by tourists than guided walk leaflets, were available to be seen by all tourists visiting the attractions at which they were available. The variation between attractions in tourist awareness of maps and prints clearly illustrates the importance of site-specific factors in the location and design of presentations. The redesign of the presentation of Castle Rushen would seem to have largely had the effect of removing those media of which tourists had been least aware, and of sustaining awareness of other media types into the new presentation. Most of the media at Castle Rushen had in fact been seen by *all* or almost all of the tourists interviewed for the Interpretation Survey in 1991, and as such the redesigned presentation can be adjudged an unambiguous success in terms of tourist awareness.

Table 9.6 Attention paid to presentational media provided at attractions by adult holiday tourists who had seen or heard these media during visits to different Manx heritage sites

Holiday tourists visiting the sites having seen or heard presentational media, reporting having examined, listened to or watched media carefully or casually:

Key: (a) carefully (b) casually	Peel Castle 1990 (a) %	(b) %	Castle Rushen 1990 (a) %	(b) %	Interpretation Survey 1991 (a) %	(b) %	Cregneash 1990 (a) %	(b) %
Guidebook(s)	31.6	68.4	4.9	47.5	—	—	20.3	70.7
Guide leaflet	47.5	46.3	53.5	44.7	—	—	60.6	35.0
Guided walk leaflet	*	*	—	—	—	—	59.4	34.4
Directional signs	—	—	84.7	15.3	88.0	12.0	—	26.7
Tape player for personal tour	—	—	—	—	—	—	40.0	9.9
Introductory film/video	—	—	—	—	96.8	2.6	89.4	13.4
Exhibition panels introducing site	—	—	—	—	60.7	38.7	86.6	—
Information panels around site	46.6	50.6	98.4	1.6	65.3/38.5	33.7/52.6	—	50.0
Model(s)/costumed figure(s)	—	—	98.3	1.7	88.0	12.0	49.3	56.0
Print(s), photograph(s), painting(s)	—	—	93.8	6.2	—	—	42.4	27.2
Map(s)/plan(s)	—	—	87.9	12.1	—	—	71.5	14.9
Other displayed item(s)	—	—	96.9	3.1	—	—	84.5	24.8
Furnished room(s)	—	—	74.4	25.6	92.2	7.8	74.4	17.2
Person(s) in period dress	—	—	—	—	—	—	81.6	—
Demonstration of crafts	—	—	—	—	—	—	—	—
Music	—	—	—	—	30.7	67.2	—	—
'Voices' of costumed figures	—	—	—	—	57.3	41.1	—	—
Live animals	—	—	—	—	—	—	88.2	11.8
Reconstructed wooden buildings	—	—	—	—	14.0	72.1	—	—

N = varies, derived from Table 9.5

Source: unpublished surveys undertaken by author for Manx National Heritage

Notes: (a) Tourists ignoring media are not tabulated, but their number can be found by subtracting the figures for careful and casual attention from 100%; (b) * indicates a sample size too small to safely permit analysis

N = sample size

Few tourists ignored the presentational media at the Manx attractions if they had seen or heard them during their visit (Table 9.6). The Manx surveys relied on self-reporting of the attention given to those media seen or heard by tourists, using three similar scales to record attention:

- examine it carefully/just glance at it/ignore it;
- listen to it carefully/listen to it casually/ignore it; and
- watch it carefully/watch it casually/ignore it.

The most widely ignored presentational medium was found to be the tape players at Cregneash, with a third of the minority of tourists who claimed in 1990 to have seen these saying that they had ignored them. In 1990 guidebooks were also ignored by a fifth of those tourists who had seen them, once again suggesting the weakness of this traditional means of interpretation. Other media were only ignored in 1990 by very few tourists, and some by none at all. Similarly, at Castle Rushen in 1991 media were infrequently ignored, the most frequent case being that of the reconstructed wooden buildings which were set in a part of the castle informally visited by the mass of tourists, and not fully integrated into the 'managed' visitor flow at the refurbished attraction. One in seven tourists claimed to have ignored these buildings. The information panels around the castle were also less popular than the other media, about one in ten tourists claiming to have ignored either sort of panel during their visit. The same did not apply to the introductory exhibition of similar panels, and this may imply that a minority of tourists had seen sufficient written information by early in their visit, and were enjoying the other media used. In other words, for a minority of tourists a substitution effect was apparent, of one medium by another, similar to that identified in the Kidwelly Castle study already noted (Prentice 1991). The design of the new presentation can be said to have been successful in this regard, for tourists wanting more information had it available in written form, but the small minority not wanting so much written material could readily ignore it, these additional panels being sited in small rooms off the main displays.

Although the presentational media used at the Manx attractions were found generally not to be ignored by the tourists visiting the attractions surveyed, it would be wrong to assume that all media had equal impacts in holding the attention of holiday tourists. Further reference to Table 9.6 shows that some media were only casually examined, listened to or watched by many tourists, most notably guidebooks, music, reconstructed buildings, and at some attractions, information panels around the site, prints, maps, introductory exhibition panels and guide leaflets. For example, of all tourists claiming to have seen the guidebook at Peel Castle in 1990, nearly seven out of ten said that they had glanced at it, rather than having examined it carefully, and of the information panels around the site at this castle, almost exactly half of those tourists who had seen them had just glanced at them. The latter might result from the traditional labelling use of these site notices, rather than their use for fuller explanation, but this cannot be advanced as an explanation of the lack of interest in the guidebook. A fear of implicit compulsion to purchase this booklet might account for the lack of attention, however. In general, those media most frequently attended to carefully by tourists would seem from the Manx surveys to include furnished rooms, other displayed items, models including costumed figures, an introductory film or video, directional signs, live animals and craft demonstrations. However, at certain attractions prints, maps and information panels were also important. A comparison of the figures set out in Tables 9.5 and 9.6 suggests that some presentational media do not only catch the attention of tourists more than others, they also hold this attention more, most notably furnished rooms, models including costumed figures, directional signs and live animals, supplemented by an introductory film or video, introductory exhibitions and information panels around the site. Assuming that the Manx findings stand up to subsequent generalisation as other studies are undertaken elsewhere, heritage attraction operators seeking to inform or entertain their tourist visitors would seem well advised to consider a presentational strategy combining these key attributes. Such a strategy notably contrasts with the usual manner in which State monuments in Britain, for example, are presented.

In planning interpretative strategies it would be useful to know for which types of tourist particular media may be more or less effective in gaining and retaining attention. The Manx surveys suggest that such linkages are ambiguous and need much further research before useful generalisations may be made. Surprisingly, despite its utility as a surrogate for reasons for visiting, whether or not a tourist was a member of a heritage organisation, and thus presumably more or less familiar with presentational media being developed by these organisations, had no effect on the attention paid to media types. This was with one exception, directional signs, which heritage organisation members were more inclined to pay careful attention to, although the size of this effect was not substantial. Quite how far this may be taken as indicative of heritage organisation members having become used to being guided around sites on their visits to attractions must await further research, but this may indicate that the consumers of heritage can become accepting of at least some techniques of visitor management. As such, this topic may be worthy of further study.

The 1990 survey at the Manx attractions found formal educational attainment to be one determinant of the attention paid by tourists to presentational media. However, the effect may not be as supposed from a characterisation of the more formally educated tourists as 'readers' and their less formally educated counterparts as 'viewers'. Tourists who had completed their continuous full-time education by the age of nineteen years were *more* likely than their more highly educated counterparts to report having paid careful attention to prints and paintings, maps and plans, other displayed items, and to information panels. For other presentational media educational attainment did not affect a tourist's likely attention paid, except for guidebooks, for which the previous situation was reversed: a quarter of tourists educated to above nineteen years of age reporting having paid careful attention to the site guidebook, compared to one in ten of their less formally educated counterparts. Considered together, these findings for 1990 would caution against an over-hasty assertion that higher educational attainment brings with it greater response by holiday-makers visiting heritage attractions to the kinds of media used in further and higher education, namely, written and graphical media. Equally, it should be noted that as in 1990 many of the information panels at the sites surveyed contained only minimal information, the more literate tourist may have glanced at them rather than read them as the amount of information presented was less than expected from contemporary displays at some attractions elsewhere in the British Isles. However, a similar explanation could not be advanced for the graphical media at the attractions.

Surprisingly, tourists claiming to visit the Manx attractions out of a particular interest in the sites were not found to report having paid more attention to the presentational media than other tourists visiting the same attractions, despite the content of the media being substantially historical, architectural or cultural in emphasis. Notably, although most of those tourists expressing a particular interest in historic sites at Cregneash were found to report having paid careful attention to the introductory exhibition, a greater proportion of those tourists not visiting for this reason also reported having paid careful attention to this, eight out of ten and nine out of ten tourists respectively. Although the size of this difference is not substantial, its direction might be thought surprising, and statistically it is likely to be wrong through sampling error fewer than twice in a hundred times. Likewise, fewer tourists with a particular interest in historic sites reported paying careful attention to the information panels around the two castles than did other tourists, and the few tourists reporting having paid careful attention to the guided walk leaflets were disproportionately those tourists without a particular historic interest in the sites. The overall impression gained from the analysis of reasons for visiting and attention paid to media at the attractions is that where careful attention was disproportionately paid to these media, this was generally by general interest tourists, even at Cregneash where substantial displays of written and graphical information was presented.

The findings for Castle Rushen in 1991 partly support and partly contradict those for the sites surveyed in 1990. First, in support of the 1990 findings, those at Castle Rushen in 1991 would confirm the need for caution in thinking that the more educated tourist is most likely to pay attention to written material. Whereas this was found to be the case for reported reading of the introductory exhibition panels at the castle, the effect was not strong, and, in contrast, the less formally educated tourists interviewed more frequently reported careful attention to the panels around the castle, as well as to the castle's refurbished rooms. Second, the tourist with a declared particular interest in castles was found to be more likely than other tourists to report having paid careful attention to the refubished rooms, costumed figures, the introductory exhibition panels, and those panels around the site. Although the sizes of these differences were not great, they do contradict the findings for 1990 for which the general interest tourist was if anything the more attentive. The reasons for these differences between the surveys in terms of the effect of reason for visiting on attention paid to media are unclear. However, looked at together the findings from the surveys of 1990 and 1991 would suggest that the identification of types of tourist in terms of likely response to presentational media is far from straightforward, and will likely require many more studies before general rules can be meaningfully proposed. One firm conclusion can be drawn: simplistic notions of response to media by tourists in terms of commitment to heritage, declared interest in subject matter expressed in reasons for visiting and educational attainment are likely to be erroneous. In particular, the difficult context of prior knowledge may need to be considered in future research, for it may be that the more literate or enthusiastic tourists consider themselves pre-informed about attractions, and thus feel less need to attend carefully to on-site media, unless it is novel, such as at Castle Rushen in 1991. Similarly, the benefits a tourist seeks to gain when on holiday may affect attention levels at attractions: the more literate tourist may be seeking to escape from a daily routine of processing written and graphical material. A future research agenda will need to consider the somewhat diffuse nature of possible determinants of this kind.

As site guidebooks have been a traditional form of site interpretation they, perhaps, warrant particular attention in an agenda for research into heritage tourism. As so few tourists interviewed at the Manx attractions had actually bought the guidebooks, the sample size of readers available here for analysis is small. However, the general impression from the Manx surveys is that if tourists buy guidebooks they are unlikely, in their own terms, to have read them carefully while at an attraction, but rather in most cases to have glanced through their purchase while on site. Even for those tourists buying a guidebook, therefore, it is unlikely in consequence to have been an effective medium through which to interpret while at the site the significance of the attraction which they have visited. As such, guidebooks should be regarded as specialist products supplementing other presentational media, and not as a principal means of interpreting an attraction. The extent of non-use of guidebooks while at attractions is revealing from the Manx database. At Cregneash, only a quarter of the minority of tourists interviewed in 1990 who had bought the site guidebook claimed to have read it carefully around the site, as opposed to having examined a copy carefully when deciding to purchase it; at Peel Castle only one in seven tourists who had bought the 'Ancient Centres of Government of the Isle of Man' guidebook claimed to have read it carefully when going around the site, and likewise only one in five tourists who had bought the same guidebook at Castle Rushen. However, in some contrast, half of the minority of tourists at Castle Rushen who had bought the guidebook specific to the castle, did say in 1990 that they had read it carefully while going around the castle. As this latter guidebook was not for sale in 1991 the impact on guidebook purchase of the new forms of site presentation at the castle can not be established. In particular, questions of media substitution might arise, the other on-site media removing the need for guidebook purchase. Alternatively, the new media may prompt souvenir purchases through which the visit may be remembered, of which guidebook purchase might benefit. Impacts of this kind need to form part of a research agenda into the presentation of European heritage attractions.

Although guidebooks may not be carefully read at attractions by those tourist visitors purchasing them, they may be read more widely subsequent to the visit, either during the remainder of a tourist's holiday or subsequently at home. The Manx evidence, however, is ambiguous in this regard. Half of those tourists interviewed in 1990 at Peel Castle and Castle Rushen who had bought the Cregneash guidebook earlier in their holiday when visiting the attraction claimed to have read it carefully, compared to, as noted above, a quarter interviewed when leaving the attraction. The general guidebook to Manx heritage, '100 Years of Heritage' (Harrison 1986), was claimed to have been read carefully by three-quarters of those few tourists who had earlier purchased it on their holiday. However, careful readership of the site guidebook to Castle Rushen was no more extensive among its purchasers interviewed at the other sites than those interviewed leaving the castle. The unread guidebooks, or those simply glanced at, may be read more carefully after a holiday; alternatively, they may be kept as souvenirs, or at most glanced at, before subsequent storage or disposal. The use of guidebooks after they leave heritage attractions is unknown. For retailing development this is perhaps not a pertinent issue, but the same cannot be said for interpretative strategies. For the minority of holiday tourists buying guidebooks, the lasting meaning of these guidebooks to their purchasers and their off-site interpretative effectiveness, if any, are important issues for any interpretative strategy at a heritage attraction. For ideals of European cultural integration through the creation of a common European heritage, the subsequent use of guidebooks, and of other off-site interpretative material, is of quite fundamental relevance. Non-use of this material may mean that even for those Europeans sufficiently interested in European heritage to purchase literature at the built manifestations of the European past, that their experience is transitory and not subsequently reinforced other than in general when visiting other attractions of the same or different types. For the wider European ideal to succeed, issues such as this are highly pertinent. Not of the same high ideals, the issue of the subsequent use of guidebooks also has a commercial pertinence; guidebooks may serve as media through which the friends and relatives of past tourist visitors are prompted to holiday at a destination area, and to visit the same attractions as their predecessors. The extent of this effect warrants inclusion in a promotional research agenda for heritage tourism, for it may be that many guidebooks are alternatively consigned to bookshelves or drawers and not shown to friends and relatives.

TOURISTS' RATING OF THE IMPORTANCE OF PRESENTATIONAL MEDIA TO HERITAGE INTERPRETATION

In an era which emphasises customer satisfaction the importance given by visitors to heritage attractions to the media which they see or hear is an important indicator of success or failure. The nineteen types of media used at the Manx attractions surveyed in 1990 and 1991 provide some opportunity to explore the differing rating of media types by tourists. Certain media types may be shown to be disproportionately rated as unimportant or for which the tourists interviewed had no strong feelings either way concerning their importance or unimportance. Notable among these media were the reconstructed wooden buildings at Castle Rushen in 1991, for whom more than six out of ten tourists who had seen them thought them either to be unimportant to their understanding of the castle or towards which they had no feelings as to their importance or otherwise. A third of tourists likewise did not think the site guidebooks important to their understanding of the sites, a not unsurprising finding in view of the few tourists who had actually read these while on site. Other media were rated as unimportant by smaller minorities of tourist visitors. These included the guide leaflets, which were thought to be unimportant by a fifth of tourists who had seen them, and the tape players at Cregneash, which were similarly rated. Of the new media at Castle Rushen in 1991, not only were the wooden buildings disproportionately thought to be unimportant to an understanding of the castle, a quarter of tourists interviewed did not think that the music which they had heard had been of importance, and a tenth thought the same about the 'voices' of the costumed figures. The point earlier about the substitution of media can also be made in terms of the importance given to them by the tourist visitors interviewed. In 1991 at Castle Rushen, dependent on which information panels around the castle are considered, around one in seven and three out of ten tourists thought the panels to be unimportant, compared to no tourist saying this in the previous year's survey. This would imply, at least in terms of customer satisfaction, that at heritage attractions wall panels are of secondary preference if more visual media are available. However, we should be careful not to overemphasise a perspective of unimportance. Except for the wooden buildings, for example, at Castle Rushen in 1991 a majority of tourists, and in some cases *all* tourists, who had seen or heard the presentational media thought them to have been of some importance in their understanding of the castle. This finding is an unambiguous endorsement of not only the presentation of this castle by Manx National Heritage, but more generally of the need for heritage attraction operators to invest in a range of presentational media at their attractions, if customer satisfaction is to be maximised. Some substitution of media types by a minority of visitors does not mean that for a majority that the media can be complementary as intended by site designers.

The extent to which those tourists interviewed and who had seen or heard the interpretative media at the attractions rated them as important to their understanding of an attraction is shown in Table 9.7. To simplify the table, only the frequencies for those thinking the media very important or important are shown of the full five point rating scale used, from very important to very unimportant. Those media most frequently thought by tourists to have been *very* important to their understanding of an attraction can be seen from Table 9.7 to include an introductory film or video and models including costumed figures, supplemented by furnished rooms and 'other' displayed items. Other media frequently thought to be important by those tourists having seen or heard them include prints, maps, directional signs, a guided walk leaflet, craft demonstrations and live animals. Some care in our interpretation of these findings is again called for as some of these frequencies could result from site-specific use of media rather than from general characteristics of media types. Generalisation is prone to possible error until other studies are undertaken elsewhere in Europe. However, it would seem from the Manx evidence that several media types recur in terms of positive tourist reaction, namely in terms of catching the attention of tourists, holding that attention and being thought as important by tourists. These media types are models including costumed figures, an introductory film or video, furnished rooms, directional signs and live animals. This package of media types warrants serious attention in a research agenda as to its generality. Other media would seem from the Manx case studies to be best used to supplement this package of media types.

The analysis of self-rated attention paid by tourists to media types leads to a conclusion that dichotomy models of general interest as against particular interest, and viewers as against more literate tourists, could not be sustained as explanations of the attention paid to media. A similar conclusion has to pertain to the importance given by tourists to the media they had seen or heard, for once again the evidence is ambiguous. The 1990 Site Survey does lend support to a particular versus general interest model. Of those tourists who had

Table 9.7 Adult holiday tourists' views on the importance of presentational media seen or heard to their understanding of the sites at different Manx heritage sites

Holiday tourists visiting sites having seen or heard presentational media, considering them important or very important to their understanding of the sites:

Key: (a) very important (b) important	Peel Castle 1990 (a)%	(b)%	Castle Rushen 1990 (a)%	(b)%	Interpretation Survey 1991 (a)%	(b)%	Cregneash 1990 (a)%	(b)%
Guidebook(s)	6.3	93.8	10.0	28.3	—	—	41.6	34.4
Guide leaflet	13.5	72.9	18.1	34.4	—	—	58.6	37.9
Guided walk leaflet	*	*	—	23.9	—	—	73.5	26.5
Directional signs	—	—	74.5	—	76.6	22.4	—	—
Tape player for personal tour	—	—	—	—	—	—	42.1	36.8
Introductory film/video	—	—	—	—	88.4	10.6	79.5	18.5
Exhibition panels introducing site	—	—	—	—	45.5	49.7	76.9	21.9
Information panels around site	12.4	67.6	97.3	2.7	52.1/20.9	42.7/50.3	—	—
Model(s)/costumed figure(s)	—	—	95.6	4.4	86.5	10.9	—	—
Print(s), photograph(s), painting(s)	—	—	77.5	21.6	—	—	50.4	48.2
Map(s)/plan(s)	—	—	74.4	24.4	—	—	49.6	48.1
Other displayed item(s)	—	—	95.7	4.3	—	—	68.7	29.4
Furnished room(s)	—	—	58.1	41.0	89.6	7.3	78.2	20.6
Person(s) in period dress	—	—	—	—	—	—	66.7	33.3
Demonstration of crafts	—	—	—	—	—	—	73.9	21.7
Music	—	—	—	—	14.1	60.9	—	—
'Voices' of costumed figures	—	—	—	—	30.7	59.4	—	—
Live animals	—	—	—	—	—	—	72.4	27.0
Reconstructed wooden buildings	—	—	—	—	5.6	30.9	—	—
N = varies, derived from Table 9.5								

Source: unpublished surveys undertaken by author for Manx National Heritage
Notes: *indicates a sample size too small to safely permit analysis
N = sample size

seen or heard the media at the attractions, general interest tourists visiting out of an interest in sightseeing in 1990 were less likely than other tourists to rate as very important the following media: guidebooks, books on Manx heritage, prints and photographs, maps and plans, guide leaflets, directional signs and persons in period dress. Some of these differences in rating were quite substantial. For example, whereas only 16 per cent of sightseeing tourists who had seen the site guidebooks thought them to have been very important to their visit, half of the other tourists gave this rating (despite not all actually purchasing a copy); similarly, only a fifth of general interest tourists rated the guide leaflets as very important, compared to 46 per cent of other tourists. Likewise, where differences in rating occurred, tourists visiting as part of a day out in 1990 were generally less likely than other tourists to rate the media they had seen or heard as very important to their understanding of the site. In contrast, in 1990 tourists with a particular interest in historic places or in Manx culture were generally more likely than other tourists to rate the media they had seen or heard as very important to their visit. Again some differences were quite substantial. For example, tourists giving a particular interest in Manx culture as a reason for visiting, or a particular interest in castles and historic places, rated site guidebooks much more frequently than other tourists as very important to their visit, with 55 per cent of tourists with a particular interest in Manx culture giving this rating compared to only one in six of other tourists, and 37 per cent of tourists claiming a particular historical interest also giving this rating, compared to a fifth of other tourists who had seen the guidebooks. The same was true for other books on Manx heritage, and could also be identified although less strongly for photographs and prints, maps and plans, and for tourists with a particular interest in Manx culture, for furnished rooms, an introductory film, a guided walk leaflet, a guide leaflet, persons in period dress and craft demonstrations. Notable exceptions, as before, were the information panels around the two castles.

In contrast to the 1990 findings, those of the 1991 Interpretation Survey at Castle Rushen do not sustain the particular versus general interest model in explaining the importance given to media. Having a particular interest in castles as a reason for visiting was not an important explanatory variable for the ratings of media importance given in 1991 by tourists at the castle. However, for sightseeing tourists the furnished rooms, costumed figures, introductory film and introductory exhibition panels were between one and a half times and twice as frequently rated as very important to their visit than by other tourists, the *opposite* of what the 1990 findings would suggest as far as comparison is possible between the two surveys.

The importance of the age at which continuous full-time education was completed by tourists is a further ambiguous determinant of the ratings given of the importance of media to understanding. Generally, in 1990 this was not a factor in predicting the rating of importance given by tourists to the presentational media which they had seen or heard at the attractions. However, some exceptions may be noted. Tourists educated to the age of nineteen years or above were notably more likely to rate the site guidebooks as very important to their visit compared to other tourists, and similarly to more frequently rate guide leaflets as very important. However, at the two castles where information panels were provided around the sites more highly educated tourists were least likely to rate these as very important to their understanding of the castles, with fewer than four out of ten tourists educated to the age of nineteen years or above rating these panels as very important, compared to two-thirds of their less formally educated counterparts who had seen these panels. As noted already, in 1990 at neither castle could it be said that the panels displayed much information, and may not have met the expectations of more literate tourists. The more general conclusion from the 1990 surveys is that a viewers versus more literate tourist dichotomy model cannot be sustained.

In contrast to the general inapplicability of educational attainment to explaining the importance ascribed to media seen or heard at attractions in 1990, in 1991 at Castle Rushen tourists educated to nineteen years of age or above were generally less likely than other tourists to rate certain of the presentational media as very important to their visit. These media included the furnished rooms, the costumed model figures and the introductory film. These differences were of much the same order, with upwards of nine out of ten of the less educated tourists rating these media as very important to their understanding of the castle, compared to around seven out of ten of their more educated counterparts. These findings for 1991 would concur with a viewers versus more literate dichotomy model, but differences to sustain this model were not to be found for the written or graphical media at the refurbished castle.

Just as the Manx database cannot be used to support simplistic models of the attention paid by holiday tourists presentational media at heritage attractions, neither can it unambiguously be used to support similar models in terms of the importance given to the media seen or heard. Some evidence supports the dichotomy models of general versus particular interest tourists and viewer versus more literate tourists, other evidence is ambiguous, and yet other evidence contradicts the direction of the differences which would be expected from these models. Further research at attractions elsewhere in Europe is needed before any general models of the determinants of the importance given by tourists to presentational media can be developed. As such models are of potential importance to the developers of heritage attractions in their formulation of appropriate presentational strategies, the priority for such studies within a research agenda for heritage tourism is clearly implied, if this agenda is to assist in interpretative and commercial success.

TOURIST EXPECTATIONS AND PREFERENCES FOR HERITAGE PRESENTATION

The expectations of tourists about the presentation of attractions are largely unknown, despite their unambiguous importance to heritage attraction development. Likewise, the preferences of tourists for presentational media are similarly unknown. These are surprising omissions, for one way of assessing customer endorsement of the presentation of an attraction is in terms of how that attraction is perceived as measuring up to expectations and preferences. The Marketing Survey at Castle Rushen in 1991 attempted to answer this question in a summary way, asking tourists whether the presentation of the castle had equalled, exceeded or failed to come up to their expectations. An overwhelming 82 per cent thought that the presentation of the castle had exceeded their pre-visit expectations, with only a single tourist among those interviewed thinking the attraction had failed to meet expectations. Whilst this is an unambiguous endorsement of the new presentation of Castle Rushen by its tourist visitors, summary assessments of this kind neither show the dimensions of tourists' expectations about attractions nor do they illustrate any variation between these dimensions in the achievement of attraction operators in meeting such expectations. A similar comment may be made about a recent summary assessment of how far visitors' expectations at Scottish folk festivals had been met (Scottish Tourist Board 1991b). As published, this analysis, although differentiating between satisfaction with the artists taking part in the festivals and the organisation of the events, did not systematically differentiate assessments by the dimensions of expectation pertinent to each. The finding that the majority of visitors to the festivals thought them to have been much as expected can really only be interpreted in terms of in what

Table 9.8 Opinions of adult holiday tourists visiting different heritage sites on the Isle of Man that, 'Historic sites should be rebuilt to show their former splendour'

| | *Holiday tourists visiting sites in 1990:* | | | |
	Peel Castle %	*Castle Rushen* %	*Cregneash* %	*All sites* %
Strongly agree	11.4	3.8	13.6	9.5
Agree	10.3	30.3	27.7	22.7
No strong feelings	19.0	17.3	20.3	18.9
Disagree	44.6	45.9	33.9	41.6
Strongly disagree	14.7	2.7	4.5	7.3
N =	184	185	177	546

Source: unpublished survey undertaken by author for Manx National Heritage
Note: N = sample size

ways either the festivals' artists or organisers failed to exceed expectations. Assessments of this kind form a basis from which the delimitation of dimensions of expectation and preference can begin; such definition needs as a priority to form part of a research agenda for heritage tourism if tourists are to be fully considered to be customers of the attractions and not simply visitors or spectators.

The Manx database enables some limited elaboration of the dimensions of tourists' preferences but not of their expectations. The 1990 Site Survey included the opinion statement, 'Historic sites should be rebuilt to show their former splendour'. Opinion was divided as reference to Table 9.8 shows. Disagreement was greatest at Peel Castle, but at no attraction did a majority of tourists interviewed agree with reconstruction. Indeed, at the two castles either a majority or a near majority disagreed with the idea. Such division of views was irrespective of social class, educational attainment or declared reasons for visiting. However, a slight tendency was noted for members of heritage organisations to be more in favour of rebuilding than were non-members, with 36 per cent of members either agreeing or strongly agreeing with rebuilding compared to 26 per cent of non-members. This difference might be interpreted as concurring with a view that heritage enthusiasts tend more towards enthusiasm for heritage as an interpretation of history, rather than for the history from which heritage is produced. Equally, a majority of neither type of tourist was in favour of reconstruction, so this difference should not be over-emphasised.

The 1991 Marketing Survey at Castle Rushen included the opinion statement, 'More historic sites should be presented in ways similar to what has been done at this castle'. This statement was intended to gain views on the new presentation in the context of tourists' experiences of other heritage attractions. More than eight out of ten tourists were in agreement with this statement, with only two tourists among those interviewed disagreeing with it, the other one in six having no strong feelings on the matter. Considered together with the previous findings on rebuilding, this would suggest that tourists wish to see monuments refurbished but not rebuilt, or at least not completely rebuilt. This would in turn imply a differentiation in the minds of many tourists between site presentation and the fabric of the site itself, a further dimension of site conservation to those discussed in Chapter 8. The same Marketing Survey asked tourists visiting the castle who had visited it before how the presentation in 1991 compared to that previously experienced. Of the tourists interviewed, only twenty were repeat visitors, but all bar one thought the presentation to be better than before, the other tourist thinking it to have been worse. Again, although this is an endorsement of the new presentation of this particular attraction, summary measures of this kind are of limited analytical use in seeking to generalise about the likely success of presentational improvements elsewhere as the dimensions of preference and expectation are absent. As noted above, these dimensions should form part of a research agenda for heritage tourism, for they underpin customer satisfaction as much as the attributes of site provision.

CONCLUSIONS

This chapter has emphasised the need in heritage tourism for the evaluation of heritage presentation to be placed as a priority on a research agenda, and has illustrated ways in which such assessments may be made. Heritage presentation at attractions, and in particular the interpretation of their meaning to visiting tourists, has to date been largely reliant on intuition and experience; formal evaluation has been generally lacking. This is despite the increasing emphasis on consumer-defined products in contemporary heritage tourism, an emphasis which might otherwise be supposed to have led to formal market research.

The starting point for evaluating the effectiveness of promotional media at heritage attractions should be the recognition that many tourists are only generally interested in a particular site and that few are likely to come pre-informed about an environment, culture or history distinct, if not different, from their own. It should also recognise that summary measures of satisfaction are of little analytical use other than in informing attraction managers of the overall effectiveness of their presentations. More detailed analysis by media type has to be undertaken if more informed decisions are to be made about likely 'successful' media mixes at attractions. Success can likewise be measured in several ways: for example, in terms of tourist awareness of media, the attention paid by them to these media and the importance they ascribe to these media in terms of the understanding they have gained of the significance of an attraction. Such an analysis should also include reference to the dimensions of tourists' expectations about attraction presentation, for which at present almost nothing is known, despite the importance of meeting such expectations if tourists as customers of attractions are to be satisfied by their visit.

Off-site media, such as a gateway interpretative introduction to an area's heritage, are unlikely to attract the volume of casual tourists who visit heritage attractions. Instead, they should be regarded as enhancing the visitor experience of heritage enthusiasts who increasingly will from their experiences of attractions elsewhere expect more elaborate presentations. Such gateway presentations may also be regarded as attractions in their own right, rather than gateways to site visits.

On-site media show great variation in the reported awareness of tourists of these media, the attention reportedly paid to them and the importance ascribed to them in terms of understanding the meaning of an attraction. Certain types of media, however, recur as most likely to catch the attention of tourists, to hold this attention and to be rated as important by tourists. These media in particular warrant further appraisal elsewhere for as at present it is difficult through the limited number of attractions surveyed to unambiguously separate effective site-specific use of a medium from more general effectiveness. The media recurrent as important in gaining and holding attention, and in terms of tourists' ratings, are as follows: models including costumed figures; an introductory film or video; furnished rooms; directional signs; and, live animals. From the Manx surveys, at least for the present, these media would seem central to customer understanding of attractions; other media would seem supplementary in importance. This conclusion has particular pertinence for the presentation of monuments in Britain, for these presentations rarely combine these media found to be of importance on the Isle of Man. As such, tourists visiting many monument attractions may not be benefiting as much as they could from their visit in terms of their understanding of the heritages of the British Isles.

10 Benefits gained by tourists from visiting heritage attractions

TOURIST ENJOYMENT OF ATTRACTIONS

Other than assertions that nostalgia is important in attracting visitors to heritage attractions (Chapter 2) and differentiations of visitors into essentially self-ascribed general and particular interest groups, our understanding of the benefits gained by visitors, including among them tourist visitors, is largely unknown. That is, the nature of what tourists and other visitors actually 'consume' by visiting attractions is as yet largely unresearched. This might seem most surprising, for it is unlikely that other 'manufacturers' know so little about their customers. As such, heritage tourism stands in contrast to much marketing debate of the 1980s which emphasized the segmentation of consumers into groups in terms of the benefits gained from consuming a product (Chapter 1).

Clearly, tourists visiting heritage attractions do not 'buy' the attractions themselves, but rather an experience generated by the visit, an experience represented by the attraction. Each heritage attraction may generate a range of experiences for it is not the site itself which alone provides this, but also its meaning to visitors, in the present case, tourists. These meanings may be derived from a variety of sources and be particular to the individual tourist. However, certain more general benefits might be supposed to result from visiting, in particular a feeling for the 'history' of a site and enjoyment of the visit to it. The Isle of Man database enables these benefits to be investigated.

In 1991 the Marketing Survey at Castle Rushen included the opinion statement, 'My visit to this castle has given me a feeling for its history'. All but three of the 146 tourists asked to respond to this statement agreed with it, a quarter of tourists strongly agreeing. As a question of this kind had not been asked in the other Manx surveys the effect of the new presentation of the castle cannot be assessed from comparison with the previous situation, nor can the generality of this feeling be shown for other of the Manx attractions. As such a statement represents one 'bottom line' for the presentation of 'authentic' attractions its further investigation elsewhere is important. However, enjoyment was more generally investigated in the Manx surveys. Few tourists did not, it would seem from the findings set out in Table 10.1, enjoy their visit to the Manx attractions. The extent of enjoyment does appear, however, to vary between the attractions, with the greatest enjoyment expressed at the Manx Museum, Laxey Wheel and in 1991 at Castle Rushen, and least expressed at Odin's Raven and in 1990 at Castle Rushen. The effects of the presentational refurbishment of Castle Rushen may account for its low rating in 1990. However, a summary analysis of this kind tells us little other than generalised customer satisfaction with a visit: in particular, it tells us nothing of the aspects of satisfaction or dissatisfaction. Recommendation is also a summary indicator of this kind. Further reference to Table 10.1 shows that few tourists visiting the Manx heritage attractions would not recommend them, most notably at Laxey Wheel, the Manx Museum and at Cregneash. The determinants of these summary indicators of enjoyment may provide some indication of at least which tourists are benefiting most from their visits, and so set a generalised baseline from which enjoyment elsewhere may be compared as further studies are undertaken. In this way these essentially summary indicators may be used to provide some further insight into customer satisfaction at heritage sites.

Strength of enjoyment and recommendation of the Manx heritage attractions was irrespective of the social class of their tourist visitors, although this does not necessarily imply that the different social classes enjoyed or would recommend the attractions for the same reasons, for enjoyment and recommendation were strongest among those tourists visiting out of a particular interest in historic places or in Manx culture. The effect of having a particular, rather than a general, interest on a tourist's likely strength of satisfaction or recommendation was found by the 1988 Site Survey to be quite pervasive. For example, four out of ten tourists giving a particular interest in Manx culture as their reason for visiting an attraction strongly agreed that they had enjoyed their visit, compared to fewer than three out of ten other tourists, and likewise 46 per cent compared to a quarter strongly disagreed that they would not recommend an attraction. We can conclude that for 1988 at least it was those tourists with a particular historic or cultural interest who were most likely to be the most satisfied with their visits.

Another indicator of satisfaction used in the Manx surveys was the

Table 10.1 Enjoyment of visits to different Manx heritage attractions by adult holiday tourists

Holiday tourists visiting sites:

Statements:	Peel Castle 1988 %	Peel Castle 1990 %	Castle Rushen 1988 %	Castle Rushen 1990 %	Castle Rushen Marketing Survey 1991 %	Manx Museum 1988 %	Nautical Museum 1988 %	Grove Museum 1988 %	Laxey Wheel 1988 %	Cregneash 1988 %	Cregneash 1990 %	Odin's Raven 1988 %
'All in all, I enjoyed my visit to. . .'												
• strongly agree	24.0	29.5	34.3	8.1	50.0	55.4	26.0	20.0	55.2	28.0	41.5	5.9
• agree	74.8	64.5	65.0	91.9	49.3	43.8	72.3	80.0	43.9	70.7	56.3	91.6
• other	1.2	6.0	0.7	0.0	0.7	0.8	1.7	0.0	0.9	1.3	2.2	2.5
'I would NOT recommend a friend to visit this site if visiting the island'												
• strongly disagree	30.3	9.9	25.2	9.7	–	45.1	24.9	23.6	47.0	43.2	33.9	10.4
• disagree	68.5	86.8	64.3	87.0	–	52.6	70.1	73.8	49.1	53.9	65.0	87.6
• other	1.2	3.3	10.5	3.3	–	2.3	5.0	2.6	3.9	2.9	1.1	2.0
N=	254	183	306	185	146	267	277	195	230	307	176	202

Source: unpublished surveys undertaken by author for Manx National Heritage
Notes: N = sample size

opinion statement, 'My visit to this castle has made me want to visit other heritage sites on the island'. This statement was included as part of the Marketing Survey at Castle Rushen in 1991. Fewer than one in ten tourists presented with this statement disagreed with it, although a further quarter expressed no strong feelings about it. Likewise, few tourists strongly agreed with the statement. As this statement was only used at this one attraction, comparison with responses at other of the Manx attractions is impossible. The statement is also limited by its summary nature, namely, it does not inform us about the individual components of satisfaction felt by the tourist visitors interviewed.

Much the same comment could be made about the length of stay tourists would recommend others to stay at attractions, for this again is a summary measure. Whereas only one in seven tourists visiting Castle Rushen in 1991 stayed over two hours at the castle, a third of all tourists interviewed said that they would recommend a friend visiting the castle to plan to stay for over two hours. This would suggest that some of the tourists visiting the castle in 1991 had under-estimated the extent of the attraction which the newly refurbished presentation of the castle represented.

Some indication of the types of benefits expected by tourists from their visit may be seen in terms of the information required by them. Asked in 1990 about the need for all historic attractions to have information available for visitors, fewer than one in a hundred tourists did not agree with some provision of this kind. Clearly, one benefit is that of an *informed* visitor experience, and not simply enjoyment of the ambience of or views obtainable from castles and other similar attractions. Of the tourists asked this question in 1990, an overwhelming seven out of ten strongly agreed with the need for information at attractions, suggesting a priority in meeting customers' needs for attraction operators. If we are to understand the attributes of benefits gained by tourists from their visits to heritage attractions, once an attraction has been shown in general to have been enjoyed by its tourist visitors, much more attention will have to be paid to disaggregated indicators of enjoyment, of this kind. Such indicators are an essential component of a research agenda for heritage tourism.

TOURIST LEARNING FROM THE PRESENTATION OF HERITAGE ATTRACTIONS

The informed visitor experience demanded by tourists visiting heritage attractions presenting past themes implies that tourists wish to benefit from their visit by increasing their understanding of how people in the past lived and how those buildings which have survived to be presented today as sites to visit, functioned. How far heritage attractions meet this desire to increase personal understanding as a recreational experience has been largely unknown, other than in the presumptive sense that as visitor numbers have increased at attractions, visitors must at least think that they are having this need met.

The extent to which tourists learnt information on their visits was included as part of the 1990 Site Survey at the Manx attractions, and also as the 1991 Interpretation Survey at Castle Rushen in 1991. Recognition tests were developed to measure tourists' 'recall' of the information which had been presented to them by the presentational media at the attractions. The recognition tests were constructed as multiple choice questions (Miles *et al.* 1988; Prentice 1991), the respondent choosing one response to each question from a set of five. The use of the latter number of choices counters the effect of guessing by tourists wishing to conceal their ignorance of an answer, despite being asked not to guess (Prentice and Prentice 1989). The location of the correct choice within the sets of five choices was varied to avoid spotting by respondent tourists. Seven multiple choice recognition tests were used at each attraction surveyed, namely at Peel Castle and Cregneash in 1990, and at Castle Rushen in 1990 and 1991. At each attraction, the questions were drawn from around the sites, each tourist interviewed being asked at any one attraction the same questions, thereby producing a summary picture of tourists' knowledge when leaving each attraction (Chapter 9). Tourists were asked to indicate any prior knowledge of the answers selected in the recognition tests. As the information presented at Castle Rushen had changed in both content and presentation between the two surveys, the recognition tests had of necessity to be changed. The resultant problem of strict incomparability between the tests was reduced at Castle Rushen by retaining three of the 1990 questions in the 1991 survey, their retention being appropriate to the refurbished presentation. The four sets of recognition tests are set out below, with the correct response in terms of Manx National Heritage's on-site interpretation indicated by italics:

Peel Castle 1990
1 With what country does the herringbone masonry found in St Patrick's Church suggest a link in the eleventh century?
   - Ireland
   - Scotland
   - *England*

- Norway
- Denmark
- do not know/unsure

2 To what use was this site put to in the twelfth century?
- *centre of government of Norse Kings*
- base for Scottish rule of island
- fort to guard against raids from Ireland
- stronghold of the native Manx
- English garrison
- do not know/unsure

3 To what use was the site put to in the nineteenth century?
- gaol
- workhouse
- asylum
- lighthouse
- *naval battery*
- do not know/unsure

4 On what landscape feature is the castle sited?
- headland
- reef
- spit
- *island*
- beach
- do not know/unsure

5 What was the principal use of the round tower?
- chapel
- *belfry*
- dovecot
- folly
- beacon
- do not know/unsure

6 What evidence of links with Viking Ireland were found by archaeologists working on the site in the 1980s?
- *silver hoard*
- monastic keeil
- jewellery
- Viking cross
- decorated pottery
- do not know/unsure

7 What unusual jewellery was found by archaeologists in the grave of the 'Pagan Lady of Peel'?
- brooch

- clasp
- *necklace*
- hair comb
- ring
- do not know/unsure

Castle Rushen 1990

1 Who rebuilt the castle in the fourteenth century?
  - the Scots
  - the Norsemen
  - the native Manx
  - *the English*
  - the Irish
  - do not know/unsure
2 From where is it thought the craftsmen came who built the castle?
  - *Wales*
  - England
  - France
  - Scotland
  - Ireland
  - do not know/unsure
3 Of what stone is the castle mainly constructed?
  - sandstone
  - slate
  - granite
  - *limestone*
  - basalt
  - do not know/unsure
4 What was the function of the sloping grass bank on the outside of the curtain wall?
  - obstacle to attackers seeking to surmount walls by ladders
  - *protection against cannon*
  - remains of a former wall
  - bank of castle moat
  - protection against undermining
  - do not know/unsure
5 What was the function of the bends in the barbican (the entrance passageway to the castle)?
  - to slow down a charge by footsoldiers
  - to enhance observation by defenders
  - *to deter attackers using battering rams*
  - to ease the gradient into the castle for carts

- ceremonial entrance
- do not know/unsure

6 What was the main function of the outer courtyard of the castle?
- refuge for population of Castletown in time of war
- to enhance fire power from keep if outer wall breached
- parade ground
- private gardens for the ladies of the castle
- *filled with buildings*
- do not know/unsure

7 For what purpose was the castle used in the nineteenth century?
- island governor's palace
- workhouse
- Tynwald parliament building
- brewery
- *gaol*
- do not know/unsure

Castle Rushen 1991

1 For whom was the present castle built?
- the King of Scotland
- the Viking Lords
- the King of England
- *the Kings and Lords of Mann*
- the Earls of Ulster
- do not know/unsure

2 Which period does the room with the peacock portray?
- *the 1500s*
- the 1700s
- the 1300s
- the 1600s
- the 1400s
- did not see room with peacock
- do not know/unsure

3 Bishop Wilson was imprisoned in this castle. What is he shown doing in the display?
- composing a poem in Manx
- writing a book
- writing a letter
- *translating the Bible from English into Manx*
- singing in Manx and English
- did not see Bishop Wilson display
- do not know/unsure

4 What was the function of the sloping grass bank on the outside of the curtain wall?
- obstacle to attackers seeking to surmount walls by ladders
- *protection against cannon*
- remains of a former wall
- bank of castle moat
- protection against undermining
- do not know/unsure

5 What was a presence chamber?
- a hall for feasting
- a robing hall
- *a place to receive important visitors*
- a bedroom
- a chapel
- do not know/unsure

6 What was the main function of the outer courtyard of the castle?
- refuge for the population of Castletown in time of war
- to enhance fire power from keep if outer wall breached
- parade ground
- private gardens for the ladies of the castle
- *filled with buildings*
- do not know/unsure

7 For what purpose was the castle used in the nineteenth century?
- island governor's palace
- workhouse
- Tynwald parliament
- brewery
- *gaol*
- do not know/unsure

Cregneash 1990

1 On what did the community's livelihood at Cregneash mainly depend?
- mainly farming
- mainly fishing
- manufacturing goods for sale to other communities
- *farming and seasonal fishing*
- smuggling goods to England
- do not know/unsure

2 How was agriculture organised at Cregneash?
- hierarchical under a landlord's agent
- *co-operative between families*

- reliant on the individual enterprise of farmers
- dependent on temporary workers from outside
- run as a single farm
- do not know/unsure

3 How was grain traditionally threshed at Cregneash?
- in the mill
- by stacking into haggards
- with grinders
- by putting into thurrans
- *with flails*
- do not know/unsure

4 What was the focal point of a Manx cottage?
- the kitchen
- the haggard
- *the open hearth*
- the cuillee
- the loft
- do not know/unsure

5 What is thought to be the age of Harry Kelly's cottage?
- nineteenth century
- *eighteenth century*
- modern reconstruction
- sixteenth century
- fourteenth century
- do not know/unsure

6 What were the cottages at Cregneash traditionally roofed with?
- reeds
- slates and tiles
- marram grass
- oat straw
- *top sod and wheat straw*
- do not know/unsure

7 What preservation activity at Cregneash preceded in the 1930s the preservation of buildings?
- rebuilding of field boundary walls
- removal of electricity wires and telegraph poles
- *recordings of Manx speech*
- restoration of a Cregneash crewed fishing boat
- declaration of the village as a national park
- do not know/unsure

The extent to which the tourists interviewed selected the correct answer is shown in Table 10.2. Some questions were much more frequently answered correctly than were others at the attractions, most notably at Peel Castle and at Castle Rushen in 1990. Although in a strict sense the frequencies are incomparable between attractions, as they are derived from differing presentations and the questions may be more or less difficult to answer correctly, it would seem reasonable to conclude that the tourists interviewed were more informed when leaving Cregneash in 1990 and when leaving Castle Rushen in 1991 than when leaving the two castles in 1990. As such, from this summary comparison, it would appear that the presentations at Cregneash in 1990 and at Castle Rushen in 1991 were more effective than at the castles in 1990. The success of the new presentation of Castle Rushen would seem also to have been confirmed, compared to that which it replaced.

At Peel Castle hardly any tourists knew either of the link with England suggested by the herringbone masonry, nor of the links with Viking Ireland suggested by the silver hoard found at the site. Only a third knew the function by which the castle had been promoted during the 1980s: namely, that in the twelfth century it was the centre of government of the Norse Kings of Mann. At Castle Rushen in both years, 1990 and 1991, few tourists on leaving the castle knew that its outer courtyard had been filled with buildings, despite the presence of reconstructed wooden buildings in this courtyard in 1991. A much more popular view was that the courtyard had served as a refuge for the population of Castletown in time of war. These incorrect understandings or failures to understand sites illustrate how easy it is to assume that tourists leave attractions having learnt about them from the promotional media used, when in reality this may not always be the case, and that some may come away with an incorrect understanding. Recognition testing of this kind has an essential role to play in a research agenda for heritage tourism, if tourist understanding is to be an objective of attraction operators.

The differing frequencies with which tourists correctly knew information when leaving the Manx attractions would, as noted above, suggest that the presentations of Cregneash in 1990 and of Castle Rushen in 1991 were more successful in conveying information than those at the two castles in 1990. However, before such a conclusion can be unambiguously drawn certain other possible effects need to be considered. In particular, we cannot assume that tourists visiting the attractions were equally uninformed about them prior to their visit. It may be that at some attractions tourists arrive with substantial prior knowledge, but at others, with little. If this is in fact the case at the

Manx attractions, it might be incorrect to ascribe all knowledge measured when leaving the attractions to on-site learning during a visit, and thus to the effects of the on-site presentational media. Reference to Table 10.3 shows that for most of the recognition questions asked the extent of prior knowledge admitted to by tourists who chose to answer a question was generally slight. However, certain exceptions may be noted, in particular at Peel Castle, where the questions concerning links with Viking Ireland, the 'Pagan Lady's' jewellery, the herringbone masonry and the topographical significance of the site received comparatively high ratings for admitted prior knowledge. Likewise, the function of the outer courtyard at Castle Rushen was similarly rated in 1991. However, with the exception of the topographical significance of the site of Peel Castle these more frequent admissions of prior knowledge are generally associated with questions for which the correct answer in terms of the on-site interpretation was either unknown or incorrectly known. In particular, at Castle Rushen tourists' prior 'knowledge' of the function of the outer courtyard was largely the cause of its incorrect interpretation by them as a refuge for the town's population. As such, the varying extent of admitted prior knowledge among the tourists surveyed at the Manx attractions cannot be said to deny an overall conclusion about the comparative effectiveness in terms of tourist learning of the site presentations at Cregneash and at the refurbished Castle Rushen, and the comparative ineffectiveness of the presentations of the two castles in 1990. What of course is unknown is the extent to which this enhanced learning was retained after leaving the attraction, and subsequent to the tourists' holidays on the island.

A preliminary conclusion that the presentations of Cregneash and in 1991 of Castle Rushen are most effective in terms of tourist learning of the four presentations assessed may be taken as evidence of the worth of contemporary integrated multi-media presentations. Both of these attractions are of this kind, whereas in 1990 the two castles were only presented in the style of many ancient monuments, largely by wall panels naming rooms and walls, and by guidebooks available if purchased in addition to payment for admission. Reference back to Chapter 9 indicates the more extensive use of media at Cregneash and the refurbished Castle Rushen than at the two castles in 1990. Equally, it would be foolish to conclude from the Manx findings that all, or most, contemporary multi-media presentations are similarly effective in promoting tourist learning: such a conclusion must await further research elsewhere in Europe.

The characteristics of tourists likely to promote their learning from

Table 10.2 Recognition of interpretative information by adult holiday tourists when leaving Manx heritage sites

	Tourists giving correct answer %
Peel 1990 (N = 184)	
1 With what country does the herringbone masonry found in St Patrick's Church suggest a link in the eleventh century?	1.1
2 To what use was this site put to in the twelfth century?	33.7
3 To what use was the site put to in the nineteenth century?	62.5
4 On what landscape feature is the castle sited?	64.1
5 What was the principal use of the round tower?	62.0
6 What evidence of links with Viking Ireland were found by archaeologists working on the site in the 1980s?	1.6
7 What unusual jewellery was found by archaeologists in the grave of the 'Pagan Lady of Peel'?	27.2
Castle Rushen 1990 (N = 185)	
1 Who rebuilt the castle in the fourteenth century?	38.4
2 From where is it thought the craftsmen came who built the castle?	10.3
3 Of what stone is the castle mainly constructed?	74.1
4 What was the function of the sloping grass bank on the outside of the curtain wall?	31.9
5 What was the function of the bends in the barbican (the entrance passageway to the castle)?	41.6
6 What was the main function of the outer courtyard of the castle?	5.4
7 For what purpose was the castle used in the nineteenth century?	84.3
Castle Rushen 1991 (N = 192)	
1 For whom was the present castle built?	65.6
2 Which period does the room with the peacock portray?	43.2
3 Bishop Wilson was imprisoned in this castle. What is he shown doing in the display?	87.5
4 What was the function of the sloping grass bank on the outside of the curtain wall?	74.5
5 What was a presence chamber?	83.3
6 What was the main function of the outer courtyard of the castle?	7.8
7 For what purpose was the castle used in the nineteenth century?	63.0

Continued

Table 10.2 Continued

Cregneash 1990 (*N* = 178)

1 On what did the community's livelihood at Cregneash mainly depend?	91.0
2 How was agriculture organised at Cregneash?	85.4
3 How was grain traditionally threshed at Cregneash?	88.2
4 What was the focal point of a Manx cottage?	77.0
5 What is thought to be the age of Harry Kelly's cottage?	45.5
6 What were the cottages at Cregneash traditionally roofed with?	70.8
7 What preservation activity at Cregneash preceded in the 1930s the preservation of buildings?	66.9

Source: unpublished surveys undertaken by author for Manx National Heritage
Note: N = sample size

heritage attraction presentations is of fundamental importance to the design of presentations, if these are to promote understanding of sites. Similarly. these characteristics provide a further dimension of the assessment of site effectiveness, for if key learning characteristics of tourists can be identified and also can be found disproportionately among tourists visiting certain attractions, the presentation of these attractions could not be considered the sole factor in learning effectiveness. In short, in terms of the present discussion, are certain of the Manx sites disproportionately visited by tourists more likely to learn from on-site presentation than other of the sites?

A problem in looking for determinants of this kind among the Manx data is the strict incomparability of the recognition test scores between attractions. This may be overcome, however, by standardising between attractions in terms of the average (median) scores obtained by tourists at each site. In effect, the average score although different between attractions is the element of comparability. This enables a comparison of the characteristics of tourists attaining average or below average (median) total scores across the seven tests at the attractions with those of tourists obtaining above average (median) scores. In this way site-specific differences are countered. The median correct scores, out of a maximum of seven correct answers, were three answers correct at Peel Castle in 1990, similarly three at Castle Rushen in 1990, four at Castle Rushen in 1991, and five at Cregneash in 1990. Classifying tourists across the attractions in this way produces a sub-sample of 278 tourists in the above average scoring category, and 461 in the average or below scoring category.

Comparing the recognition test scores of tourists in this way

Table 10.3 Admitted prior knowledge of interpretative information by adult holiday tourists visiting Manx heritage sites

	Tourists selecting an answer to the recognition questions – proportion claiming prior knowledge %

Peel 1990

1	With what country does the herringbone masonry found in St Patrick's Church suggest a link in the eleventh century?	37.1
2	To what use was this site put to in the twelfth century?	11.1
3	To what use was the site put to in the nineteenth century?	2.8
4	On what landscape feature is the castle sited?	36.2
5	What was the principal use of the round tower?	5.7
6	What evidence of links with Viking Ireland were found by archaeologists working on the site in the 1980s?	57.7
7	What unusual jewellery was found by archaeologists in the grave of the 'Pagan Lady of Peel'?	73.0

Castle Rushen 1990

1	Who rebuilt the castle in the fourteenth century?	9.8
2	From where is it thought the craftsmen came who built the castle?	8.5
3	Of what stone is the castle mainly constructed?	8.8
4	What was the function of the sloping grass bank on the outside of the curtain wall?	15.6
5	What was the function of the bends in the barbican (the entrance passageway to the castle)?	13.3
6	What was the main function of the outer courtyard of the castle?	15.1
7	For what purpose was the castle used in the nineteenth century?	14.4

Castle Rushen 1991

1	For whom was the present castle built?	17.3
2	Which period does the room with the peacock portray?	2.4
3	Bishop Wilson was imprisoned in this castle. What is he shown doing in the display?	2.3
4	What was the function of the sloping grass bank on the outside of the curtain wall?	24.6
5	What was a presence chamber?	13.8
6	What was the main function of the outer courtyard of the castle?	39.2
7	For what purpose was the castle used in the nineteenth century?	19.5

Cregneash 1990

1	On what did the community's livelihood at Cregneash mainly depend?	15.9
2	How was agriculture organised at Cregneash?	13.8
3	How was grain traditionally threshed at Cregneash?	15.9

Continued

Table 10.3 Continued

4	What was the focal point of a Manx cottage?	30.1
5	What is thought to be the age of Harry Kelly's cottage?	8.0
6	What were the cottages at Cregneash traditionally roofed with?	10.2
7	What preservation activity at Cregneash preceded in the 1930s the preservation of buildings?	6.6

Source: unpublished surveys undertaken by author for Manx National Heritage
Note: N = sample size

confirms the success of the new presentation of Castle Rushen, for at the attractions surveyed in 1990 both social class and age of completion of full-time education had direct effects on learning, but not at Castle Rushen in 1991. The presentation in 1991 clearly effected on-site learning irrespective of these background determinants, and succeeded in overcoming the effect of these otherwise important factors. The importance of these determinants, and thus the success in overcoming them in the refurbished presentation, may be seen from the 1990 survey findings. For example, in the extreme cases, in 1990 just under half, or 48 per cent to be precise, of tourists educated to the age of twenty-three years or above scored above average scores in the recognition tests, compared to fewer than three out of ten tourists educated to sixteen years of age or younger. Social class was of similar importance in 1990. Whereas, in the extreme cases, 42 per cent of tourists from professional and higher managerial households achieved above average scores in 1990, only a fifth of tourists from semi-skilled or unskilled manual worker households did so. These effects were graduated through both educational levels and, in particular, social classes, with 37 per cent of tourists from intermediate managerial households attaining above average scores, 31 per cent of those from clerical backgrounds, and 24 per cent of tourists from skilled manual worker households. At Castle Rushen in 1991 these effects were not found. As such, we may conclude that not only did the new presentation of Castle Rushen enhance the recall of tourists overall, as reflected in the higher median score of 1991 compared to 1990, it particularly enhanced that of those tourists least likely to learn from the previous largely written emphasis in interpretation of the castle to its visitors. The monitoring of other multi-media developments which combine viewing with reading is clearly important for inclusion in a research agenda for heritage tourism, if learning is to be an important objective. The style of presentation now offered at Castle Rushen would appear to offer direction to an expansion of heritage understanding, and needs to be tested elsewhere in Europe as schemes to refurbish the presentation of attractions are developed. An unambiguous link between developer and researcher is implied if this wider informational effect is to be assessed.

The changed effectiveness of the presentation of Castle Rushen may also be seen in two other indicators. Whereas in 1990 general interest or sightseeing tourists were less likely than others to attain above average recognition scores, in 1991 the situation was reversed. Whereas in 1990 three out of ten general interest tourists scored above average scores, compared to four out of ten other tourists, in 1991 at Castle Rushen just over half of the general interest tourists achieved above average scores compared to a third of other tourists. The second indicator concerns the 'Story of Mann' film, the 'gateway' interpretative device of Manx National Heritage (Chapter 9). The new presentation of Castle Rushen would seem to have removed the need to have seen this film prior to visiting other sites if learning is to be enhanced on-site. Whereas only three out of ten tourists who had not seen the film in 1990 attained above average scores in the recognition tests, 47 per cent of those who had seen the film achieved such scores. In 1991 whether or not a tourist had seen this film made no difference to his or her attainment in the recognition tests. As such, we may tentatively conclude that the presentational mix at Castle Rushen in 1991 disproportionately helped the general interest tourist to learn, whether this interest is defined as a sightseeing interest or not having previously seen the central interpretative introduction to the island's heritage.

More generally, other determinants of recall may be identified as important from the Manx surveys. The 1990 Site Survey findings would suggest that membership of a heritage organisation is one such factor, members being more likely to learn from on-site interpretation than non-members. Whereas four out of ten heritage organisation members scored above average scores on the recognition tests in 1990 (membership information was not collected in 1991), only three out of ten non-members did so. Having a child or children in a personal group would also seem a factor influencing tourists' learning at heritage attractions. This was found to be the case in both 1990 and 1991. In 1990 under three out of ten tourists with a child or children in their personal group attained above average recognition test scores, compared to four out of ten other tourists. This may well imply a distractive effect of children's demands on tourists' reading, viewing or listening to presentational media. Somewhat surprisingly, however, the length of time a tourist had spent at an attraction was not found to be a determinant of recall in either year.

As noted above, the earlier preliminary conclusion that the present-ation of Cregneash was the most effective in promoting on-site learning needs to be tested in terms of the profile of tourists visiting the attraction, for it may be that Cregneash has attracted a disproportion-ately favourable mix of tourists in terms of their propensity to learn while at the site. That certain tourist characteristics may be shown to enhance learning while at attractions implies that an attraction receiving a disproportionate share of tourists more likely to learn will obtain higher overall recognition test scores than a site attracting tourists less likely to learn while at the site. Unless factors of this kind are standardised for, we may be accrediting certain mixes of presentational media as more effective than others when really tourist characteristics are the cause.

Earlier in this chapter it was shown that of the three Manx attractions surveyed in 1990, Cregneash was that at which tourists gained on average highest recognition test scores, scoring on average five correct answers out of a maximum of seven, compared to only three correct answers on average at either of the castles. However, Cregneash was also the one attraction in 1990 of the three surveyed which received the greatest proportion of tourists from professional and higher managerial households (Chapter 3), had the highest proportion of tourist visitors having already seen the 'Story of Mann' film (Chapter 9), and the lowest proportion of general interest or sightseeing tourists (Chapter 4) among its tourist visitors. From the foregoing discussion it is clear that each of these characteristics of Cregneash's profile of visiting tourists would have encouraged greater tourist learning somewhat irrespective of the particular presentation of the attraction. Cregneash was also the middle ranking attraction of the three in terms of the proportion of tourist visitors it received in 1990 who did not have a child in their personal group (Chapter 3) and also in terms of the proportion of heritage organisation members among the tourists visiting the village (Chapter 8). As such, in 1990 Cregneash cannot be said to have received a disadvantageous tourist profile, and in several respects received an advantageous profile. Quite to what *extent* these advantages are reflected in the higher recognition test scores obtained at Cregneash is less easy to estimate in view of the comparatively few attractions surveyed in 1990. However, these findings, first, demonstrate the importance of seeking to control for, or at least consider, the impact of visitor characteristics in explaining tourist learning, and, second, imply the success of the new presentation of Castle Rushen. In terms of tourist learning, the enhanced presentation of Castle Rushen may in fact be a greater success than an implicit comparison with Cregneash might imply, for Cregneash is clearly favoured by its tourist profile. This latter inference adds even greater pertinence to the inclusion of contemporary multi-media presentations within a research agenda for tourist learning at European attractions.

CONCLUSIONS

The discussion of the present chapter has raised the issue of what benefits the consumers of heritage gain from visiting heritage attractions. Benefits can be measured in summary fashion in terms of enjoyment, recommendation or propensity to visit another heritage attraction. However, although summary measures of this kind may indicate to attraction managers whether or not their customers, tourists included, are satisfied with their product, they do not indicate the dimensions of satisfaction: they do not indicate the range of benefits gained. Certain of these individual benefits would appear to be a sense of the past at historic attractions and an informed visit. However, much more work to delimit the dimensions of benefits gained is needed if we are to fully understand what heritage tourists are in fact consuming through their visits to attractions.

Learning while at attractions is one benefit which can readily be measured within the general consumer-defined requirement for an informed experience when visiting heritage attractions. The four attractions reviewed in this chapter show that tourist learning from the information presented at heritage attractions cannot be assumed. Substantial variation between attractions in tourist learning while on-site should be expected it would seem. The analysis suggests that the modern trend towards multi-media presentations can enhance tourists' learning while at attractions, and as a strategy would concur with the conclusion of Chapter 9 in terms of the attention paid to media by tourists and their rating of them. The new interpretation of Castle Rushen would seem to have not only enhanced tourists' understanding of the significance of the site but also to have disproportionately enhanced that of those tourists least likely to learn from on-site interpretative media, namely, less educated and general interest tourists, and those from manual worker households. Many more studies of this kind need to be undertaken throughout Europe before general conclusions can be made, but the Manx findings would suggest some optimism is appropriate in undertaking such studies. In particular, modern multi-media presentations involving costumed figures and the like should not be castigated for solely promoting entertainment rather than understanding as has been the stand point of several critics in the past decade (Chapter 2). Moreover, the present findings have important implications for the presentation of, in particular, state monuments throughout the British Isles. The two Manx castles surveyed in 1990 were presented very much in the tradition of state monument presentation, with wall plates and panels, limited displays of artefacts and guidebooks. Such presentation would seem from the Manx findings to be comparatively ineffective in encouraging tourists to understand the site they are wandering around. If this is in fact the case more generally it would imply that many tourists are in effect being denied the benefits they are seeking from their visits to many state monuments. In particular, it would seem that many tourists may be being denied the introduction to the heritages of Britain about which they are paying to gain by their visits.

11 Conclusion: the heritage market place summarised

THE MARKETING CONTEXT

Heritage tourism should be regarded as a series of overlapping and somewhat ill defined market places, in which potential consumers seek to benefit internally through the beneficial feelings of 'consuming' heritage, and producers present products for consumption as attractions. As a 'product', heritage is experienced by consumers as *feelings of benefit*, it is also produced through implicit or explicit *presentation* by producers who see a demand for such products. In this manner, heritage is at one and the same time consumer-defined and producer-defined. Markets have to be made and managed in heritage tourism as in other market places. Heritage tourism market places are made and managed both by public and private sector producers in the promotion of attractions which interpret heritage from history, natural history, landscape, townscape and cultural resources. Despite the *privatist* stance of the 1980s (Prentice 1992a) in which governments throughout the Western world increasingly relied on the private sector to take initiatives and to lead in economic change, the same decade saw increased local government initiatives to promote local economic redevelopment. The promotion of an area's heritage resources was frequently part of such a strategy, and urban planners took on in effect the role not only of market managers through land-use planning regulation but more directly also that of the makers of market places for their towns' heritage products (Brown and Essex 1989; Ashworth and Voogd 1990a). In effect, a legacy from the 1980s for heritage tourism is that in an era of privatism the local state increasingly became active in defining heritage for presentation and promotion. For both the public and the private sectors a nation's or community's heritage is no longer of intrinsic worth only, it has become a resource from which employment and capital accumulation may flow (Chapter 2). For urban planners heritage tourism has had the further utility of finding uses for buildings for which conservation had become an imperative long before heritage production became a mainstream land-use planning activity. However, conservation has now been extended into 'improving' the resource to fit into images thought to be desired by consumers. A landscape and townscape increasingly fashioned in a heritage image is becoming the new vernacular of the 1990s. As such, we should not forget that in this market place, market making is an explicit activity.

Despite their rapid increase in economic importance in the 1980s, the presenters of heritage have not in general demonstrated the wider marketing philosophy of that decade. Whereas promotion was, and remains, high on the list of heritage presenters' priorities, a wider understanding of the market in a systematic and formal sense has been lacking. Expansion has largely been based on experience and opportunism, rather than on market research. Similarly, many attractions which have been developed have been 'product-led' so to speak, promoting an otherwise redundant resource to a new market. Townscape and redundant historic buildings are an obvious case in point. The urban fabric is there largely already: heritage tourism development is simply one more use to which this built fabric is to be put (Ashworth and Tunbridge 1990). The danger of such an approach is that it may become *product orientated* rather than *user orientated*; for example, in the production of trails and literature to support these, rather than in an assessment of the likely use of such developments, or the monitoring of use once these products are in the market place. Product orientation has for long been a criticism of the management of state monuments, which has traditionally emphasised the values of conservators rather than the enhancement of the understanding of the volume of their customers. To take the user orientation jargon one stage further, and draw a parallel with computing, few state monuments can be thought of as 'user friendly' in their presentation. Whereas the apparently insatiable demand for heritage products in the 1980s may have implied that a user orientation was a luxury, with a potential over-supply of attractions in the 1990s and the possibility that consumers will increasingly become more demanding in their expectations as they can pick and choose where to visit, a more user orientated approach may be essential for commercial success in the 1990s. As O'Shaughnessy has commented in general on competitive marketing:

> The more competitive the market, the more a firm must meet or exceed customer expectations if it is to stay in business. Customer

orientation in the sense of trying to meet or exceed customer expectations so as to beat competition is a key posture for any firm in a competitive economy.

(O'Shaughnessy 1984: 9)

It is perhaps no accident that some of the new heritage attractions which rapidly gained substantive market shares in the 1980s relied less on the physical resource of their location and more on the presentation of this place through multi-media interpretation: quite literally constructing the resource to meet perceived demands. As noted in Chapter 9, at such attractions it is not the physical resource, as the attraction, which is interpreted as to its meaning to its visitors, but instead the interpretation itself becomes the attraction. Product-led attractions need to avoid a product orientation, and to acquire the user orientation inherent in their rivals.

Contemporary marketing theory emphasises the processes by which producers use their resources to meet the benefits sought by those in the market. A marketing orientation is essentially a user orientation in this paradigm. These processes include:

- the definition of markets or customers which fall within the firm's or other agency's business;
- the delimitation of the wants of those in the market, and of what they potentially want;
- the grouping together of those in the market into categories ('segments') on the basis of their wants;
- the selection of those categories of customers whose wants may be best served by the firm or agency than by its rivals;
- the determination of the *marketing mix* of product, price, promotion and place (location or distribution) that meets the wants of those in the customer category selected;
- the making of this marketing mix available to the market; and
- the monitoring of the marketing mix to meet changing customer wants.

In this paradigm the heritage product is set within the wider contexts of user orientation and other marketing tasks. The marketing mix has in fact been called a 'recipe for success'; inherent in it is to balance the four Ps of product, price, promotion and place and to integrate each element with the other (Cohen 1989). It is from this standpoint that it is hoped that the discussion in the preceding chapters of this book may make a contribution to the understanding of heritage tourism markets in the 1990s, and give directions for a competitive stance in presenting heritages as products.

THE CHARACTER OF HERITAGE USERS

Although perhaps inelegant, the term heritage *user* is used intentionally in the title of this section. First, it conveys the user orientation required in a competitive market; second, it emphasises that heritage is consumed to produce beneficial feelings, be they of inspiration, relaxation or whatever, by its consumers. In the presentation of heritage as attractions which tourists can visit a user orientation implies understanding the benefits expected by visitors and meeting these through the presentation made. It is the understanding of these expectations which should form the core of a research agenda into the needs of heritage tourists.

The prevalent characteristic of heritage tourists, defined as holiday tourists visiting heritage attractions as part of their holiday away from home, is that many are seeking generalist recreation: heritage enthusiasts or specialists do not form the dominant market segment of such tourists, despite such an assumption being implied in the manner in which many established heritage attractions had until the 1980s been presented, and many remaining so now. Sightseeing and a general interest in what is being presented are frequent reasons given by heritage users for visiting attractions (Chapter 4), with a particular interest in castles, historic sites or a nation's culture as less common motivation. Although more highly educated tourists would seem to be more likely to visit heritage attractions out of particular interests, it would be easy to exaggerate the extent to which this difference applies to many tourists. Similarly, the extent to which different types of heritage attractions are substituted by tourists visiting attractions would confirm this predominantly generalist stance (Chapter 4). The same point can be made from the organisations to which a minority of the tourists visiting heritage attractions belong, and whom might be thought more committed to heritage consumption. These organisations are predominantly of a *heritage* kind, rather than of the disciplines from which the heritage product is derived, for example, *history* (Chapter 8).

For many tourists visiting heritage attractions, the visit to the attraction is only one part of a day's activities. Most tourists combine other activities with their visit, and few would seem to visit several heritage attractions on the day of their visit, other than to consume the heritage represented by townscape and landscape. Shopping, eating and drinking, and a visit to a beach are common activities associated with a visit to a heritage attraction (Chapter 5). The visit to a heritage attraction can be appropriately thought of in this context as part of an implicit 'shopping list' of things to do, which is ordered by priorities, determined in part by past activities and experiences at a destination area, and which is liable to amendment by substitution as a holiday progresses. In this way, visits to heritage attractions may either be deferred by the more casual tourists if other opportunities are found, of which fine weather may be one, or brought forward if other opportunities are lost. In this sense, for many tourist visitors, heritage attractions are not competing one with another but with a far wider range of attractions and opportunities. In effect, the generalist and recreational context of visits to heritage attractions for many tourists means that for attraction operators the competitiveness of the market place is increased compared to what it would be if more particular interests in heritage consumption predominated.

Within the generalist perspective of heritage consumption at attractions, certain *segments*, or sub-groups in the market may be identified. In particular, can we identify heritage 'enthusiasts' from other heritage users among tourists? Enthusiasm could be equated with the frequency with which heritage tourists visit other heritage attractions, either as a leisure activity or when on another holiday. Even if comparatively uninformed, frequent consumers of leisure or cultural products are often termed enthusiasts, frequency in such cases being equated with zeal and sustained eagerness. This was the definition considered in Chapter 4. As tourist visitors to heritage attractions would appear to be drawn from a population which otherwise visits such attractions, frequency of visits to the range of heritage attractions, rather than necessarily to a particular attraction, would appear to have some merit as a means by which enthusiasts could be delimited from other heritage tourists. Alternatively, if length of stay at an attraction is used as a proxy for interest in the attraction, we might conclude that longer stayers are generally the enthusiasts (Chapter 5), and that length of stay becomes our criterion of enthusiasm, particularly as this would seem to be associated with other pertinent activity, such as purchasing at attractions (Chapter 7). Alternatively, if we could definitively measure a tourist's interest in an attraction in terms of a particular or general interest, reasons for visiting attractions have a utility in this delimitation. We could, for example, equate tourists with particular interests in an attraction, that is the specialists, with enthusiasts (Chapter 4). However, we may also argue that membership of a heritage organisation, or historical society and the like, are indicators of commitment and thus of enthusiasm for heritage (Chapter 8). Equally, we may reply that heritage organisation membership is a social as well as heritage phenomenon: the social meaning of formally joining an association of this kind attracts households from some social classes and deters others. In particular, non-manual households tend to join such organisations, and particularly those heritage users from professional and higher managerial backgrounds (Prentice 1989a). If the logic of the user orientated philosophy is to be pursued, our definition of enthusiasts among heritage users should involve the dimensions of benefit gained from visiting heritage attractions. Such benefits can include being informed by the presentation of attractions (Chapter 10) or being excited by the subject matter at attractions, in the case of historical attractions, the excitement of a sense of history (Chapter 8). Much more work into the segmentation of heritage tourists needs to be undertaken. The varying ways in which enthusiasm has been seen in the preceding chapters are indicative of its multi-dimensionality. As in Chapter 8 these dimensions may be interrelated, in this case by combining excitement and commitment. The delimitation of segments in this manner needs to form part of the core for a research agenda into heritage tourism if we are fully to understand the differing demands of heritage tourists, and plan presentations accordingly.

With one exception heritage users reflect much of the socio-demographic heterogeneity to be found in Western societies (Chapter 3). The exception is social class. With this one exception, heritage consumption may be considered a widespread activity throughout different groups in the population. However, some age groups are less likely to be found among heritage tourists than others. Aged adults are commonly reported as under-represented among these groups, and sometimes young adults. Family groups should not be assumed to be the major type of heritage tourist group, despite the frequent promotion of such attractions as destinations for family days out. Despite a similar inclination on the part of many in the tourism industry to equate heritage consumption with secondary holidays, this would not seem sustainable from actual visiting patterns (Chapter 1). Heritage is consumed by both primary and secondary holiday-makers.

The heterogeneity of consumers' socio-demographic characteristics is not, however, found in terms of their social class. Heritage users are almost always disproportionately likely to be from non-manual worker households rather than from manual households, and within the non-manuals, to be from professional or senior managerial households. This is the case among tourists and other visitors alike

(Chapter 3). Even at industrial heritage attractions presenting primary production such a social bias may frequently be found. Certain attractions may differ somewhat from this general picture, for example, the National Railway Museum at York or Laxey Wheel on the Isle of Man, but the general profile is repeatedly found. It is impossible but to conclude that heritage tourism is socially selective. A derivative question then becomes how semi-skilled and unskilled households in particular appropriate heritages. Heritage tourism may reflect a particular social class view of heritage, namely that it has to be in part at least consumed by visiting attractions; equally, it may be that other social classes feel little need to use heritage, but rather enjoy the benefits of other forms of consumption. The determinants of the social selectivity of heritage use should also form part of a core agenda for heritage research, for at present this pronounced feature of consumption cannot be explained in other than behavioural terms.

That heritage consumption is socially selective in the ways measured in this book is unambiguous. Whether or not it is nationally selective is less clear. Do some nationalities consume heritage more than others? Some evidence would suggest that heritage consumption is a feature generally throughout the Western world. For example, the Atlantic Provinces of Canada promote their heritage products to tourists from the United States of America and from the rest of Canada. Of the seven segments of Belgian holiday-makers identified by Vanhoe (1989), three could be labelled heritage users, tourists seeking contacts with local populations, those loving scenery and landscapes, and those seeking to discover cultural enrichment. Heritage themes predominate among Swiss holiday choices (Schmidhauser 1989). Within Great Britain, preferences for heritage demonstrated through behaviour would seem to be general across the populations of England, Scotland and Wales (Chapter 1). However, this perspective of generality may be countered somewhat by looking at participation rates in heritage consumption at a destination area, in present case, the Isle of Man. Compared to their English counterparts, Irish tourists on the island would seem to be less likely to be heritage tourists (Chapter 3). Much more work needs to be done into potential national differences in heritage use before generalisations across different types of destination area can be made. In the particular case of the Isle of Man it may be that Irish residents are visiting it as essentially a different place to English residents; in other words, it may be that different segments are disproportionately being attracted from the two countries, rather than that national propensities to consume heritage exist between the two nationalities in general. Although Europe may be increasingly defined as a cultural area (Cuisenier 1979) this does not necessarily imply that all nationalities appropriate their cultural heritage to the same extent. Similarly, the provinciality inherent in nineteenth-century culture, although masked by centralist cultural traditions in the twentieth century (Kumar 1981), may imply that regional differences in the appropriation of heritages may occur within nationalities. Such possible variations in heritage appropriation have particular relevance for a geographical agenda for heritage tourism.

Issues of social selectivity and possible national selectivity in heritage use are part of a wider argument as to *whose* heritage is being consumed in the heritage market place. In part, this definition is consumer-defined. Issues such as authenticity (Light and Prentice forthcoming) and beauty are measured in the mind of the beholder. We know that heritage tourists and other tourists tend to have quite different views of the roles of heritage attractions (Chapter 4), although all tend to agree on the appropriateness of charging for admission to built heritage attractions in order to pay for the upkeep of sites. What we as yet do not know is whether such differences extend to how heritage in general is perceived and appropriated. In that heritage use is consumer-defined, what the consumer wants can be expected in a user orientated presentation to qualify what is presented. Such qualification may tend to be middle class in perspective simply because many heritage users are from non-manual households. This has been a criticism of many user orientated heritage developments of a decade ago (Bennett 1988; West 1988). Such a qualification has been viewed as implying objects rather than processes of social change as the focus of presentation. Some more recent presentations have sought to avoid such an emphasis, notably the 'Black Gold' presentation of the processes of social change in the Rhondda, at the Rhondda Heritage Park, but this is not a common feature of presentation. How successful such attractions will be in overcoming the qualification inherent in their market will not be known until further into the present decade when they have become more widely known.

More generally, in the contemporary 'post-modern' era, cultural diversity is increasing, and in consequence, heritages are being offered as products outside of their places of origin (Chapter 2). In this, we are seeing the beginnings of a separation of heritage from place. The heritage of colonialism further illustrates the question of whose heritage: those of the settlers or of the aboriginal populations? But the issue of whose heritage is more pervasive than the starkness of conqueror and subject would imply. If heritage users can be thought of as demonstrating a preference to be informed about heritages, their own and those of others, these demands would seem not to be met by the manner in which many attractions have been traditionally presented (Chapter 10). With the dominance of product orientated presentation, the traditional presentation of attractions cannot be said to have fostered a general understanding of attractions among the volume of heritage tourists visiting them, and thus of the heritages tourists are paying to find out about. In this sense, the presentation of heritage can deny tourists the heritage they seek, however general such demands may be. In effect, as was noted at the outset of this chapter, heritage is at both one and the same time consumer-defined and producer-defined.

THE SUPPLY OF HERITAGE PRODUCTS

An essential feature of the supply of heritage products as attractions for tourists to visit, is their heterogeneity. Such attractions range across natural history, built environment, cultural heritage and land-scape (Chapter 2). It would be wrong to equate heritage attractions with particular sites, for heritage use clearly includes more extensive places than sites alone, notably countryside and, in particular, treasured landscapes within the countryside (Chapter 1). Yet despite the heterogeneity of heritage attractions, the term *heritage industry* has been commonly used in recent years, most notably by Hewison (1987; 1989). It might be argued that the present definition of heritage attractions is broader than that implied by Hewison and others, who tend to exclude landscape and natural history heritage from their discussion. If this is accepted, the heterogeneity of built heritage to which the term is unambiguously applied still defies being termed a single industry, for to categorise it as such implies some commonness of purpose and method. By so categorising heritage producers as a single industry there is a tendency to ascribe the particular failings or strengths of one sector of producers to all producers. This is singularly inappropriate to producers who range in at least two dimensions from, in the first, a product orientated majority to a user orientated minority, and, in the second, from those giving priority to enhancing their customers' understanding to those providing entertainment. Rather than one industry it is more useful analytically to think of heritage *industries* if the industrial parallel is to be continued.

Contemporary multi-media presentations of heritage at attractions have in recent years attracted criticism that they are substituting entertainment for understanding. The evaluation of the effectiveness of presentational media to interpret heritage to its users has not been a common feature of heritage management (Chapter 9). Instead, good practice has tended to be inferred from experience rather than from formal assessment. This is despite the increasingly user orientation of heritage production and the predominance of this orientation in what is considered to be interpretative good practice. A research agenda for heritage tourism must attend as a priority to such evaluation if the users of heritage, the customers of attractions, are to receive the benefits of an informed visit which they are seeking, however generalistic this requirement for information might seem to professional historians or archaeologists. The means of converting academic information into popular information should not fall to professional 'interpreters' alone, for the translation of concepts into intelligible words and images also requires well grounded skills in identifying what is of relevance and setting these things within a wider context. As such, professional historians and other disciplines have a role in the interpretation of heritage (Hardy 1988). The general lack of assessment of presentational media to date is largely a legacy of regarding the interpretation of heritage as an 'art'; if our understanding of the effects of interpretation is to be based on anything other than surmise or casual observation a more scientific approach to evaluation is called for. This should be the style of evaluation to form part of the research agenda being defined. With the substantial investments some agencies and companies are now making in presentational media developments, such formal assessment becomes all the more important if money is not to be wasted when experience elsewhere could have warned of any inadequacies in similar strategies.

The analysis undertaken on the Isle of Man has suggested that contemporary multi-media presentations of heritage are not only popular with the users of heritage, they are used by them more frequently than the more traditional forms of attraction presentation (Chapter 9). The Manx findings must be regarded as preliminary until further studies are undertaken throughout Europe. However, they suggest that certain packages of media not only attract the attention of tourist visitors more, they are also attended to by these tourists more and thought most popular by them. These media include: models including costumed figures; an introductory film or video; furnished rooms; directional signs; and, live animals. These media would appear to be associated with attractions where tourists learn more from the presentations than at more traditionally presented sites (Chapter 10). As such, these packages warrant serious consideration elsewhere as a means of introducing tourists to the heritages they are seeking familiarity with. In particular, the Manx surveys have shown that contemporary multi-media presentations can have a substantive informational impact, and should not be regarded as necessarily replacing education with entertainment. Because of the pertinence of these findings, the inclusion of like research elsewhere as part of a contemporary research agenda for heritage tourism is imperative.

Constraints on product development by heritage attraction operators should not be equated with resource or professional constraints alone, however: other constraints, properly in a user orientated approach, derive from the market to be found among tourists and others for such attractions. For example, the market area of many attractions would seem to be quite limited (Chapter 5), a limitation which may be presumed to increase with the increasing number of attractions. As heritage tourists seem quite prepared to substitute types of heritage attractions within an overall system of preferences (the implicit 'shopping list' referred to above), the need to travel to visit attractions can readily be overcome through substituting a nearer attraction for one less accessible. In destination areas where tourists are largely without their own private transport, such an effect can be expected to be of even greater importance. A further constraint is the time tourists may budget to stay at attractions; budgets which in part can be assumed to derive from experience of visiting like attractions elsewhere. Investment in enhanced presentation of attractions may not bring commensurate increases in the length of tourists' stays at them, particularly as many tourists are on a general day out. The pertinence of constraints of this kind are important core elements of a research agenda for heritage presentation to tourists.

A further constraint on development is posed by the use of information sources by heritage tourists. Personal and social sources of information predominate (Chapter 6). Formal advertising media would seem of little direct relevance in bringing tourists to attractions. However, in that formal information sources may be of importance in some localities suggests that the design and distribution of promotional material has some effect on consumer use. The Manx surveys, for example, would suggest that although personal and social sources of information are of general importance, they may not be the single most important source. Much past research into the use of media has failed to ask *when* in the decision-making process different types of media have been used. As large numbers of tourists to destinations such as the Isle of Man would appear to choose their destination area without specific recourse to detailed formal information, the need to inform them on arrival at their destination area is all the greater. However, it would seem to be these tourists who rely disproportionately on informal sources of information about attractions after their arrival at their destination area. How this situation may be overcome warrants inclusion within a research agenda for heritage tourism, for it may offer one key to increasing the market share (if not market size) of attractions in an increasingly competitive environment. Equally, advertising needs more formally to be evaluated in terms of systems of objectives (Chapter 6) in this research agenda, and not to rely essentially on the reported use of media. Such an assessment needs to take into account the background determinants of personal and social knowledge, to find how such awareness originates. At destination areas such as the Isle of Man, where many tourists are repeat visitors, past histories of holidaying need to be investigated as part of this strategy.

Retailing sales from heritage attractions have increasingly been seen as means by which additional income can be raised. Once again attraction operators face constraints on such developments from their market. Tourists visiting attractions do so as one part of a day out; their interest is mostly generalistic. As such, souvenir purchases are frequently limited to small items (Chapter 7). However, tourists are more likely than day-trippers to make purchases at attractions. More widely, the impact of attractions in bringing tourists to their vicinity has only infrequently been studied. The evidence of spending outside of attractions which does exist suggests that it is generally quite localised to the immediate vicinity of the attraction, and not in large volume when measured in terms of the spending on average by tourist groups. A degree of segmentation in spending between tourists with a particular and those with a general interest would seem to exist: the former are more likely to spend inside the site, the latter in the vicinity of the attraction. These findings should, however, be regarded as highly tentative for they are based on the survey evidence largely from a single attraction. Before general conclusions can be drawn much greater research attention needs to be paid to the extent and determinants of retailing within attractions, and particularly of retailing induced in the vicinity of attractions. Ideally, a segmentation of heritage tourists in terms of the benefits they are expecting from a holiday needs to form the base for such an expenditure analysis. More fundamentally, the manner in which official statistics are collated need to be reviewed to allow analysis by the type of activities undertaken by tourists.

THE CENTRAL RESEARCH AGENDA OF BENEFITS AND EFFECTIVENESS

The above paragraphs of this chapter, and indeed those in many places throughout this book, have identified the need for future research if our understanding of heritage tourism is to progress. It is not the intention here to repeat all of these needs, for this would simply duplicate what has been said already. Instead, a brief overview of what are the most pressing research needs is intended.

The paradigm in which this research agenda should be effected is that of a user orientation seeking to identify and meet the benefits desired by tourists consuming heritage products. The concept of *heritage user* is an invaluable if inelegant shorthand in this regard. Tourists *use* heritage to gain *benefits*. For this approach to be applied the benefits heritage users seek through visiting attractions need to be delimited and applied as the basis of segmenting tourists into groups of heritage users. This is the over-riding research priority. Some dimensions of benefit have been identified in this book, most notably that of an informed visitor experience, and the present findings form one base from which such research may develop. But it is insufficient only to identify the benefits sought by the users of heritage attractions and to cluster them into groups on the basis of these benefits; the *effectiveness* by which these expected benefits are met needs also as a priority to be systematically evaluated for the differing segments of consumers. The present book has sought to illustrate how such evaluations may be undertaken; in the present case, using the learning achieved by tourists as a measure of the comparative success of attraction presentation in terms of the information benefit of heritage consumption sought by the users of heritage attractions. Such evaluations need, as in this book, to look towards how the benefits sought by the users of heritage attractions can be more effectively met: that is, how the visitor's experience can be best enhanced. The twin concepts of benefits and effectiveness are the central core of a research agenda around which the other core research needs should be placed: this is the principal content of the heritage tourism research agenda which is needed for the 1990s.

Bibliography

Abbot Hall Art Gallery (1985) *Wainwright in Lakeland*, Kendal: Westmorland Gazette.

Achmatowicz-Otok, A. and Goggins, L. (1990) 'Stan Hywet Hall as a cultural memorial in American perception', pp. 131–44 in Otok, S. (ed.) *Environment in Policy of the State*, Warsaw: University of Warsaw.

Addyman, P. and Gaynor, A. (1984) 'The Jorvik Viking Centre. An experiment in archaeological site interpretation', *International Journal of Museum Management and Curatorship* 3: 7–18.

Alderson, W. T. and Low, S. P. (1986) *Interpretation of Historic Sites*, second edition, Nashville: American Association for State and Local History.

Aldridge, D. (1975) *Principles of Countryside Interpretation and Interpretive Planning*, Edinburgh: HMSO.

An Foras Forbartha (1969) *The Protection of the National Heritage*, Dublin: An Foras Forbartha.

—— (1985) *The State of the Environment*, Dublin: An Foras Forbartha.

Art Gallery of Nova Scotia (1989) *Nova Scotia Art*, Halifax N.S.: Art Gallery of Nova Scotia.

Ashworth, G. (1990) 'The historic cities of Groningen: which is sold to whom?', pp. 138–55 in Ashworth, G. and Goodall, B. (eds) *Marketing Tourism Places*, London: Routledge.

Ashworth, G. J. and Tunbridge, J. E. (1990) *The Tourist-Historic City*, London: Belhaven.

Ashworth, G. J. and Voogd, H. (1990a) *Selling the City: Marketing Approaches in Public Sector Urban Planning*, London: Belhaven.

—— (1990b) 'Can places be sold for tourism?', pp. 1–16 in Ashworth, G. and Goodall, B. (eds) *Marketing Tourism Places*, London: Routledge.

Atlantic Provinces Economic Council (1987) *Atlantic Canada Today*, Halifax N.S.: Formac.

Barrow, G. L. (1979) *The Round Towers of Ireland*, Dublin: Academy.

Bennett, T. (1988) 'Museums and "the people"', in Lumley, R. (ed.) *The Museum Time Machine: Putting Cultures on Display*, London: Routledge.

Boyd, B. (1986) *A Heritage from Stone*, Belfast: Ulster Television.

Brasnett, H. (1990) *Thomas Hardy. A Pictorial Guide*, Wimborne: Lodge Copse Press.

British Tourist Authority (1992) 'Tourism forecasts 1990–1995', *Tourism Intelligence Quarterly* 13(3): 50–2.

Brown, G. P. and Essex, S. J. (1989) 'Tourism policies in the public sector', pp. 533–9 in Witt, S. F. and Moutinho, L. (eds) *Tourism Marketing and Management Handbook*, Hemel Hempstead: Prentice Hall.

Cannon, T. (1986) *Basic Marketing. Principles and Practice*, second edition, London:, Holt, Rinehart and Winston.

Cathedral Tourism Advisory Group (1979) *English Cathedrals and Tourism*, London: English Tourist Board.

Central Statistical Office (1991) *Family Expenditure Survey 1989*, London: HMSO.

Chippindale, C. (1990) 'The Stonehenge phenomenon', pp. 9–34 in Chippindale, C., Devereux, P., Fowler, P., Jones, R. and Sebastian, T. (eds) *Who Owns Stonehenge?*, London: Batsford.

Chippindale, C. and Fowler, P. (1990) 'Stonehenge tomorrow', pp. 160–71 in Chippindale, C., Devereux, P., Fowler, P., Jones, R. and Sebastian, T. (eds) *Who Owns Stonehenge?*, London: Batsford.

Chippindale, C., Devereux, P., Fowler, P., Jones, R. and Sebastian, T. (eds) (1990) *Who Owns Stonehenge?*, London: Batsford.

Clark, A. H. (1968) *Acadia*, Madison: University of Wisconsin Press.

Clark, M. (1988) 'The need for a more critical approach to dockland renewal', pp. 222–31 in Hoyle, B. S., Pinder, D. A. and Husain, M. S. (eds) *Revitalising the Waterfront*, London: Belhaven.

Cohen, A. P. (1982) 'Belonging: the experience of culture', pp. 1–17 in Cohen, A. P. (ed.) *Belonging. Identity and Social Organisation in British Rural Cultures*, Manchester: Manchester University Press.

Cohen, J. (1989) 'Tourism marketing mix', pp. 517–19 in Witt, S. F. and Moutinho, L. (eds) *Tourism Marketing and Management Handbook*, Hemel Hempstead: Prentice Hall.

Commission of the European Communities (1982) 'A Community policy on tourism – initial guidelines', *Bulletin of the European Communities*, Supplement 4/82.

Conrad, M. (ed.) (1988) *They Planted Well*, Fredericton NB: Acadiensis Press.

Cooper, C., Latham, J. and Westlake, P. (1987) *A Five Year Strategy for Tourism on the Isle of Man*, Guildford: University of Surrey, Department of Management Studies for Tourism and Hotel Industries.

Countryside Commission (1989) *Policies for Enjoying the Countryside*, CCP234, Cheltenham: Countryside Commission.

—— (1991a) *Visitors to the Countryside*, CCP341, Cheltenham: Countryside Commission.

—— (1991b) *An Agenda for the Countryside*, CCP336, Cheltenham: Countryside Commission.

Cuisenier, J. (ed.) (1979) *Europe as a Cultural Area*, The Hague: Mouton.

Daigle, J. (ed.) (1982) *The Acadians of the Maritimes*, Moncton NS: Centre d'Etudes Acadiennes.

Dower, M. (1978) *The Tourist and the Historic Heritage*, Dublin: European Travel Commission.

Draper, J. (1989) *Thomas Hardy. A Life in Pictures*, Wimborne: Dovecote Press.

Eastaugh, A. and Weiss, N. (1989) 'Broadening the market', pp. 58–67 in Uzzell, D. (ed.) *Heritage Interpretation*, vol. 2, London: Belhaven.

Edwards, A. M. (1989) *In the Steps of Thomas Hardy*, Newbury: Countryside Books.

Edwards, B. (1986) *Scottish Seaside Towns*, London: British Broadcasting Corporation.

Edwards, J. A. E. (1989) 'Historic sites and their local environments', pp. 272–93 in Herbert, D. T., Prentice, R. C. and Thomas, C. J. (eds) *Heritage Sites: Strategies for Marketing and Development*, Aldershot: Avebury.

English Heritage (1988) *Directory of Public Sources of Grants for the Repair and Conservation of Historic Buildings*, London: Historic Buildings and Monuments Commission for England.

English Tourist Board (1991) *English Heritage Monitor*, London: English Tourist Board.

English Tourist Board, Northern Ireland Tourist Board, Scottish Tourist Board and Wales Tourist Board (1991a) *Sightseeing in the UK 1990*, London: English Tourist Board.

—— (1991b) *The UK Tourist Statistics 1990*, London: English Tourist Board.

European Centre for Traditional and Regional Cultures (1988) *Study of the Social, Cultural and Linguistic Impact of Tourism in and upon Wales*, Cardiff: Wales Tourist Board.

Fielding, A. J. (1989) 'Inter-regional migration and social change', *Transactions of the Institute of British Geographers*, 14: 24–36, London: Institute of British Geographers.

Fowler, P. (1981) 'Archaeology, the public and the sense of the past', pp. 56–69 in Lowenthal, D. and Binney, M. (eds) *Our Past Before Us*, London: Temple Smith.

—— (1990a) 'Stonehenge in a democratic society', pp. 139–59 in Chippindale, C., Devereux, P., Fowler, P., Jones, R. and Sebastian, T. (eds) *Who Owns Stonehenge?*, London: Batsford.

—— (1990b) 'Stonehenge: academic claims and responsibilities', pp. 120–38 in Chippindale, C., Devereux, P., Fowler, P., Jones, R. and Sebastian, T. (eds) *Who Owns Stonehenge?*, London: Batsford.

Frain, J. (1986) *Principles and Practice of Marketing*, London: Pitman.

Fraser, D. (1982) *Historic Fife*, Perth: Melven.

Goodall, B. (1990) 'The dynamics of tourism place marketing', pp. 259–79 in Ashworth, G. and Goodall, B. (eds) *Marketing Tourism Places*, London: Routledge.

Gordon, G. (1985) 'Management and conservation of the historic city', pp. 236–79 in Gordon, G. (ed.) *Perspectives of the Scottish City*, Aberdeen: Aberdeen University Press.

Hanna, M. and Hall, M.A. (1984) *English Churches and Visitors*, London: English Tourist Board.

Hardy, D. (1988) 'Historical geography and heritage studies', *Area* 20: 333–8.

Harrison, A. (1976) 'Problems: vandalism and depreciative behaviour', pp. 490–1 in Sharpe, G. W. *Interpreting the Environment*, London: John Wiley.

Harrison, S. (ed.) (1986) *100 Years of Heritage*, Douglas: Manx Museum and National Trust.

Heady, P. (1984) *Visiting Museums*, OPCS SS1147, London: HMSO.

Herbert, D. T. (1989) 'Does interpretation help?', pp. 191–230 in Herbert, D.

T., Prentice, R. C. and Thomas, C. J. (eds) *Heritage Sites: Strategies for Marketing and Development*, Aldershot: Avebury.

Herbert, D. T., Prentice, R. C. and Thomas, C. J. (eds) (1989) *Heritage Sites: Strategies for Marketing and Development*, Aldershot: Avebury.

Hewison, R. (1987) *The Heritage Industry. Britain in a Climate of Decline*, London: Methuen.

—— (1989) 'Heritage: an interpretation', pp. 15–24 in Uzzell, D. (ed.) *Heritage Interpretation*, vol. 1, London: Belhaven.

Historic Buildings and Monuments (1987) *A Queen's Progress*, Edinburgh: HMSO.

Hunter, M. (1981) 'The preconditions of preservation', pp. 22–32 in Lowenthal, D. and Binney, M. (eds) *Our Past Before Us*, London: Temple Smith.

Irwin, F., Wilton, A., Finley, G., Wigley, T. and Huckstep, N. (1982) *Turner in Scotland*, Aberdeen: Aberdeen Art Gallery and Museum.

Isle of Man Economic Advisor's Office (1988) *Isle of Man Digest of Economic and Social Statistics*, Douglas: Isle of Man Government.

Isle of Man Treasury (1989) *Isle of Man National Income 1987/1988*, Douglas: Isle of Man Government.

Jansen-Verbeke, M. (1990) 'Leisure + Shopping = Tourism Product mix', pp. 128–37 in Ashworth, G. and Goodall, B. (eds) *Marketing Tourism Places*, London: Routledge.

Johnson, P. and Thomas, B. (1990a) *A Report on a Survey of Visitors to Beamish Museum*, Tourism Working Paper no. 9, Durham: University of Durham, Department of Economics.

—— (1990b) 'Measuring the local employment impact of a tourist attraction', *Regional Studies*, 24: 395–403, Abingdon: Carfax Publishing Company.

Jones, A. (1987) *Tewkesbury*, Chichester: Phillimore.

Kaye, K. J. (1990) 'Use of the countryside by the urban state: Scotland's north-west seaboard and islands', *Scottish Geographical Magazine*, 106: 89–98, Edinburgh: Royal Scottish Geographical Society.

Kaynak, E. and Yavas, U. (1981) 'Segmenting the tourism market by purpose of trip', *International Journal of Tourism Management*, 105–12.

Kent, P. (1990) 'People, places and priorities', pp. 42–62 in Ashworth, G. and Goodall, B. (eds) *Marketing Tourism Places*, London: Routledge.

Kightly, C. (1988) *A Mirror of Medieval Wales*, Cardiff: Cadw.

Kumar, K. (1981) 'The nationalization of British culture', pp. 117–31 in Hoffman, S. and Kitromilides, P. (eds) *Culture and Society in Contemporary Europe*, London: George Allen and Unwin.

Laenen, M. (1989) 'Looking for the future through the past', pp. 88–95 in Uzzell, D. (ed.) *Heritage Interpretation*, vol. 1, London: Belhaven.

Lewis, J. and Townsend, A. (eds) (1989) *The North-South Divide. Regional Change in Britain in the 1980s*, London: Paul Chapman.

Light, D. (1987) 'Interpretation at historic buildings', *Swansea Geographer*, 24: 34–43, Swansea: University College of Swansea.

—— (1988) 'Problems encountered with evaluating the educational effectiveness of interpretation', *Swansea Geographer* 25: 79–87, Swansea: University College of Swansea.

—— (1989) 'The contribution of the geographer to the study of heritage', *Cambria* 15: 127–36, Swansea: University College of Swansea.

—— (1991) 'The development of heritage interpretation in Britain', *Swansea Geographer*, 28: 1–13, Swansea: University College of Swansea.

Light, D. F. and Prentice, R. C. (forthcoming) 'Who consumes the heritage product?', in Ashworth, G. J. and Larkham, P. J. (eds) *A New Heritage for a New Europe*, London: Routledge.

Lowenthal, D. (1981) 'Dilemmas of preservation', pp. 213–37 in Lowenthal, D. and Binney, M. (eds) *Our Past Before Us*, London: Temple Smith.

Mackay Consultants (1989) *Economic Importance of Salmon Fishing and Netting in Scotland*, Edinburgh: Scottish Tourist Board.

McManus, P. (1989) 'What people say and how they think in a science museum', pp. 156–65 in Uzzell, D. (ed.) *Heritage Interpretation*, vol. 2, London: Belhaven.

Mair, C. (1988) *Mercat Cross and Tolbooth*, Edinburgh: John Donald.

Medlik, S. (1989) *Tourism Employment in Wales*, Cardiff: Wales Tourist Board.

Mew Research (1990) *Scottish Domestic Home Holiday Study*, Edinburgh: Scottish Tourist Board.

Middleton, V. T. C. (1988) *Marketing in Travel and Tourism*, Oxford: Heinemann.

Miles, R. S., Alt, M. B., Gosling, D. C., Lewis, B. N. and Tout, A. F. (1988) *The Design of Educational Exhibits*, second edition, London: Unwin Hyman.

Monmouth District Council (1987) *Vale of Usk and Wye Valley Tourism Research Scheme 1985–1987. Project Report*, Pontypool: Monmouth District Council.

Moore, A. W. (1971) *The Folk-Lore of the Isle of Man*, Wakefield:, S.R. Publishers.

National Committee for European Architectural Heritage Year (1975) *Irish Architecture. A Future for Our Heritage*, Dublin: National Committee for European Architectural Heritage Year.

National Parks Review Panel (1991) *Fit for the Future*, CCP 334, Cheltenham: Countryside Commission.

National Trust for Scotland (c. 1985) *Little Houses*, Edinburgh: National Trust for Scotland.

—— (1992a) *Guide to Over 100 Properties*, Edinburgh: National Trust for Scotland.

—— (1992b) *Events*, Edinburgh: National Trust for Scotland.

Northcott, J. (1991) *Britain in 2010*, London: Policy Studies Institute.

Nova Scotian Department of Culture, Recreation and Fitness (published sometime in 1980s) *A Nova Scotian's Guide to Built Heritage. Architectural Styles 1604–1930*, Halifax N.S.: Nova Scotian Department of Culture, Recreation and Fitness.

Nova Scotian Department of Lands and Forests (1987) *Wildlife. A New Policy for Nova Scotia*, Halifax N.S.: Nova Scotian Department of Lands and Forests.

—— (1988) *Forest/Wildlife Guidelines and Standards for Nova Scotia*, Halifax N.S.: Nova Scotian Department of Lands and Forests.

Nova Scotian Department of Small Business Development (1989a) *Mainstreet Program. Program Guide 1989/90*, Halifax N.S.: Nova Scotian Department of Small Business Development.

—— (1989b) *Village Square Program. Program Guide 1989/90*, Halifax N.S.: Nova Scotian Department of Small Business Development.

O'Cleirigh, N. (1985) *Carrickmacross Lace*, Mountrath: Dolmen.

Office of Population Censuses and Surveys (1989) *General Household Survey 1986*, SS4570, London: HMSO.

Oliver, N. (1991) 'The Tarka project', *Interpretation Journal* 49: 8–9.

O'Shaughnessy, J. (1984) *Competitive Marketing: A Strategic Approach*, Boston, Mass.: Allen and Unwin.

Parks Canada (undated) *Parks Canada Policy*, Ottawa: Parks Canada.

Pattinson, G. (1990) 'Place promotion by tourist boards', pp. 209–26 in Ashworth, G. and Goodall, B. (eds) *Marketing Tourism Places*, London: Routledge.

Pearce, D. (1987) *Tourism Today*, Harlow: Longman.

Pennyfather, K. (1975) *Guide to Countryside Interpretation. Part Two. Interpretive Media and Facilities*, Edinburgh: HMSO.

Prentice, M. M. and Prentice, R. C. (1989) 'The heritage market of historic sites as educational resources', pp. 143–90 in Herbert, D. T., Prentice, R. C. and Thomas, C. J. (eds) *Heritage Sites: Strategies for Marketing and Development*, Aldershot: Avebury.

Prentice, R. C. (1989a) 'Visitors to heritage sites', pp. 15–61 in Herbert, D. T., Prentice, R. C. and Thomas, C. J. (eds) *Heritage Sites: Strategies for Marketing and Development*, Aldershot: Avebury.

—— (1989b) 'Pricing policy at heritage sites', pp. 231–71 in Herbert, D. T., Prentice, R. C. and Thomas, C. J. (eds) *Heritage Sites: Strategies for Marketing and Development*, Aldershot: Avebury.

—— (1989c) 'Sales promotion in tourism', pp. 375–9 in Witt, S. F. and Moutinho, L. (eds) *Tourism Marketing and Management Handbook*, Hemel Hempstead: Prentice Hall.

—— (1990a) 'Tourism', pp. 248–67 in Robinson, V. and McCarroll, D. (eds) *The Isle of Man. Celebrating a Sense of Place*, Liverpool: Liverpool University Press.

—— (1990b) 'Social infrastructure', pp. 163–76 in Robinson, V. and McCarroll, D. (eds) *The Isle of Man. Celebrating a Sense of Place*, Liverpool: Liverpool University Press.

—— (1990c) 'The 'Manxness of Mann': renewed immigration to the Isle of Man and the nationalist response', *Scottish Geographical Magazine* 106: 75–88, Edinburgh: Royal Scottish Geographical Society.

—— (1991) 'Measuring the educational effectiveness of on-site interpretation designed for tourists', *Area* 23: 297–308, London: Institute of British Geographers.

—— (1992a) *Change and Policy in Contemporary Wales*, Llandysul: Gomer.

—— (1992b) 'Market segmentation and the prediction of tourist destinations', pp. 73–93 in Johnson, P. and Thomas, B. (eds) *Choice and Demand in Tourism*, London: Cassell.

Public Attitudes Surveys Research Ltd (1986) *Visitors to Attractions in Wales*, Cardiff: Wales Tourist Board.

Risk, P. (1989) 'On-site real-time observational techniques and responses to visitor needs', pp. 120–8 in Uzzell, D. (ed.) *Heritage Interpretation*, vol. 2, London: Belhaven.

Robinson, T. (1989) 'Marketing in visitor centres', pp. 51–7 in Uzzell, D. (ed.) *Heritage Interpretation*, vol. 2, London: Belhaven.

Robinson, V. (1990) 'Social demography', pp. 133–59 in Robinson, V. and McCarroll, D. (eds) *The Isle of Man. Celebrating a Sense of Place*, Liverpool: Liverpool University Press.

Russell, F. M. (1992) 'Close encounters', *Scots Magazine* 136: 527–33, Dundee.

Russell, T. (1989) 'The formative evaluation of interactive science and technology centres', pp. 191–202 in Uzzell, D. (ed.) *Heritage Interpretation*, vol. 2, London: Belhaven.

Schmidhauser, H. (1989) 'Tourist needs and motivations', pp. 569– 72 in Witt, S. F. and Moutinho, L. (eds) *Tourism Marketing and Management Handbook*, Hemel Hempstead: Prentice Hall.

Scottish Tourist Board (1990a) *Visitor Attractions Survey 1989*, Edinburgh: Scottish Tourist Board.

—— (1990b) *Visits to Attractions Survey*, Market Research Results RH9, Edinburgh: Scottish Tourist Board.

—— (1991a) *Scottish Leisure Day Trips Survey: 1990*, Market Research Results RH8, Edinburgh: Scottish Tourist Board.

—— (1991b) *Survey of Scottish Folk Festivals 1990*, Market Research Results RH4, Edinburgh: Scottish Tourist Board.

—— (1992) *Activities Undertaken by British Tourists to Scotland in 1990*, Market Research Results RH12, Edinburgh: Scottish Tourist Board.

Sealey, G. (1987) 'Interpretation. Five basic needs and a new definition', *Heritage Communicator* 1(1): 23–4.

Seekings, J. (1989) 'Components of tourism', pp. 57–62 in Witt, S. F. and Moutinho, L. (eds) *Tourism Marketing and Management Handbook*, Hemel Hempstead: Prentice Hall.

Shettel, H. (1989) 'Evaluation in museums', pp. 129–37 in Uzzell, D. (ed.) *Heritage Interpretation*, vol. 2, London: Belhaven.

Simpson, J. (1976) *The Folklore of the Welsh Border*, London: Batsford.

Solomon, P. J. and George, W. R. (1977) 'The Bicentennial traveler: a lifestyle analysis of the historian segment', *Journal of Travel Research* 15(3): 14–17, Boulder, CO: University of Colorado.

Soulsby, I. (1983) *The Towns of Medieval Wales*, Chichester: Phillimore.

Sports Council for Wales (1989) *Sports Update. Sports Participation in Wales 1987/88*, Cardiff: Sports Council for Wales.

Survey Research Associates Limited (1988) *Survey of Holiday and Day Visitors to Wales 1987*, Cardiff: Wales Tourist Board.

Thomas, C. J. (1989a) 'The roles of historic sites and reasons for visiting', pp. 62–93 in Herbert, D. T., Prentice, R. C. and Thomas, C. J. (eds) *Heritage Sites: Strategies for Marketing and Development*, Aldershot: Avebury.

Thomas, C. J. (1989b) 'Marketing and advertising', pp. 94–142 in Herbert, D. T., Prentice, R. C. and Thomas, C. J. (eds) *Heritage Sites: Strategies for Marketing and Development*, Aldershot: Avebury.

Tilden, F. (1977) *Interpreting Our Heritage*, third edition, Chapel Hill: University of North Carolina Press.

Tunbridge, J. (1988) 'Policy convergence on the waterfront?', pp. 67–91 in Hoyle, B. S., Pinder, D. A. and Husain, M. S. (eds) *Revitalising the*

Waterfront, London: Belhaven.

Uzzell, D. (1989) 'The hot interpretation of war and conflict', pp. 33–47 in Uzzell, D. (ed.) *Heritage Interpretation*, vol. 1, London: Belhaven.

Uzzell, D. L., Henderson, J. and Lee, T. R. (1981) *Problems and Policies in Forestry Interpretation*, Guildford: University of Surrey, Department of Psychology.

Vander Stoep, T. (1989) 'Time-lapse photography', pp. 179–90 in Uzzell, D. (ed.) *Heritage Interpretation*, vol. 2, London: Belhaven.

Vanhoe, N. (1989) 'Tourist market segmentation', pp. 563–8 in Witt, S. F. and Moutinho, L. (eds) *Tourism Marketing and Management Handbook*, Hemel Hempstead: Prentice Hall.

Wales Tourist Board (1984a) *Survey of Visitors to Dylan Thomas' Boathouse, Laugharne*, Cardiff: Wales Tourist Board.

—— (1984b) *Survey of Visitors to Big Pit Mining Museum, Blaenafon*, Cardiff: Wales Tourist Board.

—— (1985) *Attitudes to Wales as a Tourist Destination*, Cardiff: Wales Tourist Board.

—— (1991a) *Tourism in the United Kingdom*, Cardiff: Wales Tourist Board.

—— (1991b) *Analysis of the Domestic (UK) Visitor to Wales*, Cardiff: Wales Tourist Board.

—— (1991c) *Visitors to Tourist Attractions in Wales 1990*, Cardiff: Wales Tourist Board.

Walker, F. (1985) 'National romanticism and the architecture of the city', pp. 125–59 in Gordon, G. (ed.) *Perspectives of the Scottish City*, Aberdeen: Aberdeen University Press.

Walsh-Heron, J. and Stevens, T. (1990) *The Management of Visitor Attractions and Events*, Englewood Cliffs, NJ: Prentice Hall.

West, B. (1988) 'The making of the English working past', pp. 36–62 in Lumley, R. (ed.) *The Museum Time Machine: Putting Cultures on Display*, London: Routledge.

Willsher, B. (1985) *Understanding Scottish Graveyards*, Edinburgh: Chambers.

Wilton, A. (1984) *Turner in Wales*, Llandudno: Mostyn Art Gallery.

Wood, M. (1991) 'Interpretation – Its role in South Somerset's tourism strategy', *Interpretation Journal* 49: 6–7, Oxford: Society for the Interpretation of Britain's Heritage.

Young, K. (1986) 'A green and pleasant land?', pp. 59–88 in Jowell, R., Witherspoon, S. and Brook, L. (eds) *British Social Attitudes. The 1986 Report*, Aldershot: Gower.

—— (1987) 'Interim report: the countryside', pp. 153–69 in Jowell, R., Witherspoon, S. and Brook, L. (eds) *British Social Attitudes. The 1987 Report*, Aldershot: Gower.

—— (1988) 'Interim report: rural prospects', pp. 155–74 in Jowell, R., Witherspoon, S. and Brook, L. (eds) *British Social Attitudes. The 5th Report*, Aldershot: Gower.

—— (1990) ' Living under threat', pp. 77–103 in Jowell, R., Witherspoon, S., Brook, L. and Taylor, B. (eds) *British Social Attitudes. The 7th Report*, Aldershot: Gower.

Index

abbey attractions: locational clustering of gift shops around 139–40, 142

accessibility of heritage sites: and social class 57; tourist perceptions of 107–8; and visitor numbers 103, 108

accommodation choice, and advertising 125

accommodation industry: as a beneficiary of tourist spending 141; and gross domestic product 49

accommodation origin areas of tourists 102–6

accommodation profiles 72–3

admission charges *see* entrance fees

advertising: and accommodation choice 125; and awareness of heritage attractions 123–5; effectiveness and objectives of 119–21; *see also* promotional media

age profiles: of Scottish domestic tourists 10–11; of visitors to heritage sites 58–63, 227

air passengers, and their heritage tourism preferences 77

airlines, as beneficiaries of tourist spending 141

allocentrics 8–9

An Foras Forbartha 22–4

Antigonish (Nova Scotia) 29

Atlantic Canada *see* Canada

attitudinal analysis of tourists 9–10

attractions *see* heritage attractions

Audley End House: social class of visitors to 53

Beamish Museum 36; job creation at 139; length of visit to 96, 97, 98; spending at 138–9, 147, 151

bedroom browsers (promotional leaflets) 131

behaviour patterns of tourists 87

Belgian holiday-makers: segmentation of perceived benefits to 7, 51, 228

benefits: of holidays 7; of segmentation in tourism 7–11; of visiting attractions 202–21, 234

Big Pit Mining Museum: age of visitors to 60; guidebook purchases at 144; length of visit to 96; reasons for visiting 79, 81; social class of visitors at 53–4, 55; sources of information for visitors to 121; visitor group size at 62; visitors' spending at 138; visits to similar attractions 87, 110

Bishop's Palace (St David's): reasons for visiting 81

Brasnett, H. 21–2

Brewers Quay 36–7

Cadw (Welsh Historic Monuments): theming of heritage sites by 28

Caerleon Roman Sites 16

Caernarfon Castle: length of visit to 96; reasons for visiting 81; visitor numbers at 43

café facilities at heritage sites 150

Canada: and employment due to tourism 1; heritage inventories in

Nova Scotia 24; *Mainstreet* and *Village Square* refurbishment programmes 17–18; presentation of heritage in 32; promotion of heritage in 228; theming of heritage areas in Nova Scotia 28–9, 30

car use, influence on tourists visiting attractions 106–8, 116, 118; *see also* transport

Carrickmacross lace 25

Castle Rushen 44; accessibility of 57, 103; age profile of visitors to 62, 63; attitudes to rebuilding 199; educational attainment of visitors 58, 59, 100; effectiveness of presentational media at 185–6, 189, 192, 195; effects of refurbishment 97, 118, 175, 182–5, 203, 212, 218, 219; enjoyment of visits to 150, 203, 205; expenditure by tourists in the vicinity of 151–2; function of 158–60; group profile of tourists visiting 65, 66, 67; guidebook purchases at 143, 146, 147, 190–1; holiday type of visitors 69, 70; inclusive entrance fees at 145; length and number of visits to 86, 97, 98, 100, 118; multiple choice recognition tests at 206, 208–10, 212–20; promotional media portraying 132, 180–1; reasons for visiting 81, 82; social class of visitors to 56, 57, 58; sources of information for visitors to 122, 128, 131–2; souvenir sales at 147–50; specificness of visits to 95, 133; surveys involving 46; visitor expectations at 197; visitor satisfaction at 177–9; visits to other heritage sites by visitors to 88, 89, 90, 91

castles: functions of 76; locational clustering of gift shops around 139–41; and their interest to children 78, 93

Castletown 95, 101, 133, 151

cathedral visiting: age of visitors 60; with children 62; educational

attainment 57; and shopping trips 110; spending by visitors when 137; and visitor management 156

cathedrals 110

central interpretative facilities 180–2, 200, 218

Chepstow Castle 16; locational clustering of gift shops around 139–41

children: impact of presence on multiple choice recognition test scores of parents 218; perception of heritage attractions by 78, 93; presence in adult groups visiting Manx heritage sites 64–6, 73; visiting cathedrals 62

Chippindale, C. 32

churches: reasons for visiting 79; and visits to other attractions 110

clachan (village) 47, 177

class *see* social class

classification of heritage attractions 37–41, 44, 47

Colonial Williamsburg *see* Williamsburg

Commission of the European Communities 6

commitment to history/heritage, and visitor profiles 166

conservation: of historic sites 154–70; tourists preparedness to pay for 167–8, 169

consumer decision-making 119

consumers of heritage: character of 225–30; needs of 33; spatial distance from attractions 17

consumption of products 202

Conwy Castle: guidebook purchases at 144

countries of residence: of tourists to the Isle of Man and its heritage sites 68; *see also* nationalities

Countryside Commission, The: classification of countryside tourists by 13; conservation initiatives by 154; and expenditure by tourists 137; purpose of countryside recreational trips 12

countryside management 157

Cregneash (folk village) 44, 103; age
  profile of visitors 62, 63;
  educational attainment of visitors
  58, 59; enjoyment of visits to 150,
  203; function of 158–60; group
  profile of visitors 65, 67;
  guidebook purchases at 143,
  190–1; holiday type of visitors 70;
  inclusive entrance fees at 145;
  length and number of visits to 86,
  98; multiple choice recognition
  tests at 206, 210–20;
  presentational media at 177,
  185–6, 188, 192; reasons for
  visiting 81, 82; social class of
  visitors 56; souvenir sales at 147;
  visits to other heritage sites by
  visitors to 88, 89, 90, 91
culinary diversity 31–2, 50
cultural diversity 229
cultural integration policy in Europe
  44
culture and history (Manx):
  acceptance of entrance charges
  and an interest in 168; and
  awareness of heritage attractions
  123; expenditure of visitors with
  an interest in 148, 152, 153; as
  reasons for visiting heritage
  attractions 80, 81, 157–66; the
  'Story of Mann' film as an
  introduction to 180

damage caused to heritage sites, by
  tourists 155
databases (Manx Summer Holiday
  Tourist Surveys) 44–7
day-trippers 89, 101, 121, 137–9, 152
decision-making 75–93; and
  homogeneity of tourists 92–3; and
  the importance of information
  sources 134; main influences on
  119–35
demand for heritage consumption
  1–20
'Discover the Story of Mann' leaflet
  131–3; awareness of admission
  passports provided with 132
distances travelled to reach heritage
  sites 101–6

distribution of tourists at Manx
  heritage sites as percentage
  indices 104–6
Dorset, and links with Thomas
  Hardy 28
Douglas: proportion of visitors
  without cars in 107
Douglas Sea Front Survey (1988)
  46, 47; social class of respondents
  55
Durham Cathedral 110

educational attainment: of heritage
  tourists 57–8, 225; length of stay
  at heritage attractions and
  98–100; multiple choice
  recognition tests and 217; reasons
  for visiting attractions and 79, 81,
  83, 84; specificness of visiting
  intentions and 95; use of
  presentational media and 188,
  189, 196; variations in visitors to
  heritage sites and 57–8, 74
educational gain, as a reason for
  visiting heritage attractions
  157–66
Ely 26–7
employment: economic impact of
  tourist expenditure on 138–9;
  generated by tourism 1–2
England: diversity of heritage
  features in 23
English Heritage 25; and
  management of Stonehenge 156;
  size of groups visiting attractions
  owned by 62; social class of
  membership 133
enjoyment of visits to different
  Manx heritage attractions 202–5
entrance fees: and inclusive rates
  145–6; as a proportion of visitor
  expenditure 137; social class and
  acceptance of 167–8, 169, 229; to
  attractions on the Isle of Man 142
environmental degradation 17
environmental enhancement 154
Environmentally Sensitive Areas of
  Britain 154
ethnography of locality 10
Europe: impact of tourists on

artefacts in 156; range of heritage attractions in 38; tourist expenditure analysis in 142; use of guidebooks in 147, 191

European Architectural Heritage Year (1975) 21

European Community: growth in tourism in 2–3

evaluations, of promotional campaigns 119–20

expectation as a factor in accepting entrance fees 167

expenditure: around heritage attractions 139; by tourists on Isle of Man 140–53; by visitors to heritage sites 136–53, 233; and household income 3–5; regional inequalities in United Kingdom tourism 4–5; on tourism 1–5

ferries, as a beneficiary of tourist spending on the Isle of Man 141

films: the 'Story of Mann' 180, 181–2, 218, 219

folk villages *see* Cregneash

food and drink expenditure by tourists at heritage sites 150, 152

foreign holidays: British adults taking 2–3

functional specialism, and the concentration of souvenir shops in towns and cities 139

functions of historic sites on the Isle of Man 157–61

gallery visits in the United Kingdom 11, 12

garden visits in the United Kingdom 11

gateway presentations 180–2, 200, 218

General Election Campaign in Great Britain (1992): predominance of economic issues in 19

general interest versus particular interest: and awareness of heritage attractions 123; as reasons for visiting heritage attractions 79–83, 92–3, 95, 115; and spending at sites by visitors 233

gift shops: locational clustering around attractions in heritage towns 139–42, 153

Glastonbury Abbey: locational clustering of gift shops around 139–40, 142

gross domestic product (GDP), generated by the Isle of Man tourist accommodation industry 49

group size and composition profile of tourists at Isle of Man heritage sites 62–6, 67, 73

Grove Museum 103; age profile of visitors 62, 63; function of 158–60; group profile of visitors to 65, 67; number of visits to 85, 86; reasons for visiting 81, 82; social class of visitors to 56; souvenir sales at 149; visits to other heritage sites by visitors to 88, 90

guidebook purchases 143–7

guidebook use: at heritage sites 190, 192; and educational attainment 188

guided tours: popularity with tourists 175–6

Halifax (Nova Scotia): refurbishment of 17; *see also* Canada

Hardy, Thomas 22

heritage: definitions of 5–6, 24

heritage attractions: accessibility of 57, 103, 107–8; age profile of visitors 62; awareness of 123–5; benefits gained from visits to 202–21; and children 78; classification of 37–41, 44, 47; damage by tourists at 155; and decision-making 75–93; definitions of 35–7; development and presentation of 47, 48; disposition of tourists to visit other 114; heterogeneity of 21–50; interpretation of 171–5; length of stay at 96–101, 118, 226; and links with other attractions 111–12; major Isle of Man 44, 47,

48; market areas of 101–6, 232; market size for visits to 115–18; popularity indicators of 85; promotion of 119–35; reasons for visiting 79–83; refurbishment of 45; repeat visiting of 83–92; socio-demographic characteristics of tourists at 51–74; specificness of visits to 94–5; tourist expenditure around 139; types of tourist at 69–72; visits to, and other holiday activities 108–15, 225–6

heritage consumption: history of 21; social selectivity of 73, 228; tourists' demands for 1–20

heritage enthusiasts 20, 87, 93, 161–4, 198, 226–7

heritage and history 161–6, 169

heritage industry 36, 40, 43, 230

heritage integration 45

heritage interpretation: importance of presentational media for 192–7

heritage organisation members: and attitudes to rebuilding of sites 198; and multiple choice recognition tests 218; socio-demographic characteristics of 52, 133, 226–7; use of presentational media by 187–8

heritage products: supply of 230–3

heritage specialists 93

heritage tourists: accommodation origin areas of 102–6; behaviour patterns of 87; damage caused to heritage sites by 155; definition of 1, 20, 45, 51, 76; educational profile of 53–8; enjoyment of attractions visited by 202–5; heterogeneity of 73–4; longer staying 72; preferences of 75, 77, 197–9, 200; preparedness to pay for heritage conservation 167–8, 169; reasons for visiting heritage attractions 79–83; segmentation of 51, 113; site-specific segmentation of 117; social class of 53–8, socio-demographic characteristics of 51–74; *see also* tourists

heritage users 225–30, 234

heterogeneity: of heritage 21–35; of heritage attractions 35–43, 62, 73, 81, 98; of heritage consumption 85; of heritage tourists 73–4

Hewison, R. 22, 34–5, 42

Hexham Abbey: locational clustering of gift shops around 139–40, 142

hierarchies of preference for heritage attractions 117

historic buildings visits in the United Kingdom 11, 12

Historic Scotland: theming of historic buildings by 28

history and heritage 161–6, 169

holiday type: and the effect of seasonality 71; of tourists visiting heritage attractions 69–72

homogeneity, in tourists' general decision-making processes 92–3

Huntingdonshire 26

images of heritage attractions, as perceived by visitors on Isle of Man 75–9, 93

immigration to the Isle of Man 31

income levels and expenditure on tourism 3–5

indices, percentage distribution of tourists by area 104–6

industrial archaeology, as a reason for visiting heritage attractions 79

industrial attractions: Big Pit 53

industrial change and heritage opportunities 32–3

industrial monuments: Laxey Wheel 44

information recall by tourists, of presentational media 206–19

information sources 120–1, 232–3; main sources used by tourists on Isle of Man 126–9; and social class 130, 134

informational content, as a reason for visiting heritage attractions 157–61

intentions to visit heritage attractions 116

interpretation of heritage attractions 171–5

interview-based surveys 45–9
inventories: of heritage in Nova
   Scotia 24; of Irish heritage 23–4
Ireland: diversity of heritage
   features in 22–3; National Parks
   in 23
Isle of Man, The: expenditure by
   tourists on 140–53; location of
   major heritage sites on 44–8;
   Passenger Surveys on 47;
   promotion of attractions in the
   Victorian era on 21; size of 101

jobs *see* employment
Jorvik Viking Centre (York) 36,
   155–6

Kent, P. 8–9
Kidwelly Castle: student recall of
   the interpretative display at 174;
   substitution effect of
   presentational media at 186

Larkhill (near Stonehenge) 156–7
Laugharne, Dyfed (Dylan Thomas's
   boathouse): activities in
   combination with visit to 110; age
   of visitors to 60; children visiting
   62; length of visit to 96; reasons
   for visiting 79; repeat visiting at
   83; size of visiting groups at 62;
   social class of visitors to 53;
   sources of information for visitors
   to 121; spending by visitors to
   138; visitors visiting similar
   properties to 87, 89
Laxey Glen 112
Laxey Wheel (industrial monument)
   44; accessibility of 57; age profile
   of visitors at 62, 63; enjoyment of
   visit to 203; entrance charges at
   145, 167, 168; group profile of
   visitors 64, 65, 66, 67; guidebook
   purchases at 143; length and
   number of visits to 85, 86, 87, 98;
   reasons for visiting 81, 82; social
   class of visitors to 56, 57, 228;
   sources of information for visitors
   to 128; souvenir sales at 147, 149;
   visits to other heritage sites by
   visitors to 88, 89, 90

leaflets *see* promotional leaflets
learning by tourists, from the
   presentation of heritage
   attractions 205–20
length of stay at attractions:
   determinants of 96–101, 118, 232;
   guidebook purchases and 144,
   147; multiple choice recognition
   test scores and 219; souvenir
   purchases and 148, 150
length of stay on the Isle of Man by
   heritage tourists 71
Light, D. 155, 172, 173–4
linkages, between heritage site visits
   and other holiday activities
   108–15
Little Houses projects (National
   Trust for Scotland) 24–5
Llanthony Priory 16
localisation of market areas 101–6
localisation of shops around
   heritage attractions 139–42
Lowenthal, D. 22

Machynlleth 27–8
Mainstreet and *Village Square*
   refurbishment programmes,
   Atlantic Canada 17–18; *see also*
   Canada
Manchester: culinary diversity in
   31–2
Manx culture and history *see*
   culture and history
Manx Museum 44, 103; age profile
   of visitors to 62, 63; central
   interpretative facility at 180;
   enjoyment of visit to 203;
   entrance charges at 167; function
   of 158–60; group profile of
   visitors to 65, 67; number of visits
   to 85, 86; one hundredth
   anniversary of 146; reasons for
   visiting 81, 82; social class of
   visitors to 56; souvenir sales at
   147–8; visitor attitudes to displays
   at 177; visits to other heritage
   sites by visitors to 88, 90
Manx Museum and National Trust
   see Manx National Heritage
Manx National Heritage (formerly

the Manx Museum and National Trust) 45, 131, 193; central interpretative facility 180; purchase of the 'One Hundred Years of Heritage' book by tourists 146

Manx National Trust *see* Manx National Heritage

Manx Summer Holiday Tourist Database 44–7

Manx Surveys 44–9

Manx Tourist Trophy motor cycle races 49

market areas of heritage attractions 101–6, 118, 232

market segmentation 5–11

market size for heritage attraction visits 115–18

marketing context 222–5

marketing of heritage 41, 49

marketing mix 224

marketing theory, and techniques of segmentation 7

media presentation type, and length of stay by visitors 97

members of heritage organisations: attitudes to rebuilding of sites 198; presentational media used by 187–8; socio-demographic characteristics of 52, 133, 226–7; visits to heritage attractions by 163–6, 169

Middleton, V.T.C. 7–8

modes of travel, and accessibility to heritage sites 106–10

Morwellham Quay 36

multi-holiday behaviour 87

multi-media presentational attractions 37, 230–2; importance of 184; value of 213, 220–1

multiple choice recognition texts 206–19

museums 44; Science, social class of visitors to 55; and their interest to children 78, 93; Victoria and Albert, social class of visitors to 55; visits in the United Kingdom to 11, 12

National Parks in Ireland 23

National Railway Museum (York), and social class of visitors 55, 228

National Trust (England and Wales) 13, 156, 163

National Trust for Scotland: classification of heritage attractions by 38; *Little Houses* projects 24–5; magazine of 25

nationalities, of heritage tourists 66–9, 73, 228

Nautical Museum 44; accessibility of 103; age profile of visitors to 62, 63; group profile of visitors to 65, 67; number of visits to 85, 86; reasons for visiting 82; social class of visitors to 56; sources of information for visitors to 128; souvenir sales at 147, 149; visits to other heritage sites by visitors to 88, 90

neighbouring attractions, and age profile of visitors 60

Netherlands: promotional image of destinations in 26

Newfoundland, employment due to tourism 1; *see also* Canada

Nicholson, J. H. (Manx artist) 31

North of England Open Air Museum *see* Beamish Museum

North–South divide 5

Northern Ireland: household spending on tourism in 4; purpose of long stay holidays in 14

Norwich Cathedral 110

Nova Scotia: inventory of heritage 24; theming of heritage areas in 28–9, 30; *see also* Canada

objectives, of advertising 119–21

Odin's Raven (reproduction Viking boat) 44; age profile of visitors to 63; enjoyment of visit to 203; function of 158–60; group profile of visitors to 65, 67; number of visits to 85, 86; reasons for visiting 81, 82; social class of visitors to 56; souvenir sales at 147, 149; visits to other heritage sites by visitors to 88, 90

off-site presentational media: tourist satisfaction of 180–2, 200

oil industry as a heritage theme 32–3

on-site presentational media: tourist assessment on the Isle of Man 182–91; tourist satisfaction at Manx heritage attractions 175–9

on-street surveys 45–9

'One Hundred Years of Heritage' (Manx National Heritage) 146, 191

O'Shaughnessy, J. 223–4

other holiday activities, and linkages between visits to heritage attractions 108–15

overseas tourists: activities undertaken on holiday by 15–16; expenditure in the United Kingdom by 2

particular interest versus general interest: and awareness of heritage attractions 123; as reasons for visiting heritage attractions 79–83, 92–3, 95, 115; and spending at sites by visitors 233

Passenger Surveys 47

passports (promotional tickets), to heritage sites on the Isle of Man 132–3

Pearce, D. 8–9

Peel Castle 44; accessibility of 103; age profile of visitors to 62, 63; educational attainment of visitors to 58, 59; function of 158–60; group profile of visitors to 65, 67; guidebook purchases at 143, 190–1; holiday type of visitors at 70; inclusive entrance fees at 145; multiple choice recognition tests at 206–8, 212–19; number of visits to 86, 87; presentational media at 187; reasons for visiting 81, 82; social class of visitors to 56; souvenir sales at 147, 149; and suggestions to rebuild 198; visits to other heritage sites by visitors to 88, 89, 90, 91

perceptions: of accessibility to heritage sites 107–8; of boredom and images of heritage sites 78; of the functions of historic sites on the Isle of Man 157–61

place-products 3, 5

planning gains 17

popularity indicators of heritage sites 85

Port Erin 103, 104, 106, 107

preferences: hierarchies of 117; of tourists 77

Prentice, R. C. 51–2

presentational change: and effect on tourist response at Castle Rushen 182–5

presentational media: awareness of 183; diversity of at Isle of Man heritage sites 182; effectiveness of 171–5, 183, 185–6, 206–19; importance to heritage interpretation 184, 192–7; key attributes for the success of 187, 193, 200; tourist expectations of and preferences for 197–9; tourist responses to 171–201; tourist satisfaction with off-site media 180–2; tourist satisfaction with on-site media 175–9, 182–91

Prince Edward Island (Canada), employment due to tourism 1; *see also* Canada

prior knowledge, of interpretative information by tourists 216

private transport *see* transport

privatism 222

product life cycle 33

promotion of heritage attractions 119–35; effect of hierarchies of visiting preference on 117

promotional campaigns: evaluations of 119–20

promotional expenditure: maximising the effectiveness of 119–21

promotional films: 'Story of Mann' 180, 181–2, 218, 219

promotional leaflets: 'Discover the Story of Mann' 131, 132, 133; role in encouraging tourists to

visit heritage sites 130–5; and specificness of trips 133; 'Visitors Sightseeing' 131, 133
promotional media: and determination of tourist trip making 119–21, 232–3; stage when most important 128–30; used after arrival 125–30; used prior to arrival 121–5, 129
promotional tickets *see* passports
psychocentrics 8–9
public transport *see* transport
push and pull factors in holiday choice 8

Raglan Castle 16
railways: social class of visitors to National Railway Museum (York) 55; theming of Exeter to Barnstaple line 28; use by visitors to heritage attractions 107, 108; vintage Isle of Man steam 103, 107; visits by tourists to Welsh steam 15–16; *see also* transport
Ramsey 103, 104
reasons for visiting heritage attractions 79–83, 225; and educational background 81, 83, 84
rebuilding of heritage sites: tourist attitudes to 198–9
recession 3
recognition tests 206–19
recreational activities: participation rates in 11–12
refurbishment: of Castle Rushen 118, 148–9, 175; of heritage sites 45, 97; of urban townscapes 17
regional inequalities in tourism spending 4–5
repeat visits: to heritage attractions 83–92; and the use of promotional media 121–2
research agenda for heritage tourism: suggestions for inclusion in 222–34; typology of attraction types for inclusion in 39–40
restructuring of British tourist industry 2–3

retailing role of heritage attractions 136–53, 233
retired households, as proportion of visitors 55
Rhonda Heritage Park 36, 229
Richmond Castle: locational clustering of gift shops around 139–41
Royal Society for the Protection of Birds 13

St. Paul's Cathedral 110
salmon fishing in Scotland, and employment 139
sample sizes of Manx surveys 46–7
Science Museum (London): social class of visitors to 55
Scotland: age profiles of domestic tourists in 10–11; employment in historic houses and museums 138; heritage features promoted in 41; importance of heritage for visitors 6; purpose of day trips 12; purpose of long stay holidays 14; salmon fishing and employment 139; socio-demographic and socio-economic segmentations of tourists 10–11
Scotland's Border Heritage 25
Scottish domestic tourists, socio-demographic and socio-economic segmentations 10–11
sea passengers, and their heritage tourism preferences 77
Sealey, G. 33
seasonality, and holiday type taken 71
secondary holidays: by British adults 2–3, 6; by heritage tourists 69–72, 73
segmentation: of demand for heritage products 5–11; site specific 117, 233; of visitor types 13
sightseeing, as a reason for visiting heritage attractions 81, 92–3, 157–66
Site Surveys (1988, 1990) 46
site-specific factors 117, 184, 233
social class: accessibility of heritage

sites and 57; admission fees and 167–8, 169; functions of heritage attractions and 160–1; guidebook and souvenir purchases and 130, 144, 147, 150; links between leisure and tourist activities and 12, 91–3; membership of heritage organisations and 133, 163–6, 169; multiple choice recognition tests and 217; profile of heritage tourists 54, 56; specificness of visiting intentions and 95; of tourists 14, 53–8, 74, 227–9; use of information sources and 130

social selectivity of heritage consumption 73, 228

socio-demographic characteristics, of heritage tourists 51–74

socio-demographic and socio-economic segmentations, of Scottish domestic tourists 10–11

Solomon, P. J. and George, W. R. 9–10

South Somerset District Council: interpretative objectives of 172

souvenir sales, as a source of income to heritage attraction operators 147–50, 152–3

spatial differences in tourism demand 4–5

spatial localisation of tourism 104

spatial segmentations 118

specificness of visits to heritage attractions 94–5; and use of leaflets 133

spending by tourists *see* expenditure

Sports Council for Wales, report on popularity of long distance walking and social class 12

staff roles, in aiding visitor interpretation 177–9

Stan Hywet Hall (Ohio): age profile of visitors to 58; expenditure on souvenirs at 138; sources of information for visitors to 121

state monuments 221; repeat visiting to Welsh 83

Stonehenge 10, 21–2; visitor pressure at 156–7

'Story of Mann' film 180, 218, 219; visitor satisfaction 181–2

sulphuric acid: damage caused by 155

supply, of heritage products 230–3

surveys 18–19, 44–9

Switzerland: purpose of holidays in 13

television, as a form of advertising 119, 126, 129

Tewkesbury 21

Tewkesbury Abbey: locational clustering of gift shops around 139–40, 142

theming of heritage areas 28–30, 37

Theobald, A. D. 31

time spent in vicinity of attractions 118

Tintern Abbey 16, 43

tourism: definition of 2; spatial differences in demand for 4–5

Tourist Information Centres in Wales: proposals to rename 26

tourist learning, from the presentation of heritage attractions 205–20

tourists, decline in numbers visiting the Isle of Man 49; *see also* heritage tourists

transport: influence on accessibility to heritage sites 103, 106–8, 110, 116, 118, 232; modes used by visitors 106–9; *see also* railways

Turner, J. M. W. 21

Tynwald Mills 29–31

unemployed households, as a proportion of visitors to the Isle of Man 55

United Kingdom, The: expenditure on tourism in 1–5; purpose of holiday trips in 13; regional inequalities in tourism spending in 4–5; social class profile of short break holidaymakers in 14; visitor numbers at heritage sites in 11

urban refurbishment of townscapes 17

Uzzell, D. 38–9

Vale of Usk 16, 43
Vanhoe, N. 7
'Vermuyden Country' (fenland) 27
Victoria and Albert Museum
    (London): social class of visitors
    to 55
Viking boat (reproduction) 47
Village Square and *Mainstreet*
    refurbishment programmes,
    Atlantic Canada 17–18; *see also*
    Canada
visitor numbers 43, 103, 108
visitor profiles, and commitment of
    tourists to history/heritage 166
visitors: area of origin on the Isle of
    Man 102; classification by the
    Countryside Commission 13
'Visitors Sightseeing' leaflet 131, 133

Wainwright, A. 25–6
Wales: activities of holiday-makers
    in 15–16; age profile of visitors to
    heritage attractions in 60;
    employment due to tourism in 2;
    expenditure by tourists and day-
    trippers in 138; guidebook sales at
attractions in 144; heritage
    features promoted in 41; localised
    market areas of tourist attractions
    in 101; recreational context of
    visits to heritage attractions in
    110; secondary holidays to 2–3, 6;
    visitors preferences for
    presentational media in 173, 174
walking as a holiday activity 14–15
Walsh-Heron, J. and Stevens, T.
    35–6, 155
waterfront revitalisation 17
White Castle 43
Wigan Pier 36
Williamsburg: age profile of visitors
    to 58; educational attainment of
    visitors to 57; repeat visiting of 83
Wood, M. 172
Wye Valley 16, 43

York: Jorvik Viking Centre 36,
    155–6; social class of visitors to
    the National Railway Museum
    55, 228
Young, K. 18–19